2068148

'Ziya Meral challenges our assumptions about religious violence, drawing from a broad range of scholarship and grounding it all on a deep analysis of case studies in Nigeria and Egypt. The result is a fascinating reminder of how narratives promoted particularly in the West impact local conflicts and narrow our understanding of the relationship between religion and violence in human history.'

Reza Aslan, author of *Zealot and God: A Human History*

'Ziya Meral has written an eye-opening study that explains how religion and violence interact in conflicts, particularly in Africa and the Middle East. It challenges the reader to think beyond common arguments that either make religion the cause of violence or brush away the role played by religion in violent conflicts. It is a must-read for anyone who seeks a deeper understanding of this complex topic.'

Hassan Hassan, co-author of *New York Times* bestseller *ISIS: Inside the Army of Terror*

'A fascinating book which highlights the need for the West to recognize the critical relevance of religion in the 21st-century world. Ziya argues that religion permeates and resonates with profound significance across the world view of billions of people, shapes our understanding of an uncertain world, with alternately constructive and highly destructive narratives. We should never be surprised by the human capacity to tend towards violence. It is in our fallen human nature. But the true beauty of this book lies in the account that, through networks and the communities of the faithful, extraordinary stories of forgiveness, truth and reconciliation can be found, yielding the very foundations for re-building broken lives.'

Justin Welby, Archbishop of Canterbury

'In *How Violence Shapes Religion*, Ziya Meral turns conventional assumptions about the relationship between religion and militancy on their head. His careful and thorough case studies demonstrate that the question – indeed, the very direction – of causality between faith and violence is anything but straightforward. This is a must-read for anyone – scholars, students, policymakers – wishing to understand the complex sociology of religion and violence in the contemporary world.'

Peter Mandaville, George Mason University

How Violence Shapes Religion

Is there an inevitable global violent clash unfolding between the world's largest religions: Islam and Christianity? Do religions cause violent conflicts, or are there other factors at play? How can we make sense of increasing reports of violence between Christian and Muslim ethnic communities around the world? By seeking to answer such questions about the relationship between religion and violence in today's world, Ziya Meral challenges popular theories and offers an alternative explanation, based on insights inferred from real cases of ethno-religious violence in Africa and the Middle East. The relationship between religion and violence runs deep, and both are intrinsic to the human story. Violence leads to and shapes religion, while religion acts to enable violence as well as providing responses that contain and prevent it. However, with religious violence being one of the most serious challenges facing the modern world, Meral shows that we need to de-globalise our analysis and focus on individual conflicts, instead of attempting to provide single answers to complex questions.

Dr Ziya Meral is a senior resident fellow at the British Army's Centre for Historical Analysis and Conflict Research, based at the Royal Military Academy Sandhurst. He is also the director of the Centre on Religion and Global Affairs. He frequently gives television and radio interviews for British and international media outlets, and he has been cited by leading newspapers, including *The Financial Times* and *The New York Times*. He has given expert testimonies before the House of Commons Foreign Affairs Committee, as well as lectures at the British Foreign and Commonwealth Office, US State Department, NATO Defence College and the European Commission. He holds a PhD from the University of Cambridge in political science, a MSc in sociology from the London School of Economics, a Masters of Divinity from the International School of Theology Asia in Manila, Philippines and a 1st Class BA from Brunel University. He has also taken short-term courses around the world, including classes on genocides and prevention in Canada and introduction to Chinese language and culture in China.

How Violence
Shapes Religion

Belief and Conflict in the Middle East
and Africa

ZIYA MERAL

CAMBRIDGE
UNIVERSITY PRESS

CAMBRIDGE
UNIVERSITY PRESS

University Printing House, Cambridge CB2 8BS, United Kingdom

One Liberty Plaza, 20th Floor, New York, NY 10006, USA

477 Williamstown Road, Port Melbourne, VIC 3207, Australia

314–321, 3rd Floor, Plot 3, Splendor Forum, Jasola District Centre,
New Delhi – 110025, India

79 Anson Road, #06–04/06, Singapore 079906

Cambridge University Press is part of the University of Cambridge.

It furthers the University's mission by disseminating knowledge in the pursuit of
education, learning, and research at the highest international levels of excellence.

www.cambridge.org
Information on this title: www.cambridge.org/9781108429009
DOI: 10.1017/9781108553964

© Ziya Meral 2018

First published 2018

Printed and bound in Great Britain by Clays Ltd, Elcograf S.p.A.

A catalogue record for this publication is available from the British Library.

Library of Congress Cataloging-in-Publication Data
Names: Meral, Ziya, author.
Title: How violence shapes religion : belief and conflict in the Middle East
   and Africa / Ziya Meral.
Description: First [edition].. | New York : Cambridge University Press, 2018. |
   Includes bibliographical references and index.
Identifiers: LCCN 2018021296 | ISBN 9781108429009 (harback : alk. paper) |
   ISBN 9781108452854 (pbk. : alk. paper)
Subjects: LCSH: Violence–Religious aspects. | Violence–Egypt. |
   Violence–Nigeria. | Christianity. | Islam.
Classification: LCC BL65.V55 M47 2018 | DDC 201/.76332–dc23
LC record available at https://lccn.loc.gov/2018021296

ISBN 978-1-108-42900-9 Hardback
ISBN 978-1-108-45285-4 Paperback

To Dylan:
Noli timere

Contents

Acknowledgements

While the myth that you can be all you want to be if only you believe in yourself might help self-help book sales, I have been able to fare forward in my personal, professional and academic life only because of the people who believed in me, supported me, opened doors and opportunities for me. Writing might be a solitary process, but there are many people behind a book besides the author that make it all possible. I am deeply thankful to friends and contacts who enabled my research trips in Egypt and Nigeria and helped tremendously in arranging meetings, translating and offering logistic support. Many thanks to the colleagues at the Centre for Historical Analysis and Conflict Research for giving me ample space and time to work on this book. Grateful to Dr Harald Wydra for his friendship and guidance over the years, and to Dr Devon Curtis and Dr Roberto Farneti as well as the anonymous reviewers of this manuscript who gave valuable feedback on how to structure my thoughts. This manuscript would not have emerged as a book without the support and vision of its editor, Maria Marsh. At the personal level, the list is much longer with family and friends. I am sincerely grateful to all of them for the part they played in the long journey behind this book: Amanda Gray Meral, the Creber family and friends in Cornwall, Steve and Sue McGowan, Denis and Tina Alexander, Ard and Mary Louis, Gamze Ates and Joel Ackerman and many more who are not listed here.

1 | Introduction

We are afraid. The loud voices that dominate television channels, social media posts and popular politics provide very little by way of actual solutions. Instead, with each new terror attack and with each news report of violent religious conflicts in the Middle East and Africa, we are garnished with the same petrifying commentaries. A cosmic war is said to be unfolding across the world, not simply between local communities or nations but between Muslims and Christians, the 'Islamic world' and 'Judeo-Christian West', 'us' versus 'them'. Myriad of events, conflicts and terror attacks are claimed to be intrinsically linked to each other. A thread is said to run across issues surrounding migration to social cohesion, female genital mutilation, honour killings, domestic abuse, civil wars, violent conflicts and failed states. It is claimed to be historic, primordial, timeless and sets 'them' apart from 'us' eternally, leaving no chance for things to change and improve but only bringing us closer each day to an inevitable global clash. Distances melt, long dead histories become here and now, geographies disappear along with distinctly different localities, individuals, languages, backgrounds and beliefs. A single factor, a single cause captures the complexity. One narrative to explain them all. Variations of this can be heard frequently and bluntly on American cable infotainment shows and lectures at worried European capitals as well as mosques in the Middle East and Africa. The only difference is who the antagonist is, who 'them' is in a given conversation, not the declared bankrupt and innate qualities of the 'other' who is always seeking to destroy 'us'.

There is a reason why such explanations persist and find willing audiences. Terror is a real threat, and terror groups that ground their activities in religious calls, particularly Islamic, constitute most of the increase in terror attacks across the world.[1] Yet, the larger picture is much more worrying than the relatively small number of individuals that are attracted to committing terrorist acts in European or North American cities. The Pew Research Center notes that 'religious hostilities increased in every major region of the world', particularly in the Middle East and North Africa, with 33 per cent of the 198 countries surveyed by Pew having high religious hostilities in 2012, up from 29 per cent in 2011 and 20 per cent in 2007.[2] Since some of the countries where there are social hostilities involving religion are among the most populous in the world, Pew calculates that the percentage of the world's population that live in countries with religious hostilities went up from 45 per cent in 2007 to 74 per cent in 2012. Subsequent Pew studies continued to record worrying levels of social hostilities involving religion across the world, noting the increase of use of violence or threat of violence to enforce religious norms in 16 countries in sub-Saharan Africa in 2015.[3] The same study also noted that 17 countries in Europe saw mob violence related to religion and assaults on individuals in 28 countries, a sharp increase from nine countries in 2014.

While such studies suggest a recent intensification, violent conflicts involving religious actors and causes are not a new phenomenon. There have been widespread incidents of ethno-religious violence since the mid-twentieth century.[4] Rapport notes that 'after World War II half of the internal struggles were ethno-religious; by the 1960s ethno-religious violence outstripped all others put together' (Rapport 2007:275). He estimates that some three-quarters of conflicts globally from 1960 to 1990 were instigated by religious tensions (Rapport 2007:259). Steve Bruce also claims that three-quarters of violent conflicts in the world had religious characteristics and argues that many who were involved in these conflicts 'explain or justify their causes by reference to their religion' (as quoted by Ruane & Todd 2011:67). In his study of the State Failure Data Set, Jonathan Fox observes that 'throughout the 1960–96 period, religious conflicts constituted between about 33 per cent and 47 per cent of all conflicts' (Fox 2004:64). The last ten years have seen further examples of this worrying trend with violent ethno-religious conflicts across Africa and the Middle East, including in Sudan,[5] Central African Republic (CAR),[6] Egypt,[7] Nigeria,[8] Syria,[9] Afghanistan[10] and Iraq.[11]

It is true that the events in distant places are no longer tragedies separated from our day-to-day lives. Conflicts spill over; terrorism is contagious. As Rene Girard observes, each violent act creates another one as rivals mimic one another and retaliate in a 'planetary principle of reciprocity' (Girard 2010:40). An act of violence in one part of the world triggers further violence and animosities in another, and religious identities and solidarities seem to provide an effective global channel for that to happen. Girard notes that 'the world is caught up in an escalation to extremes and that people today do not see that it can be stopped' (Girard 2010:197). It is a petrifying thought. But is that true? Can we really not stop this escalation to extremes? Are we really facing a global war between the adherents of two of the world's largest religions and identities and nations that are deeply shaped by them? Is this an inevitable clash? Are the terror attacks in Western cities linked to conflicts and grievances elsewhere? What leads human beings to pursue violence? Is it religions that cause violence? If they do so, how? Or are there other factors in play? Are some religious communities and nations more violent than others? And most importantly, are these even the right questions to ask?

These thoughts have haunted me personally for a very long time and have shaped my personal, academic and professional journey thus far. Over the years, I have witnessed first-hand the suffering of countless people, for no other reason than their religious identities and their beliefs. I have sat across from people who have suffered immensely from torture, from imprisonment, from arbitrary state violence and communal conflicts. Those experiences have given me a personal agenda that will be clear to the reader rather quickly: the need for a better understanding of the conflicts the world is facing, so that we can also explore ways to contain and prevent them. This is a difficult task in an age that is more interested in sound bites asserted most confidently rather than conclusions from studies that take a long time to mature, or in sensational arguments providing you with more proof of what you already believe rather than challenging you with your assumptions and even questions you ask before giving you an answer.

Popular Explanations

This is particularly the case for the topic of religion and violence. The resurgence of violent conflicts with religious characteristics has triggered an avalanche of popular explanations that argue that religions, if not particularly Islam, are the primary causes of such violence. A prominent example of this has been the 'clash of civilisations' language provided by Samuel Huntington. Huntington argued that 'in the post-Cold War world, the most important distinctions among peoples are not ideological, political or economic. They are cultural'

(Huntington 1996:21). He attributed this to the fact that 'improve-
ments in transportation and communication have produced more frequent, more intense, more symmetrical and more inclusive interactions
among people of different civilizations. As a result, their civilizational
identities become increasingly salient' (Huntington 1996:129). Thus,
not only enforcing sharper 'civilizational identities' but also 'deeper
consciousness of civilizational differences and of the need to protect
what distinguishes "us"' (Huntington 1996:129). Huntington saw
Sinic, Japanese, Hindu, Islamic, Orthodox, Western (Europe, North
America and Australia and New Zealand), Latin American and 'possibly African' to be the major civilizations in the world (Huntington
1996:45, 46, 47). While predicting particularly a clash between Christian Western and Islamic civilizations, Huntington noted that conflicts
have not been evenly distributed among world's civilizations: 'the overwhelming majority of fault line conflicts have taken place along the
boundary looping across Eurasia and Africa that separates Muslims
from non-Muslims' (Huntington 1996:255). In fact, some of the dead-
liest examples of ethno-religious violence take place in countries that
have mixed religious populations and are located between Muslim-
majority North Africa and non-Muslim-majority sub-Saharan Africa.
Since the overwhelming majority of religion-related violence over the
last couple of decades has involved Muslims, Huntington argued that
there was a 'Muslim propensity to violence' due to the historic origins of doctrines of jihad and warfare seen in the life of the Prophet
Muhammad and early formation of Islam (Huntington 1996:258).

Huntington's conceptualization of a clash of civilizations – and his
argument that there is an intrinsic aspect of Islam that promotes
violence – has remained influential as it seems to have provided an
intellectual framing to many who see a Manichean battle unfolding
between an imagined Christian West with an equally imagined Islamic
world. Bernard Lewis, in his widely cited essay 'The Roots of Muslim
Rage' (1990) took Huntington's theory further and argued that there is
a thread in Islam that links violence to the emergence of Islam with a
prophet who was a statesman and a warrior and Islamic beliefs that
deny a separation between religion and politics, divide the world into
the 'World of Islam' versus the 'World of War' and does not grant
equality between believers and non-believers. Lewis noted that 'we are
facing a mood and a movement far transcending the level of issues and

policies and the governments that pursue them. This is no less than a
clash of civilizations: the perhaps irrational but surely historic reaction
of an ancient rival to our Judeo-Christian heritage, our secular present,
and the worldwide expansion of both' (Lewis 1990:60). Sam Harris,
an American author who frequents television news and commentary
and popular publications, argues that we have to leave political cor-
rectness behind and face the 'reality of Islam', which is 'a civilization
with an arrested history', and as he warns about Muslim migration to
Europe, he argues that it is time we recognized 'and obliged the Muslim
world to recognize that "Muslim extremism" is not extreme among
Muslims' (Harris 2006). By this line of reasoning, the root cause of
religious violence in the world is Islam and Muslims, who are intrinsically violent, unlike Christians (if not Europeans or North Americans),
who, by implication, are not so. As the refugee crisis of the summer of
2015 meant hundreds of thousands of Muslims from the Middle East
and North Africa sought asylum in Europe, concerns over religious
clashes in Europe became a common topic for debate in the mass
media. German sociologist Hans-Georg Soeffner warned that 'the
refugees bring political and religious conflicts from their countries of
origin to Germany like the conflicts between Sunnis and Shiites, or
liberal Muslims and Salafists' (Deutsche Welle 2015). Therefore, it was
no surprise that there were calls both in Europe[12] and in the United
States[13] for the Western countries to accept only Christian refugees,
not Muslims.

Another kind of popular explanation for the relationship between
religion and violence in the world has been provided by the so-called
New Atheists headed by celebrity figures such as Richard Dawkins.
Their arguments have focused on not just Islam and Muslims as the
cause behind violence in the world, but on the very idea of religion
as the root cause of all that is wrong in the world. This underlying
assumption is clear in Dawkins' adaptation of the song 'Imagine' by
John Lennon:

Imagine, with John Lennon, a world with no religion. Imagine no suicide
bombers, no 9/11, no 7/7, no Crusades, no witch-hunts, no Gunpowder Plot,
no Indian partition, no Israeli/Palestinian wars, no Serb/Croat/Muslim mas-
sacres, no persecution of Jews as 'Christ-killers', no Northern Ireland
'troubles', no 'honour killings', no shiny-suited bouffant-haired televangel-
ists fleecing gullible people of their money. Imagine no Taliban to blow up

ancient statues, no public beheadings of blasphemers, no flogging of female skin for the crime of showing an inch of it. (Dawkins 2006:23–24)

While Dawkins accepts that 'patriotic love of country and ethnic group' can also produce extremism and violence, 'religious faith is an especially potent silencer of rational calculation, which usually seems to trump all others', 'because of the easy and beguiling promise that death is not the end, and that a martyr's heaven is especially glorious. But it is also partly because it discourages questioning, by its very nature' (Dawkins 2006:306). Dawkins boldly states:

Faith is an evil precisely because it requires no justification and brooks no argument. Teaching children that unquestioned faith is a virtue primes them – given certain other ingredients that are not hard to come by – to grow up into potentially lethal weapons for future jihads or crusades. Immunized against fear by the promise of a martyr's paradise, the authentic faith-head deserves a high place in the history of armaments, alongside the longbow, the war-horse, the tank and the cluster bomb. If children were taught to question and think through their beliefs, instead of being taught the superior virtue of faith without question, it is a good bet that there would be no suicide bombers. (Dawkins 2006:308)

Thus, for Dawkins, a return to the idealized vision of rational critical thinking, scientific method and secular education would stop the violence unleashed in the world under the banner of religion. The imagined civilizational fault line is once again drawn, not between the constructs of a Christian West and Islamic World as distinct cultural entities as Huntington did, but through the Enlightenment narratives of an advanced world versus a backward world still in the shackles of religion. Therefore, the violence we see is simply caused by religions, and those who hold religious beliefs represent the unfinished task of liberation provided by scientific advancement. However, for Dawkins, and those who share his ideological belief in science, there is a difference between Islam and Christianity, which is benign and has at least a cultural role to play. As the scientist dean of an elite college in the United Kingdom put to me in a conversation: the solution to religious conflict is ultimately Muslims converting to 'a mild religion like Anglicanism'.

A similar linear construct of the advancement of humanity, and thus by implication its lapse in the illogical endurance of religion, can be seen in liberal views that neither share the modernist narratives of scientific truth and objective rationality like the New Atheists, nor accept the essentialization of any culture and people as we see in arguments about a claimed Muslim propensity for violence, but instead follows the postmodern impulse to see absolute truth-claims as the root of problems. In his book, *A God of One's Own*, Ulrick Beck (2010) starts with the assumption that monotheism leads to violence and conflict due to its exclusive truth-claims and unshaken belief in them. Beck asks, 'the question that counts today is: how are we to civilize the global potential for conflict between the monotheistic world religions?' (Beck 2010:44). Beck is worried that a worldwide tension is emerging since there is a cosmopolitan given to religions which move beyond boundaries of nation-states and form global solidarities based on shared beliefs. Beck exhorts the religious believer to let go of a rigid 'truth' to be able to establish 'peace', and to see other beliefs as an enrichment rather than a confrontation, which he refers as the 'clash of universalisms' (Beck 2010:164ff). Beck provides the example of Japan, which he argues, demonstrates the positive example of a 'syncretic tolerance' due to its polytheistic traditional beliefs which accommodate other deities (Beck 2010:62).

The argument that monotheism leads to violence whereas polytheism leads to accommodation of others is not new. Jonathan Kirsch argued that there was a 'war of God against gods', which 'has been fought with heart-shaking cruelty over the last thirty centuries, and it is a war that is still being fought today' (Kirsch 2004:2). Kirsch notes:

Monotheism turned out to inspire a ferocity and even a fanaticism that are mostly absent from polytheism. At the heart of polytheism is an open-minded and easy going approach to religious belief and practice, a willingness to entertain the idea that there are many gods and many ways to worship them. At the heart of monotheism, by contrast, is the sure conviction that only a single god exists, a tendency to regard one's own rituals and practices as the only proper way to worship the one true god. (Kirsch 2004:2)

As convincing as this argument sounds within its reasoning, it faces serious problems when tested against the history of violence in the world. While praising Japanese polytheism, for example, Beck ignores the fact that historically Christianity in Japan was wiped out with mass killings of thousands of Christians. In fact, 'Roman Catholics maintain that the campaign against Christianity which took place in Japan in the early 1600s was more ferocious than any other religious persecution in the history of the Church. They estimate that tens of thousands of Japanese Christians were put to death, many after being tortured' (Bartlett 2008). Similarly, widespread ethno-religious violence we see in Hindu (World Bulletin 2013) and Buddhist (Strathern 2013) communities today as well as in the violent history of many of the polytheistic pre-Abrahamic religions are simply left out (Timmer 2013). Beck universalizes an assumed intrinsic nature of religious beliefs and concludes an outcome, regardless of the context in which such beliefs emerge and are held, and projects a 'clash' between those who hold monotheistic beliefs and those who do not, whether in Europe or the Middle East, which leads him to see a global conflict unfolding. While not explicitly stated, Beck's argument also implies a lapse in human advancement that should by now have demonstrated a cosmopolitan accommodation and move beyond absolutisms. Thus, the religious believer finds him or herself once again as the root cause of violence, by virtue of their failure to adapt to the milieu we live in.

What all of these popular attempts to explain violence with religious characteristics in the world share is their fundamental belief that it is religions, religious beliefs, and identities that cause violence due to a claimed intrinsic nature they have. While attempting to explain a wide range of issues including conflicts in Africa and the Middle East, terrorism and the cohesion of migrant populations in Europe through a single variable, i.e., religion, these explanations construct a global fault line between 'us' and 'them'. The 'them' in this is often Islam and Muslims with their unbridgeable differences from 'us'. Those who hold religious beliefs in general represent a lapse in human advancement as embodied both by modernity (scientific advancement) and late modernity (cosmopolitan accommodation). Thus, it is no surprise that the reality of a resurgence of violence in the world only seems to prove the narrative they promote.

Deconstructing Assumptions

Awareness of assumptions that lead to such conclusions are crucial before one can even attempt to provide explanations. In fact, assumptions that are not examined and simply taken for granted as 'plain truths' are often exactly where explanations to complex matters start to go wrong. That is why the work of German philosopher Hans-Georg Gadamer on hermeneutics is vitally important in interpreting a 'text' as well as developments in the world. Gadamer argued that a person trying to understand a text often projects a meaning into it as soon as some meaning in the text is observed, and such an 'initial meaning emerges only because he is reading the text with particular expectations in regard to a certain meaning'. (Gadamer 2014:279). That is because, the way we understand the world before us is deeply affected by our context at a particular historic moment. Such a historic positioning 'determines in advance both what seems to us worth inquiring about and what will appear as an object of investigation' (Gadamer 2014:311). This conditioning gives us our prejudices: a judgement we hold before examining a situation (Gadamer 2014:283). As Gadamer warns, 'it is impossible to make ourselves aware of a prejudice while it is constantly operating unnoticed' (Gadamer 2014:310). That is why the interpreter and the text – the subject that seeks understanding and the object that is subjected to understanding – lives within horizons. Thus, the interpretation is ultimately an understanding of both of the two horizons: our own and that of the text (Gadamer 2014:313). It is, therefore, not a coincidence that the popular explanations on the relationship between religion and violence cited above contain declared and undeclared political visions, teleologies of linear human progress and *a priori* beliefs held about the place of religion and violence in the world. Incidentally, the horizon that all these views share is profoundly shaped by a particular form of European and North American modernity. This manifests itself as prejudices or assumptions in three critical areas that are central for this book: *religion, violence* and *constructs of civilization.*

Assumptions on Religion

A key prejudice is the perception of religion as an anomaly, and a factor that somehow represents the impediment to human progress, whether in advancement of a more liberal outlook (e.g., Ulrich Beck) or in scientific rationality (e.g., Richard Dawkins) or civilizational achievement (e.g., Huntington). The increase in religious terror attacks in the world since the 9/11 attacks have once again demonstrated this prejudice, widely held in Europe and North America. Islam and

Muslims have not fitted into common projections onto the world, in which religion ought to be a matter of personal belief, away from the public and political space, only dealing with the world to come, and declining as the person achieves education, scientific knowledge and liberalization. This belief in what the place of religion in the world ought to be can be seen throughout the history of the Enlightenment and have been integral in the project of modernity. They have been actively promoted as inescapable outcomes in much of the twentieth-century scholarly literature on secularization.

Jose Casanova distinguishes three different connotations of secularization: 'a) Secularization as the decline of religious beliefs and practices in modern societies, often postulated as a universal, human, developmental process'; 'b) Secularization as the privatization of religion, often understood both as a general modern historical trend and as a normative condition, indeed as a precondition for modern liberal democratic politics'; and 'c) Secularization as the differentiation of the secular spheres (state, economy, science), usually understood as 'emancipation' from religious institutions and norms' (Casanova 2006:7). All these three connotations can be seen as declared and undeclared assumptions about the role of religion in today's world in the arguments cited in the introduction. These were assumed to be a given by many scholars. In fact, in 1968, Berger had famously stated that by the '21st century, religious believers are likely to be found only in small sects, huddled together to resist a worldwide secular culture' (Stark & Finke 2000:58). This projection had a convincing rationale: the process of modernization meant that religion's role in providing an overarching meaning for the society and individual has been shaken. In the process, religious traditions have lost their monopoly and became just one of the contenders in a pluralistic market that have been limited to 'specific enclaves of social life' (Berger 1990:135). As the individual is exposed to multiple views beyond religion, 'the plausibility of religious definitions of reality is threatened from within, that is, within the subjective consciousness of the individual' (Berger, Berger & Kellner 1977:75). When the individual interacts with others from other traditions, or realizes the legitimacy of other interpretations of the world, 'the hold of religion on society and on the individual' is weakened (Berger, Berger & Kellner 1977:76). Therefore, as a result of the pluralism brought by secularization, religions should be in decline and significance.

Such a trajectory was seen to be inevitable, but developments across the world from the 1970s and onwards deeply challenged these assumptions. As Gilles Kepel notes in his *The Revenge of God* 'the 1970s was a decade of cardinal importance for the relationship between religion and politics, which has changed in unexpected ways during the last quarter of the twentieth century' (Kepel 2004:1). He notes that after World War II, it seemed that the realm of politics had broken away from religion, and that 'the influence of religion became restricted to the private or family sphere, and now seemed to have only an indirect effect on the way society was organised, like a leftover from the past' (Kepel 2004:1). He notes that 'around 1975 this whole process went into reverse. A new religious approach took shape, aimed no longer at adapting to secular values but as recovering a sacred foundation for the organization of society – by changing if necessary', which varies from 'Cairo or Algiers to Prague, from the American Evangelicals to the zealots of Gush Emunim, from Islamic militants to Catholic charismatics, from the Lubavitch to Communion and Liberation' (Kepel 2004:2). This reality pushed Peter Berger to abandon his earlier views on religions. He acknowledged that the idea that 'modernization necessarily leads to a decline of religion, both in society and in the minds of the individuals ... has turned out to be wrong' (Berger 1999:3). According to Berger, 'by and large, religious communities have survived and even flourished to the degree that they have not tried to adopt themselves to the alleged requirements of a secularized world' (Berger 1999:4). The world remains as 'furiously religious as it ever was, and in some places more so than ever' and this automatically means 'that a whole body of literature by historians and social scientists loosely labelled 'secularization theory' is essentially mistaken' (Berger 1999:2). Berger presents two main reasons for this unseen outcome. First of all, since the modernization process has underlined 'taken for granted' realities which people held and left them in an uncomfortable place, religions that provide strong certainty have gained great appeal. Secondly, the secular worldview is located in an elite intellectual group, which excludes many people, who out of resentment choose to join religions that have a strong anti-secular bent (Berger 1999:11).

In some sense, this should not have been surprising. Nietzsche came to realize that most of the secular ideals presupposed a moral ideal which was clearly Christian in origin. With his declaration of the metaphorical death of God in the *The Gay Science*, he called for a total break from the past (Nietzsche 1974:181–182, 279–280). The shadow of God, which lingered long after the death of God, had to be eradicated: human beings had to take up the task of the revaluation of all values. A similar view was shared by Auguste Comte, whose beliefs in scientific positivism have had tremendous impact on European views on secularization.[14] Comte shared Nietzsche's need for a revaluation of all values after the death of God, yet came to a different conclusion: the establishment of a positivist religion, with no deity but priests, sacraments, beliefs and services. In other words, the most radical attempts to declare an end to religion had resulted in only mimicking religion. Thus, when Ulrich Beck states that 'modern humanity is tormented by the idea that religious people might be utterly serious about their faith' (Beck 2010:63), he places his fingers on a deep pulse in particular readings of the world in Europe and North America that still hold onto an incoherent and now proven shaky teleology of secularization that is only reinvented and reapplied in frantic efforts to make sense of ethno-religious violence and religiously motivated terrorism in the world. The widespread presence of religion in the world is perceived as an alien factor that takes control of human beings in a powerful grip, disrupting a journey into the utopian perfection of modernity, lapsing humanity into the dark ages. What makes it all more interesting is that religious believers still make up the vast majority of the world numerically and it is the lack of religiosity in particular countries in Europe that remains as a global anomaly. Given that Europe enjoys a certain level of educational, scientific and economic achievement, it becomes tempting to explain the global importance of religion in terms of the lack of such achievements. In fact, economist Lester Thurow states that 'those who lose out economically or who cannot stand the economic uncertainty of not knowing what it takes to succeed in the new era ahead retreat into religious fundamentalism' (Quoted in Smith 1998:70). These historic views shape the prejudices and historical conditions through and within which much of the discussion on religion and its relationship with violent conflicts is made, thus posing serious problems in interpretation of the reality out there by starting from the assumptions of our own horizons. That is why religion and those who hold religious beliefs are seen as possessing lesser rationality and primitive attitudes. This inevitably frames the question as 'does religion lead to violence?' when faced with complex reports of conflicts with religious characteristics.

Assumptions on Violence

A similar problem of unspoken beliefs show itself in the treatment and perceptions of violence and violent conflict through paradigms of 'us' vs. 'them', the latter having a propensity towards violence and terror that 'we' do not have. In his *Thoughts on War and Death*, Sigmund Freud reflected on how the reality of World War I impacted European societies and noted that it had led to the 'destruction of an illusion' (Freud 1957:280). Freud stated that 'we welcome illusions because they spare us unpleasurable feelings, and enable us to enjoy satisfaction instead. We must not complain, then if not and again they come into collision with some portion of reality, and are shattered against it'. Freud argued that two things have aroused a sense of disillusionment: 'the low morality shown externally by states which in their internal relations pose as the guardians of moral standards, and the brutality shown by individuals whom, as participants in the highest human civilisation, one would have not thought capable of such behaviour' (Freud 1957:280). In fact, Freud says that the basis of disillusionment 'on account of the uncivilized behaviour of our fellow-citizens of the world' was unjustified, because it was 'based on an illusion to which we had given way. In reality our fellow-citizens have not sunk so low as we feared, because they had never risen so high as we believed' (Freud 1957:283).

The illusion of 'civilized Europe' did not merely suffer through the cognitive dissonance of perceiving events outside of its control. As Zygmunt Bauman noted, what made the Holocaust possible was the very ideals of the modern society, such as the advancement of mankind, industrial and scientific progress, a 'harmonious, orderly and deviation-free society' (Bauman 2002:51). In fact, what is most chilling about Bauman's arguments is how natural the process of exterminating millions of people in Europe seemed to be to those who planned and carried it out. In *Modernity and the Holocaust*, Bauman notes 'that most of the perpetrators of the genocide were normal people, who will freely flow through any known psychiatric sieve, however dense, is morally disturbing. It is also theoretically puzzling, particularly when seen conjointly with the "normality" of those organizational structures that co-ordinated the actions of such normal individuals into an enterprise of genocide' (Bauman 1989:19). That is why Hannah Arendt's observations on the trial of Eichmann and her concept of 'banality of evil' have stood the test of time in unmasking any constructs that see an 'evil' barbarian in the 'other'. Arendt noted that psychiatrists who examined Eichmann found him to be normal and healthy, and 'that his whole psychological outlook, his attitude towards his wife and children, mother, and father, brothers, sisters, and friends, was "not only normal but most desirable"' (Arendt 2002:94).

The conditions of World War II could be vulnerable to being relativized as an extreme experience. In his bestselling book *The Better Angels of Our Nature: Why Violence Has Declined,* Steven Pinker argues that the world is less violent than ever before in human history. This is due to historical developments such as the containment of violence by modern states, the human rights movement, trade, advancement of human knowledge and enlightenment ideals as well as further development of human potential for empathy (Pinker 2011). Pinker makes grand philosophical assumptions that result in the relativization of the unprecedented levels of violence seen in the twentieth century and the 'civilized' world that embodies these 'advancements' (Gray 2015). It is also problematic to use death rates from previous wars as the basis for arguing that comparatively lower mortality rates than from wars in previous eras mean a decline of human violence (Arquilla 2012). Simply because this is no guarantee that the next century will not be bloodier than the current one. A staggering truth remains, as Hinton points out, 'during the twentieth century alone, sixty million people were annihilated by genocidal regimes' (Hinton 2002:1). Girard noted that what made global developments worrying today is not the intensity of the violence or comparisons of the number of dead today with that of yesterday, but 'that the *unpredictability of violence* is what is new' (Girard 2010:68). In fact, new studies have demonstrated that the last decade has seen an increase in violent incidents globally. The report 'Global Peace Index 2015' released by the Institute for Economics and Peace (IEP) note that while it is in fact true that 'in Europe and in many other developed countries, homicide rates and other forms of interpersonal violence continue to drop and are at historic laws', there is a deterioration of peace across the world with some 86 countries seeing an increase in violence during the last eight years (IEP 2015:3). Similarly, a study by the International Institute for Strategic Studies found that even though there were fewer wars, there has been an 'inexorable intensification of violence', citing some 56,000 fatalities in 63 active conflicts in the world in 2008, which increased to 180,000 fatalities in the world from 42 active conflicts in 2014 (Norton-Taylor 2015). Norton-Taylor notes that the 'World Bank estimates that 1.2 billion people, roughly one-fifth of the world's population, are affected by some form of violence or insecurity' (Norton-Taylor 2015). What makes this cold fact all the more bitter is that the occurrence of violence and mass atrocities such as ethnic cleansing and genocides are 'neither particular to a specific race, class, or nation, nor rooted in any one ethnocentric view of the world' (Harff 2000:41). Michael Mann makes a startling conclusion from his research into mass atrocities:

If I have learned one thing from my research, it is that, placed in comparable situations and similar social constituencies, you or I might also commit murderous ethnic cleansing. No people are invulnerable. (Mann 2000:12)

In fact, neither the colonial history of European powers, nor the mass atrocities committed by Christian Serbs against Bosnian Muslims, the Christian priests and nuns actively partaking in the Tutsi genocide in Rwanda and currently Christian militias murdering thousands of Muslims in Central African Republic in an ethnic cleansing project allow one the comfort of constructing a sense that violence is alien to the civilized 'we' and a propensity for the 'other'.

The illusion that Freud observed, however, continues against all the odds, since contemporary human beings are exposed daily to the reality of widespread global violence. But such incidents in the news remain as dispatches from another land that is still 'developing' and somehow not at the same civilizational achievement as 'us'. Thus, what shocks a European or North American in a terror attack on their homelands is the confrontation of reality that reminds them of conditions beyond the confinements of their own horizons, fixed and managed within particular historic conditions. Wars that are fought out there, return home, and violence so eloquently kept away confronts us in our own streets. Its traumatic impact on our assumptions can only be tamed in heroic notions of the 'defence of our freedoms' and our 'way of life' and languages of 'good' and 'evil'.

A key element of this historic condition is the success of modern states in Europe and North America in managing and containing violence. Max Weber noted that 'the relation between the state and violence is an especially intimate one', and argued that 'a state is a human community that (successfully) claims the *monopoly of the legitimate use of physical force* within a given territory', thus 'the state is considered the sole source of the 'right' to use violence' (Weber 1948:78). This supports Walter Burkett's assertion that 'all orders and forms of authority in human society are founded on institutional-ized violence' (Burkett 1983:1). Whether through its military forces or security forces, the modern state seizes the use of violence from indi-viduals and promises to enforce justice and give protection both from crime and from mass violence such as wars. As Albrow put it, 'the nation-state did not simply monopolize legitimate violence, it managed it and shaped the public expression of emotion' (Albrow 1996:57). Thus, a Western individual experiences a sense of 'peace' and 'stability' as the norm and violence as a propensity of the other, while not being able to see how their own experiences of stability and security and economic progress depends on their own states and peoples use of violence across history. Thus, enquiries into violence with religious characteristics start with a "fore-projection" that violence is an alien factor and could only be seen as the outcome of a lapse in human achievement, thought and rationality, caused by religious beliefs or civilizational predispositions that are different from 'ours'. It is no surprise, therefore, that Richard Dawkins, Bernard Lewis and Samuel Huntington can easily ask the question 'Does Islam lead to violence?' when confronted with the reality of violence related to Muslims, but they do not ask 'Does Christianity lead to violence?' or 'Does scientific advancement and rationality lead to violence?' In fact, given the his-toric evidence of violence emerging in pluralistic societies such as India, or even in the ones that Ulrich Beck cites as 'proof' for his argument such as Japan, he does not seem to even entertain the question 'Does pluralism lead to violence?'

Assumptions on Civilizations

While the word 'civilization' is largely used in the public discourse in Europe and North America as a marker of accomplishment or advance-ment, Huntington distinguishes his vocabulary of 'civilisations', in the plural, from the use of 'civilisation', in the singular, with the latter being an eighteenth-century European use as an opposite of 'barbarism' and signifying advancement (Huntington 1996:40–41). For Huntington, civilizations are a complex product of culture, identity, religion and history, uniting a multiplicity of communities living in multiple states. He acknowledges the difficulty emerging from such a wide brush stroke of boundaries by stating that 'civilizations have no clear-cut boundaries and no precise beginnings and endings. People can and do define their identities and, as a result, the composition and shapes of civilizations change over time. The cultures of peoples interact and overlap' (Huntington 1996:43). For Huntington, the major contemporary civilizations are: Sinic, Japanese, Hindu, Islamic, Orthodox, Western (including Europe, North America, Australia and New Zealand), Latin American and 'possibly African' (Huntington 1996:45, 46, 47). It is striking that Huntington's typologies of civilizations are based upon religions, which automatically creates multiple problems and inconsistencies. For example, why is Western civilization separated from Latin American and Orthodox civilizations if they are all Christians? In contrast, why lump some one billion Muslims spread across the world into a single category, when South Asian, African, Middle Eastern and European Muslims have as much distinct cultural, linguistic and political differences as Latin American, Western and Orthodox Christians? The problem with such categorizations is one reason why Huntington briefly notes a 'possibly' African civilization, since the continent is divided in its religious topography. Such a project of mapping of civilizations inevitability raises more questions than any heuristic opportunities.

A most helpful critique of Huntington's theory comes from Jonathan Fox (2002b) in the form of a quantitative assessment of Huntington's predictions, particularly in the types of conflict defined by Huntington as 'fault line conflicts', which directly relate to this book as stated in the introduction. In his analysis, Fox acknowledges that there is an operationalization challenge in that Huntington's typologies of civilizations are 'in many places not nearly specific enough for use in categorizing groups, especially minority groups' (Fox 2002b:422). Fox also points out Huntington's inconsistency in regards to a Buddhist civilization, where he states there is such a civilization in some parts of his work then denies in it others, later including Buddhists in Sinic/Confucian civilization (Fox 2002b:422). Fox notes a problem of

Huntington's definitions of the African civilizations, which is 'wholly based on identity and culture and has no obvious religious component', which creates problems in where to locate African-Americans and Muslim groups in Africa (Fox 2002b:423). Does the former belong to Africa or the West? Does the latter belong to the Islamic civilization and not to the African? Fox notes that such difficulties in operationalizing Huntington's concept of civilizations raise questions about the validity of Huntington's book. While taking the theory at its face level, Fox uses yearly data from the Minorities at Risk Phase 3 (MAR3) between 1985 and 1998. Fox finds that 'civilizational conflicts make up only a minority of ethnic conflicts in the post-Cold War era, constituting 37.8 per cent (104 out of 275) of the conflicts. Almost half of the conflicts are non-civilizational constituting 47.6 per cent (131) of the conflicts. Indigenous conflicts constitute 14.5 per cent (40) of them. This situation differs little from the situation before the end of the Cold War' (Fox 2002b:427). Fox also found that the data has not supported Huntington's expectations of a Sinic/Confucian-Islamic tension with the West, as 'three of these civilizations engage in more clashes within their civilizations than with any other civilizations' and that 'there are only twelve clashes between the West and either Islamic or Sinic/Confucian groups. This constitutes only 4.4 per cent of the 275 ethnic conflicts contained in the entire MAR3 database' (Fox 2002b:429). Thus, as Fox notes, there is not an increase in claimed civilizational clashes since the end of Cold War era, and conflicts that are characterised as civilizational only constitute a small number of conflicts in the world.

It is clear that while Huntington is right in noting the significance of religion in today's world and conflicts that relate to religious themes, events in the world since the end of the Cold War do not correspond to his paradigm of dividing the world into six or seven civilizations and giving them intrinsic qualities and fixed teleologies. What is most peculiar is the horizon from which Huntington sees the world. Perhaps a clue for that is found in the fact that his entire project is built from within a framework of the Cold War with its three-category world and seeks to read the world through its continual legacy while stating the fragmentation that follows it. In fact, Huntington does not hide what he carries over from the intellectual legacy of the Cold War into his forecasts of the future:

For forty years students and practitioners of international relations thought and acted in terms of the highly simplified but very useful Cold War paradigm of world affairs. This paradigm could not account for everything that went on in world politics. There were many anomalies, to use Kuhn's term, at times the paradigm blinded scholars and statesmen to major developments, such as Sino-Soviet split. Yet as a simple model of global politics, it accounted for more important phenomena than any of its rivals, it was an essential starting point for thinking about international affairs, it came to be almost universally accepted, and it shaped thinking about world politics for two generations. (Huntington 1996:30)

Thus, the conflicts in the world and new trends are read through the lens of the Cold War, which shaped his generation profoundly. Interestingly, Huntington confirms 'the tendency to think in terms of two worlds recurs throughout human history. People are always tempted to divide people into us and them, the in-group and the other, our civilization and those barbarians', but he believes that 'depending upon how the parts are defined, a two-part world picture may in some measure correspond with reality' (Huntington 1996:32). This perception of 'reality' that is in fact the most decisive factor, and an anthropological truth which we will return to later on in the book.

All of these fore-projections on religion, violence and constructs of civilization serve as a filter through which developments in the world are to be understood. Schemes used to modify them to fit into narratives are more telling about ourselves than the events in the world. A vast array of unspoken assumptions, perceptions and anxieties drives not only the questions asked but also the answers given, and ultimately the solutions proposed. These 'prejudices', as Gadamer noted, play an important part in what Pierre Bourdieu named as 'habitus': 'a system of durable, transposable dispositions, structured structures predisposed to function as structuring structures, that is, as principles which generate and organize practices and representations that can be objectively adapted to their outcomes without presupposing a conscious aiming at ends' (quoted in Swartz 2002:625). A habitus that is formed by a narrative more than a hundred years old of the projects of modernity and enlightenment, together with the Cold War, inescapably plays an important part in any attempt to understand a world that seems to not fit in to mental schemes and assumptions deeply internalized and unquestioned. William Cavanaugh draws attention to a further utility in such assumptions.

He notes that 'in what are called "Western" societies, the attempt to create a transhistorical and transcultural concept of religion that is essentially prone to violence is one of the foundational legitimating myths of the liberal nation-states. The myth of religious violence helps to construct and marginalize a religious Other, prone to fanaticism, to contrast with the rational, peace-making, secular subject' (Cavanaugh 2009:4).

Pointing out to problematic assumptions held and thus inadequate answers provided by popular explanations of the relationship between religion and violence in today's world, however, does not necessarily take away the validity of their concerns over increasing violence across the world with religious characteristics. It is clear that we cannot simply ignore that religion is an important aspect of some violent conflicts in the world, not least because stakeholders in such conflicts say and believe it is so. Therefore, some key questions remain unanswered: What is the relationship between religion and violent conflict in today's world? Do religions in general, if not particularly Islam, cause such conflicts? Specifically, are we really witnessing an escalation to extremes at a planetary level between followers of the world's two largest religions, Islam and Christianity, showing itself in local conflicts between Muslim and Christian communities?

This book seeks to answer these questions and provide an alternative explanation that is grounded in insights inferred from actual cases of ethno-religious violence. It attempts to move on from prejudices shaped by European and North American assumptions and almost exclusive and often myopic interest on religious terrorism. It does so by first looking closely at two frequently cited cases of violence between Muslim and Christian ethnic groups in Africa and Middle East. It seeks to establish whether religion plays such a causal role in these cases as claimed by popular explanations. It then compares the cases to each other to be able to observe similarities in the factors that contribute to the emergence of ethno-religious violence before providing insights gained from such an exercise and theoretical reflections on the complex relationship between religion and violent conflict in today's world.

The book demonstrates that popular explanations of the causes of violence with religious characteristics are not sustainable when tested against actual cases of ethno-religious conflict. It argues that while there are close links between violence and religion, ultimately, religions are not the causes of such violence. It notes that violence has been an integral aspect of the history of Homo sapiens, and not simply a propensity of a particular group of people as promoted by popular explanations, and that its occurrence is an ever-present possibility if certain conditions are met. While disproving a causal role in religion's place in the emergence of violent conflicts, the book points out that religion has been an effective mechanism both to contain and enable its execution. Unlike the common question of whether religious beliefs result in violence, this book notes that religions are often shaped by exposure to violence due to religions' intrinsic role in enabling human beings to make sense of and respond to a chaotic world. The book argues that there is in fact a link between the local conflicts with global developments, though not in the way explained by popular theories. These developments trigger new forms of violence, most worryingly, and contribute to the reification of languages and imageries of cosmic wars used by ethno-religious communities in the legitimizations of violence. In return, local incidents are picked up by international networks in line with their sensitivities and agendas, promoted and used for their own local contexts, thus providing a contagion mechanism that spreads local conflicts and triggers tensions elsewhere. Thus, what we are witnessing is not an intrinsic outcome of a primordial clash between civilizations, or an inevitable clash of religions playing themselves out across the globe. Instead it is something equally petrifying: self-fulfilling prophecies of Manichean battles between 'us' and 'them' with devastating outcomes.

The Question of Method

While the reader might now jump into the following chapters analyzing the cases and offering an explanation based on them, those with a scholarly interest are probably already troubled with the complex methodological decisions that lie at the core of this book. Therefore, allow me to offer an account of methodological choices I have made while conducting the research for this book, which could be skipped by those who are less inclined to find such a preamble enticing.

Both the phenomenon this book seeks to address and the research strategy it follows in order to be able to do so pose significant conceptual and methodological challenges. First of all, any discussion of religion and violence cuts across multiple scholarly disciplines. As mentioned previously in the discussion of problematic assumptions made by popular explanations of religious violence in the world, any attempt to address the topic requires engagement with a wide range of scholarly literature in theology, history, philosophy, anthropology, sociology and political science. This is due to the complexity of the place of religion and violence in the human experience, and the scholarly compartmentalization of knowledge and methodologies that are only able to partially address aspects of the issues surrounding the relationship of religion with violence. Thus, while the basic parameters of this book are grounded within the framework of political science and political theory, it often crosses beyond the languages of both disciplines in order to be able to provide answers to the questions it sets out to answer. Secondly, the research strategy that the book follows equally demands a multidisciplinary approach in analysis and theoretical speculation from its findings. The methodological approaches the book follows can be demonstrated under three categories: choosing the cases, analyzing the cases and comparison of the cases.

Choosing the Cases

As David Collier argues, comparisons of a small number of cases – in this case only two, 'sharpens our power of description, and plays a central role in concept-formation by bringing into focus suggestive similarities and contrasts and among cases' (Collier 1993:105). In such a comparative analysis, the selection of the cases is important to ensure that they do not reflect a bias that might set itself to prove the argument put forward by the book. They also have to serve as an adequate basis to answer the research questions. In the process of finalizing the cases compared in this book, certain principles have been followed: cases must see a history of violence between Christian and Muslim communities in Africa and the Middle East; they must be accessible for research visits and have adequate scholarly work to interact with; they must share enough similarities to be able to make reasonable comparisons but also distinct structures, features and differences to be able to assess questions on the claimed universal impact of religions on conflicts and they must be among common examples cited in discussions of a global conflict between Christianity and Islam.

Based upon these principles, two countries were chosen as case studies: Nigeria, a country with a multiplicity of ethno-religious communities that sees high levels of violence between Muslims and Christians and Egypt, a country with a majority Muslim population and a Christian minority that is often targeted in violent episodes and persecuted. Both countries are the most populous countries in Africa and the Middle East. Nigeria is a major geopolitical power in West Africa, and Egypt in North Africa and the Middle East. Ethno-religious violence in both countries frequently features in international media reports, and both cases are regularly cited in public discussions on an imagined clash between Islam and Christianity, or the West and Islam.[15] Both countries have a substantial amount of scholarship written about their history, and both countries can be visited and research carried out within certain limitations unlike other countries in the regions with ongoing violent ethno-religious conflicts such as CAR, Sudan, Syria and Iraq. Both countries occupy an important place in Huntington's arguments about types of countries that see a civilizational clash.[16] Yet, the two countries differ significantly, both in political structures and characteristics of the ethno-religious violence within their borders. While in Egypt violence is directed towards an ethno-religious minority in a Muslim-majority society, in Nigeria Christian and Muslim ethnic communities have roughly the same percentage of the population. The countries are geographically, culturally and linguistically distinct from each other, thus providing a clear break from the most visible similarities of religions. Thus, the comparison of Nigeria and Egypt is not only possible within the limits of a book project, but also possible due to their comparability and accessibility and direct relevance for the research questions posed.

Analyzing the Cases

This book follows a conventional case-oriented analysis, which uses multiple methods to explore complex processes and relationships in a detailed manner (Newton & Deth 2010:404). To be able to do so, it draws analytic approaches from the literature on ethnic conflict, most particularly the highly relevant multi-layer analysis approach developed by Karl Cordell and Stefan Wolff (Cordell & Wolff 2010). They propose that there are four levels that must be addressed in a nuanced analysis of ethnic conflict: a) the local level: actors, issues and structures that impact the conflict at the sub-state or local level; b) the state level: political, economic, cultural and social dynamics at the national state level that shape and impact the conflict; c) the regional level: neighbouring states, institutions and networks as well as political, religious and cultural developments and d) the global level: international non-governmental organizations, powerful state interests, international bodies and developments that impact the conflict (Cordell & Wolff 2010:8–9). However, unique features of ethno-religious violence that distinguish it from other ethnic conflicts is the theological and theo-political thought that becomes integral, if not directly involved, in the development and responses to the conflict. Thus, this book integrates not only the four layers proposed above in its analysis of origins and dynamics of social and political tensions, but also a fifth, theo-political, level: religious ideologies and responses that impact, emerge in response to or are utilized by actors in violent conflict. This layer is particularly important to help in decoding the way in which religion, or specifically monotheism or Islam, is interwoven in ethno-religious conflict. The case study chapters narrate all these layers within a chronological order of major political developments in both countries to be able to provide an overall context before focusing closely on particular violent conflicts. They integrate available scholarship on the histories, politics, cultures, religions and conflicts in the two case-study countries, with contemporary studies, policy and news reports of violent incidents. They also draw from in-depth interviews held in Nigeria and Egypt. Given the levels of fatal violence levels and intimidation by state officials, it is no surprise that most individuals interviewed requested anonymity and no audio recording and allowed only limited transcription and quotations for public use. Such sensitivities were handled with the utmost ethical care. Though some conversations and especially identities of contacts could have provided attractive quotes for use in this book, or demonstrated first-hand exposure to issues, they have not been used or listed with biographical and geographic details to protect the participants.

Comparing the Cases

A key element of developing an answer to the questions considered in this book is the comparison of the individual cases. While the two countries selected have different political, social, cultural, religious and historical features, the outcome is the same: widespread violence between Muslim and Christian ethno-religious communities. What this book seeks to answer is whether or not such an outcome is due to an intrinsic quality of religion, religious beliefs and identities defined through imagined boundaries of so-called civilizations. Therefore, while assuming differences in variables in each case study that contributes to a shared outcome, the primary aim is to identify common features that emerge through the comparison. If the hypotheses put forward by the three theories developed by Huntington, Dawkins & Beck on why such violence occurs are correct, then it should be observed as similarities in different cases of violent conflict regardless of their local contexts. Thus, the most relevant comparative strategy for the aims of this book is the Most Different Systems Design (MDSD), which 'compares countries that do not share any common features apart from the political outcome to be explained and one or two of the explanatory factors seen to be important for that outcome' (Landman 2008:70). The MDSD is based upon the 'method of agreement' developed by John Stuart Mill. Mill distinguished between two types of comparison that seek to explain causal relations through different analytic strategies: the method of agreement and the method of difference. As Newton and Deth point out, Mill noted that 'if a phenomenon occurs in two or more situations then the explanation for the phenomenon must lie in the common features of those situations'. (Newton & Deth 2010:406)

One must acknowledge the limits and risks of any comparative study, not least of which is this book's ambitious theoretical aims. The methods and cases that are chosen have ramifications for the logic that underlines the arguments (Keman 2006:16). Similarly, 'selection bias' might result in intentional and unintentional mistaken inferences and reaching to misleading conclusions based up on choice of cases (Geddes 1990:132, 133). While, as explained previously, selecting Nigeria and Egypt as the cases to compare has a legitimate grounding; nevertheless, it is still vulnerable to such a bias. However, as Douglas Dion argues, such a bias could be dealt with if the selection of cases based on the dependent variable is for 'evaluating necessary (as opposed to sufficient) conditions' for the studied phenomenon to occur (Dion 1998:127). While warning of the potential risk of selection bias, Geddes too acknowledges that comparative analysis of a limited number of cases is ideal for in-depth insights as well as highlighting anomalies and revising theories. (Geddes 1990:149).

This is exactly what this book seeks to achieve by thorough stand-alone analysis of both cases as independent chapters, and then a comparison, inferring insights from the cases and comparison between them to challenge common assumptions and perspectives on the relationship of violent conflict with religion in today's world. It offers a unique line of enquiry by not only undertaking a comparative study, but also producing theoretical reflections that serve to move the analysis beyond one particular national context and take account of the globalization process and its impact on local ethno-religious conflicts. It also seeks to challenge the common conversations on religion and violent conflict in Europe and North America that are often limited to questions of countering violent extremism and international terrorism. Religious terrorism is only an expression of the larger question of religion and violence. Therefore, while the book is limited in its empirical basis, its theoretical formulations have a much wider use for those seeking to decode the relationship of religion and conflict in today's world.

2 | Religious Violence in Nigeria

There is simply no place like Nigeria. Its energy, complexity, history and challenges are dizzying. It is a continent turned into a country with the trick of border lines on a map. There you meet some of the funniest, most resourceful, resilient and profound people you can ever meet in the world. Yet, Nigeria mostly makes the international news with its email tricksters, corruption and violent militants. Religious violence in Nigeria has particularly attracted widespread global media attention since the summer of 2014 when Boko Haram abducted some 276 school girls in the small rural town of Chibok in northeast Nigeria on 14 April (HRW 2014a). The victims were subjected to gross violations. A campaign launched by the families of kidnapped girls and Nigerian activists, called Bring Back Our Girls, captured international attention and spread fast as an online form of solidarity expressed by millions of people around the world (Pesta 2015). However, as Chandler noted, the violence linked to Boko Haram went far beyond the April 2014 abductions: 'fifteen thousand people have died in violence related to the group's insurgency since 2009 . . . The civilian death toll since the start of 2014 alone has eclipsed 5,500' (Chandler 2015). In fact, aside from attacks by Boko Haram, the country has seen unprecedented levels of violence along ethno-religious lines, particularly in the Middle Belt region where Muslim and Christian ethnic groups live in mixed populations, or in northeastern Nigeria where non-Muslims, as well as Muslims, find themselves victims of extremist groups and mob violence.

What happens in Nigeria has substantial implications for West Africa and larger Muslim-Christian communities across the Sahel region. Nigeria is the most populous country in Africa with an estimated more than 155 million citizens and one of the continent's largest economies. More than 250 ethnic groups and around 500 languages form the country's complicated ethnic tapestry. While exact ratios of ethnic groups and religions are impossible to assert since the issue is an extremely political one, the CIA World Fact Book, in broad agreement with most other sources, breaks down the major ethnic formation of the country as Hausa and Fulani 29 per cent, Yoruba 21 per cent, Igbo (Ibo) 18 per cent, Ijaw 10 per cent, Kanuri 4 per cent, Ibibio 3.5 per cent and Tiv 2.5 per cent (Central Intelligence Agency). Islam and Christianity almost evenly compose 90 per cent of the country and the remaining 10 per cent is made of traditional African religions. The Pew Research Centre notes that 'the Muslim population in Nigeria is projected to increase by more than 50 per cent in the next 20 years, from about 76 million in 2010 to about 117 million in 2030. If current trends continue, Nigeria will have a slight Muslim majority by 2030' (Pew 2011). This means that Muslims will make up around 51 per cent of the population by 2030. The vast majority of Muslims are Sunnis, with a small portion of Shiites and smaller communities of Sufis and Ahmadiyas. The majority of Christians are Protestants, either of various Nigerian and African Evangelical denominations or Anglican. Pentecostal and independent churches are increasing fast and mega-size churches with thousands of worshippers springing up especially in southern Nigeria. The religious demography of the country is visible in geographical terms: northern Nigeria is predominantly Muslim and southern Nigeria is predominantly Christian, the so-called Middle Belt that lies between the two is evenly occupied.

Nigeria's size, as well as the complexity of its populations, religious trends and turbulent political history makes any reduction of the causes behind such extreme levels of religious violence in the country to religious beliefs alone problematic. This chapter first provides a background to the current ethno-religious violence and political tensions in the country, starting with the emergence of Nigeria under British colonial rule then into independence. It provides a history of how both ethnic identities and religious solidarities evolved along with local, national and international developments, and how these developments are linked to the violence we see in Nigeria today. It provides a multi-layered approach to decode developments that have increasingly given religion and religious actors a major role in national politics. It then focuses on religion-related violence in the country, before offering preliminary reflections as to why and how such violence emerged, and how it interacts and impacts religions. The chapter ends with a preliminary conclusion, summarising key points from the case study in line with the research questions.

Background

About 90 per cent of Nigerians identify as Muslim or Christian today, but both Islam and Christianity are relatively recent religions in the history of the people of Western Africa, which has spanned thousands of years with numerous kingdoms, tribes and local animistic and ancestral religions and customs.[1] Both religions followed trade routes, entering the area now referred to as Nigeria from different directions: Christianity from the south and west, Islam from the north and northeast. The legacy of these developments continues to show itself in the geographical dominance of these religions in modern-day Nigeria.

Adamolekun argues that the people of Nigeria's first contact with Christianity was in 1472 when Portuguese missionaries arrived in the Delta region but that until the close of the eighteenth century, Christianity did not gain any substantial ground (Adamolekun 2012:2). In fact, it was not really until late in the nineteenth century that Christian missionaries from Europe and North America began effective proselytism campaigns in the region, overlapping with both the advancement of colonial expeditions and the evangelical revival happening in missionary-sending countries. This resulted in various missionary groups, Baptists and Anglicans as well as European Catholic and North European Protestant groups, arriving in Nigeria (Komolafe 2013:39–55). Methodist and Anglican mission boards were followed by Baptists and Roman Catholics, mostly active in the southern regions of Nigeria (Adogame 2010:484). Throughout the twentieth century, the Nigerian church saw rapid nationalization with local leadership, associations and theological education. Indigenous mission movements spread local churches independent of established historic churches. It was not until the later part of twentieth century that Christianity spread rapidly across northern Nigeria, both due to conversion from animistic religions and among Hausa-Fulanis as well as migration to the Middle Belt and north from other parts of Nigeria (Gaiya 2004).

As Abiodun Aloa points out, Islamic presence in Nigeria had two distinct phases; before and after the nineteenth century (Aloa 2009:6). He notes that Islam came to the northeast of today's Nigeria in the eleventh and twelfth centuries through scholars and trade merchants from North Africa, resulting in its spread along the trade routes and becoming more significant among the elites in the Kanem Bornu Empire, particularly during the reign of Dunama Dabalemi

(1221–1259) (Aloa 2009:6). Increasingly Islam and Arabic language spread across northern Nigeria in Hausa and Kanuri lands, offering chances for further trade for local rulers, alongside a new religion that could grant them spiritual and political power over their subjects as well as new solidarities with other powerful Muslim rulers and peoples (Falola & Heaton 2008:30). However, as with Christianity, it took centuries for Islam to achieve a strong social and political significance. Even though across the north, there were Hausa and Fulani rulers and tribes who adopted Islam en masse, many were syncretic and unorthodox in their understanding and practice of Islam with a strong continuation of their pre-Islamic traditions and beliefs (Falola & Heaton 2008:32). Their unorthodox relationship with Islam and heavy-handed rule of the common people led to an Islamic renewal movement that sought to reform beliefs of the common people and challenge the abuse of power by rulers, which gave birth to the second phase of Islam's expansion in Nigeria.

This second phase began in the early nineteenth century, when the Islamic scholar and preacher Othman Dan Fodio launched a jihad with the aim of reforming what he saw to be the corruption, syncretism and unfairness of the Muslim rulers in the north. From reformist preaching, which got him into trouble and led to his brief exile from the city of Gobir, he moved on to declare a military jihad both to restore Islam and to expand and unite the diverse populations under an Islamic banner. He was joined by a wide range of Hausas and Fulanis reacting against their local rulers. He managed to bring disparate groups together, creating a Caliphate with Sokoto as its capital, eventually controlling over 1,500 square miles of northern Nigeria (Badejogbin 2013:231). He maintained tight control through appointed emirs handling particular regions with the rigid application of Shari'a laws. More than thirty emirates were subsequently created (Adogame 2010:482). A centralized governance system based on Islamic principles and using Arabic language, which was not widely known, enabled a divine legitimization for the autocratic rule of Dan Fodio, now the new Sultan of the Caliphate. His rule included the passing of the title to his son after his death and forcing of heavy taxes, discrimination, forced migration and military campaigns against any Muslim or non-Muslims who did not ascribe to the Caliphate (Ejiogu 2011:93–95).

While Dan Fodio's jihad began the unification of the northern region and its peoples under a single rule, ultimately Nigeria's emergence as a single political unit owes itself to British colonial rule. The British eventually won the competition with France for the territory. From earlier trade agreements in southern parts of the land in the late nineteenth century, British interests gradually expanded from trade through private companies into full colonial control by 1903 after conquering the Sokoto Caliphate (Falola 1998:51). The country's name was a term invented by a British journalist who had married the first Governor-General of the British colonial administration, Lord Lugard (Hill 2012:1). The journalist, Dame Flora Louisa Shaw, in an essay published by the *Times* on 8 January 1898, suggested that 'it may be permissible to coin a shorter title for the agglomeration of pagan and Mahomedan States which have been brought, by the exertion of the Royal Niger Company, within the confines of a British protectorate', which, she noted as 'Nigeria' (Adebanwi & Obadare 2010:388).

Managing such a complex territory and its peoples with limited military capacity and dubious trade agreements with local chieftains was no easy task for the British colonial engagement with Africa. Berman notes that colonial rulers, therefore, developed a 'divide and rule' strategy, which confined social activities into local administrative subdivisions, each containing a single culturally and linguistically defined community, directed by their indigenous structures and discipline processes, thus not only fragmenting the possibility of a united discontent across the land against the colonial rulers, but also drawing legitimacy and indirect control from traditional social structures (Berman 1998:315). This was the policy formulated and executed by the British administration of Nigeria. In his book *The Dual Mandate in British Tropical Africa* published in 1922, Lord Lugard not only clearly expressed his views of the peoples of Africa and Nigeria, but also spelt out his policy of indirect rule. He observed that all stages of social organization could be seen across the land, from tribes with basic units of family and social relations to highly organized ones (Lugard 1922:75). He argued that the arrival of Islam had been 'a creative and regenerating force', bringing a written language, organization, strong governance and clear guidelines; rather than revoking local customs, it contained them and provided continuation on issues such as polygamy, slavery, invasion, combat and looting of the spoils of war

(Lugard 1922:76–78). In contrast, Lugard argued that Christianity did not bring a strong social and political organization to the people, and its emphasis on sexual purity, kindness, forgiveness, humility and 'its recognition of brotherhood with the slave, the captive, and the criminal do not altogether appeal to the temperament of the negro' (Lugard 1922:78). In contrast to conversion to Islam, Lugard saw that conversion to Christianity tended to lead to a cultural rejection of older customs, and that Christianity played a 'constructive' role as it was combined with Western education (Lugard 1922:78). In fact, the issue of Christian education raising new generations of southern Nigerians for administrative posts and occupations, such as medicine and law, became increasingly a point of contention between Muslims and Christians. Falola states that 'religious tensions had started to build as early as 1930 as the Muslim elite became increasingly upset by the power and arrogance of the Christian elite', due to their own 'comparatively slow acquisition of Western education' (Falola 1998:7).

Lugard's comments on the 'educated African' included their 'desire for a larger individual and collective responsibility and liberty', which Lugard saw as 'the natural outcome of British teaching' and that this may be 'regarded as indications of progress' (Lugard 1922:83). It is in fact this 'progress' of civilization that formed the dual purpose of British rule: both a realistic acknowledgement of the trade interests of the West, and with it, the civilizational advancement of the native populations. Lugard summarized his vision for advancing Nigeria and his policy of managing such a large swath of land with the following statement:

The British Empire, as General Smuts has well said, has only one mission – for liberty and self-development on no standardised lines, so that all may feel that their interests and religion are safe under the British flag. Such liberty and self-development can be best secured to the native population by leaving them free to manage their own affairs through their own rulers, proportionately to their degree of advancement, under the guidance of the British staff, and subject to the laws and policy of the administration. (Lugard 1922:94)

His understanding of the complex human geography and how best to engage with it to secure British interests and prevent uprisings as well as to develop natives to fulfil administrative roles became a template not only for his governorship of Nigeria but for colonial rule all across the British Empire.

In 1914, the Northern and Southern Nigeria protectorates were amalgamated as Nigeria. In the late 1940s, the British colonial administration then divided the Nigerian territory into three administrative zones. The three zones – the North, East and West – implied the ruling power of the three ethnic groups that dominated those three geographical spreads, the Hausa, Igbo and Yoruba. This gave British rulers control over three major groups and indirect rule through their privileged position, which in return meant that 'the three major ethnic groups believed it was their destiny to dictate the future of Nigerian political, social and development.

Each sought to out-maneuver the others to become the dominant influence in shaping policy' (Nnoli 1995:31). Ejiogu notes that 'in contrast to the Igbo and Yoruba, members of the Fulani ruling elite were quick to reconcile themselves to British conquest. They even identified them as benefactors' (Ejiogu 2011:17). As an example, Ejiogu cites the post-independence Northern Premier, Ahmedu Bello, who stated in his autobiography, 'the British were the instrument of destiny and were fulfilling the will of God' (Ejiogu 2011:17). Ahmedu Bello saw a divine providence behind the empowerment of the traditional Hausa-Fulani northern Muslim elite and their expanding mandate to the entire northern region through the British colonial administration. In fact, far from restricting the expansion of Muslim rule and Islam in the north, the colonial administration had 'deliberately prohibited Christian evangelisation in Muslim areas', while Christian missionaries, schools and hospitals spread to other parts of Nigeria (Adogame 2010:484). The gradual accommodation of British rule by the Northern Muslim elite stood in stark contrast to the views expressed by the leadership of the Sokoto Caliphate at the time of British conquest. Attahiru dan Ahmadu, who was the Caliph of Sokoto at the time, had rejected peaceful offers by the British with the following statement in 1902: 'From us to you. I do not consent that any one from you should ever dwell with us. I will never agree with you. I will have nothing ever to do with you. Between us and you there are no dealings except as between Muslims and unbelievers, war, as God Almighty has enjoined us. There is no power or strength save in God on high' (as quoted in Levtzion 2000:210).

In January 1913, the British invaded Kano followed shortly thereafter by Sokoto. Attahiru fled the city, to be killed in a battle with the British forces pursuing him. When Lugard appointed the new Sultan of

Sokoto (replacing the position of Caliph), he declared: 'The Fulani in old times under Dan Fodio conquered this country. They took the right to rule over, to levy taxes, to depose kings and to create kings ... All the things ... do now pass to the British ... [But] all men are free to worship God as they please. Mosques and prayer places will be treated with respect by us ... You need have no fear regarding British rule, it is our wish to learn your customs and fashion' (Quoted in Levtzion 2000:211). For the British, 'Hausaland's centralised and autocratic political system, and large-scale political organization and autocratic patterns of authority made protracted military engagements beyond the initial campaigns virtually unnecessary' and they were able to quickly recognize and exploit the opportunities offered by 'easy iden-tification of a ruling class, ready and willing to turn itself into an ally, and a population of subjects who have long been conditioned to subservience' (Ejiogu 2011:104). The British faced difficulty in apply-ing their indirect rule model to the Igbos, whose complex social and political systems were often misread, resulting in resentment and anger among them, as the colonial powers appointed people whom they thought to have traditional power, but in fact did not (Ejiogu 2011:130). Ejiogu argues, that 'in the overall, while the Hausa-Fulani who cherished the preferential treatment that they received from the British in the course of colonial state building, saw themselves as rulers, the Igbo, the Yoruba and others became increasing [sic] distrustful of the resultant supra-national state and its authority' (Ejiogu 2011:186). In addition, other ethnic groups who had local majorities but were regional numerical minorities feared ethnic domination by the three privileged groups, which resulted in tensions and rebellions (Nnoli 1995:32). For example, the northern Fulani Muslim emirs sought to control the Middle Belt region and the wide range of non-Muslim communities under their own traditional leaderships. Nnoli notes that 'inevitably, the non-Muslim majority of the territory mobilised against this injustice, domination and oppression. They were resentful of the emirs for imposing Islamic norms and religion on them and for rele-gating their own rulers to an inferior second class status' (Nnoli 1995:50). For many Christians, 'at the local level the question of national independence was relatively unimportant to most of the pol-itically minded Protestants. Their main concern was to uphold their independence from the Muslim Fulani, not of the British ... They generally saw the British as their best guarantee against Fulani rule'

(Kastfelt 1994:167). Thus, many non-Muslims in the Middle Belt and North found themselves in a paradoxical position. On one hand they saw an alliance between the British and Fulani enabling the Muslim traditional rulers to expand Islam and their rule over them; on the other hand the same colonial rule was seen as their best protection against a Fulani takeover in independence from the British (Kastfelt 1994:168).

The 1954 constitution formalized the power sharing of regional governments, giving them authority over education, administration, health and public works at the local levels, while creating a federal government which handled macro-economic policies, higher education, military, foreign policy and transportation. This created multiple layers of ethnic competition: among the three dominant ethnicities of the West (Yoruba), East (Igbo) and North (Hausa-Fulani) there was competition for control of the federal government. In return, these three dominant groups competed with ethnic minorities in their own local governments for power and access (Falola 1998:53). Thus, national politics emerged as ethnic politics when the federal state was created. Colonial rule had not only united a diverse human geography under the umbrella it created, but also its governance shaped the way individuals and communities perceived and responded to emerging national space. As Berman observes in postcolonial states across Africa, 'the structures and practices of the colonial state, its demarcation of political boundaries and classification of people, as well as European expectations about African cultures and institutions, contained African political processes within the categories of 'tribe' and encouraged Africans to think ethnically' (Berman 1998:323). Berman argues that it was 'within these intersecting social, cultural, economic and political processes that the social construction of modern African ethnicities has taken place – partially deliberate and intended, and partially as their unintended and unforeseen consequence' (Berman 1998:323). As it will be explained in the section below, the consequences of colonial rule continue to impact Nigeria and are directly linked to ethno-religious violence in the country.

Nigeria since Independence

Nigeria became independent from British colonial rule on 1 October 1960 but faced major complications from the start. As Chief Obafemi

Awolowo famously said: 'Nigeria is not a nation. It is a mere geographical expression. There are no Nigerians in the same sense as there are English, Welsh or French. The word Nigerian is merely a distinctive appellation to distinguish those who live within the boundaries of Nigeria from those who do not' (Kew 2010:501). In fact, it was colonial rule that not only created the word Nigeria but also decided who was part of it and how they related to the created nation. Chinua Achebe captures the ironies of Nigeria's independence from the British colonial rule and yet dependence on its legacy in its emergence as a sovereign state in Nigeria's first national anthem: 'Our national anthem, our very hymn of deliverance from British colonial bondage, was written for us by a British woman who unfortunately had not been properly briefed on the current awkwardness of the word *tribe*. So we found ourselves on independence morning rolling our tongues around the very same trickster godling: 'Though tribe and tongue may differ, In brotherhood we stand!' It was a most ominous beginning. And not surprisingly we did not stand too long in brotherhood' (Achebe 1984:6).

In his study of postcolonial African politics, Berman asks a key question: 'What has happened to the colonial state and its links to patronage networks and ethnic development since independence?' (Berman 1998:333). He observed a paradox, that the answer is both 'very little' and also 'a very great deal' had changed. He sees a continuation of colonial power structures, bureaucratic authoritarianism and the use of local leaders to assert power and clientelism that bought allegiances along ethnic lines. (Berman 1998:333, 334). Indeed, independent Nigeria, too, has seen a paradoxical 'very little' but also 'a very great deal' changed. Since its independence, Nigeria has seen a vicious cycle of attempts to move to civilian rule paused by multiple military coups, suspending the normal functioning of the political system as well as maintaining a perpetual state of emergency in the governance of the country.

Providing a detailed account of all stages and governments in Nigeria's dynamic history would be out of the scope of this book. However, a few important stages of its political journey need to be highlighted. At independence, the country was divided into three regions roughly in line with the legacy of colonial administration: North, dominated by Hausa-Fulani; West, dominated by Yoruba; and East, dominated by Igbo. These regions were in no way homogeneous and remained home to many other ethnic groups. Falola points out that independence triggered a fierce political competition and 'the three regions and their ethnicities competed as enemies' (Falola 1999:10). Under both the Independence Constitution of 1960 and the Republican Constitution of 1963, these regional administrations had 'considerable powers, including concurrent authority with the central government over higher education, industrial and water development, the judiciary and police. In addition, the regions were responsible for all residual matters, including various socio-economic programs' (International Crisis Group 2006:2). While in principle, this might have sounded like a good way to ensure a federal structure that could maintain unity and administration of the newly created state, in practice, it fuelled deep grievances. The fact that the North had a much larger geographical share than the East and West combined fuelled deeply-held fears in the South that the northern Hausa-Fulani elite were seeking to take over and dominate the entire federal state. Similarly, smaller ethnic groups felt excluded, both regionally since they were administered by the three dominant ethnic groups, but also at the national level. Protests of minority Tiv people in the Middle Belt were met by the first use of Nigerian military force against civilians, ordered by Prime Minister Balewa (Maier 2000:12).

The 1964 national elections saw massive fraud, boycotts and political assassinations (Maier 2000:12). Fierce political divisions based on ethnic solidarities and identities and a widespread sense that elite politicians were only interested in their own financial interests and protecting their own power brought the end of the First Republic with a military coup in January 1966. It was mostly led by Igbo army officers under Major General Johnson Aguiyi-Ironsi, which killed Prime Minister Balewa and other leading figures in the First Republic. The military passed a 'Unification Decree', which abolished the regional governance system in favour of a much more centralized state. This was seen as an attempt to promote Igbo dominance. Shortly after the decree, attacks on Igbos living in the North started. Thousands died and many fled to the South. A counter-coup in July of the same year by northern military officers under Lieutenant Colonal Yakubu Gowon – a Christian – brought back federalism and with it, perceptions of northern dominance. Falola notes that attacks on Igbos in the North became more deadly after the counter-coup, and involved members of the army, with estimates of the dead ranging from 7,000 to

50,000 (Falola 1999:120). A mass exodus of Igbos and others to the South then took place, spreading news of northern brutality across the country. General Gowon declared a state of emergency and undertook the project of dividing the governance of Nigeria into twelve regions rather than the three which had been formulated at independence. This act strengthened the power of central government, since no ethnic community could declare a large challenge to its rule due to its limited scope, yet it was also seen as a northern attempt to seize the rights of other communities.

Attempts at unity and poor economic and political relations between the Gowon administration and Igbo leaders of the East did not end the increasing tensions between the central government and the Igbos. On 30 May 1967, the latter declared independence from Nigeria and the creation of the Republic of Biafra (Nixon 1972:475). While Gowon had threatened that the unity of Nigeria was paramount and no secessionism would be allowed and would in fact be met by force if necessary, 'the East believed that there were no significant military preparations on the federal side to implement these threats, and did not really believe they would be carried out' (Nixon 1972:479). Yet, on 5 July 1967, Gowon undertook military action against the newly declared Republic of Biafra, triggering what is now called the Biafran War or the Nigerian Civil War that lasted from 1967 to 1970, with a loss of life of up to 2 million people, ending only when Biafra eventually surrendered.

The Biafran War played a key part in perceptions of Muslim-Christian relations particularly in Europe and North America. Williams & Falola highlight a common view, that given that secessionist movements were primarily Christian in identity and framed the war as a genocide against Christians by Muslims, this resulted in a wide range of European Christian relief and rights agencies to support the Eastern cause for independence (Williams & Falola 1995:310). The clear narrative that this was a Muslim North pogrom against Christian southerners was complicated further by the fact that General Gowon himself was a Christian, as were many of his commanders, with a substantial number of Christian Tiv soldiers fighting for him and Christians in other parts of Nigeria also opposing Bifara's cessation (Omenla 2010:368–369). However, effective international propaganda 'convinced many that Nigeria was following a policy of genocide, that starvation in Biafra was rampant and increasing astronomically, and that the war was religiously motivated' (Williams & Falola 1995:310). Omenla argues that it was only when northern Christians started sharing their experiences of protecting southern Christians living in the North and explaining the complexity of the issue to Western European Christian audiences did the Christian church and aid agencies start acknowledging the complexity of the Biafra conflict and that this war might not be a genocide against Christians per se (Omenla 2010:373). A Catholic papal envoy that had visited Biafra and Nigeria in 1967 stated that the civil war had no religious underpinning (Omenla 2010:376). However, increasing pressure on Nigeria during the Biafran war caused a shift in Nigeria's foreign policy, which turned from the Western bloc to the Eastern bloc and the purchase of Russian arms as Britain and the United States refused to sell weapons to Nigeria, France recognized the independence of Biafra, and Nigerian leaders felt that international reporting of the war was biased (Falola 1999:124). After the war, Gowon began enjoying wide domestic and international support. He promised stability and national reconciliation, but also an end to corruption and the political back-fighting that had brought the end of the First Republic. Yet, under Gowon, corruption took a new form in the work of 'commission agents', who received financial payments from individuals and businesses seeking to access the powerful military rulers (Balogun 2007:245). Dissent and civil demands were increasingly ignored. General Gowon had promised that the military would give way to civilian rule by 1976, yet retracted his own promise in 1974, opening the door for a bloodless coup in July 1975 that resulted in the premiership of General Murtala Muhammed, a Muslim nobleman from the North (Herskovits 1979:316).

General Muhammed had wide support and set out a clear timeline to transition to civilian rule with an elected government. He set up an 'Assets Investigations' panel to look into widespread accusations of corruption in the Gowon administration. It indicted ten out of the twelve governors of the Gowon administration and confiscated their assets (Lawal & Tobi 2006:645). However, Muhammed was murdered in an aborted coup attempt in 1976. Many thought Gowon was behind the attempt, and Nigeria demanded his extradition from the United Kingdom, where he resided after his ousting from power (Aluko 1977:304, 305). The task of pursuing transition to civilian rule was left to Muhammed's successor, Lieutenant-General Obasanjo, who created an independent electoral commission, increased the number of states to nineteen, and in September 1978 lifted the ban on civilian politics. In 1979, a series of elections were announced. (Herskovits 1979:319).

The winner of the first election was Shagari, a Muslim Fulani from Sokoto, northern Nigeria, therefore reinforcing perceptions that the Northern People's Congress, which dominated pre-military rule in the First Republic, was once again set to pursue northern hegemony over the country in its successor, the National Party of Nigeria. This was particularly important as fierce debates over the place of Shari'a, particularly the issue of jurisdiction of and appeals to the decision of Shari'a courts in the North, had taken place between 1977 and 1979 in the writing of the constitution that formed the basis of the elections and creation of the Second Republic (Laitin 1982). Laitin points out that the debates had multiple reasons behind them, and in a sense 'this battle over the Sharia symbolically represented the North exerting its influence on the constitutions of the state to position itself against the economic and administrative power of the South' (Laitin 1982:413). The outcome was a compromise on the Shari'a appeal system and defusing of the situation as political parties began focusing their energy on the upcoming elections. With the victory of Shagari and new structures established by the new constitution. Nigeria was now governed in a system based on the US model, with a powerful president and two-house national assembly (Falola 1999:165). Falola notes that while the constitution of the Second Republic had addressed the issue of power sharing, a strong executive and limiting regionalism and a foundation for creation of establishment of national parties, it triggered a new level of competitive politics that turned politics into a business with limited accountability for the politicians and 'the subversion of the democratic process by the political class' (Falola 1999:166).

In fact, it was the level of corruption by the political parties, including Shagari's own party officials, which once again brought an end to civilian politics and legitimized another military coup in 1983. The coup brought the end of the Second Republic, taking Nigeria into another long spell of military rule (Othman 1984). The army's legitimization of its coup was made clear in the first military broadcast after the coup by Brigadier Sani Abacha:

Fellow countrymen and women … You are all living witnesses to the grave economic predicament and uncertainty which an inept and corrupt leadership has imposed on our beloved nation for the past four years. I am referring to the harsh, intolerable conditions under which we are now living. Our economy has been hopelessly mismanaged. We have become a debtor and a beggar nation. (Quoted in Othman 1984:44)

Major General Muhammed Buhari, the new military leader, made addressing the corruption of civilian politicians a battle cry, setting up a special tribunal that found most of the politicians from the Second Republic guilty and giving them varying jail terms (Lawal & Tobi 2006:646). He also launched a 'War against Indiscipline', that not only punished civil servants who showed up late to work, but even included disciplining the general public, such as ordering Nigerians to form queues at bus stops (BBC News 18 April 2011). While General Buhari did not follow his predecessors in finding himself allured by lucrative opportunities in governing Nigeria, his initial wide public support started to wither not long after the coup. His anti-corruption drive without a viable fiscal policy to deal with falling oil prices resulted in the dismissal of over one million workers from their jobs in the first year of his leadership, with prices of food and basic commodities seeing a 500 per cent increase in a single year and a scarcity of essentials such as cooking oil, rice, milk, sugar and salt. In addition, tuition fees for higher education which had been waived in 1972 were introduced (Ekwe-Ekwe 1985:610). Buhari's response to increasing discontent was merely to clampdown on freedom of speech and brutally punish his critics. Less than two years after he assumed leadership, Buhari was ousted in a bloodless coup and sent to prison by another military officer in 1985, General Ibrahim Babangida. He ruled Nigeria till 1993.

Under Babangida, Nigeria saw significant structural changes. He increased the number of states again from nineteen to twenty-one, and doubled the number of local government authorities to 600, which resulted in the creation of more official positions that could access power and resources. This was widely welcomed by communities and political actors who felt excluded by a narrower leading political class. Alongside this expansion, he centralized power and strengthened the presidency, giving him more direct control over the disbursement of funds to state governors (Welch 1995:596). This extended the

patron-client relationships and increased the personal power of Babangida, who personally distributed or allocated state funds according to
his interests. In 1989, the ban on political parties was lifted and dates
for the elections were set for 1992. In just two months, forty-nine
political associations had emerged with thirteen of them seeking to
run in the elections. But Babangida dissolved all groups, allowing only
two parties to run (Welch 1995:598). These two parties, the National
Republican Convention and the Social Democratic Party, were running
against each other, but their visions, rules and political aims were
written by the ruling Babangida government. Interestingly, this meant
that the South-North, Muslim-Christian and ethnic divides were not to
be as dominant in the upcoming elections, as both parties had a broad
spectrum of politicians. This was important as Babangida's dangerous
game of signing Nigeria to join the Organization of Islamic Conference
(OIC) in 1986 without even consulting his cabinet, let alone the wider
public, had triggered mass unrest across the country. It led to widespread protests by Christians who saw this to be a secret Islamization
and northern plot, which led to more than 5,000 people dead in the
early 1990s (Campbell 1994:180). While there was tension across the
country that both of the parties were putting forward Muslim candidates, when the elections were finally held in 1993, they were seen as
one of the fairest and least violent of all the elections to date in Nigeria
both by domestic and international observers.

   The winner of this election was Mashood Abiola, a famous Muslim
businessman, who had attracted substantial votes from Christians as
well. Yet, Babangida cancelled the outcome of the elections ten days
after voting, citing feeble arguments that votes were 'sold and bought'
(Welch 1995:600). Babangida was not keen to turn over power as
Abiola was seen as a strong candidate who could diminish the military
and northern stronghold over politics (Campbell 1994:190). Ikpe
points out that 'although Babangida recruited clients and supporters
all over Nigeria, his primary support came from the North. This is
because he was such an ardent believer in Northern dominance of
Nigerian politics and government that he actually used his regime to
foster this project' (Ikpe 2000:157). The government promised new
elections with new rules, in effect barring Abiola from running again,
which caused reactions both inside the country and internationally.
Eventually Babangida was forced to retire by the military and an

interim government led by Shonekan was put in place. However, it did not take long for the powerful minister of defence General Sani Abacha to assume leadership and the Shonekan government resigned, and with that the Third Republic ended before it really began, resulting in a further era of military rule from 1993 to 1999.

Reno argues, that just like Babangida, 'Abacha's rule was about the survival of Abacha in power, not about what was good or proper for Nigerians', and in order to achieve that, he 'creatively and skillfully co-opted and manipulated groups in Nigeria and abroad for personal aggrandisement' (Reno 1999:110). Abacha was notorious for awarding business contracts to his own children, friends and close allies, and in the process amassed an unparalleled fortune. Kraxberger notes that while between 1988 and 1994 some $12.2 billion was diverted from state funds to off-budget accounts, thus granting billions to Abacha's close associates, 'the percentage of people in poverty steadily increased from 28.1 per cent in 1980 to 65.6 per cent in 1996' (Kraxberger 2004:415). Abacha dissolved the national and state assemblies, the National Electoral Commission, the two political parties that competed in the 1993 elections, and banned all political activities (Ogbondah 2000:232). Abacha put Abiola, whom many saw as the rightful winner of elections, under detention until his death on accusations of 'treason'. Abacha maintained his lucrative rule by setting up a parallel security apparatus to protect himself from a possible counter-coup (in fact, he survived two coup attempts, in 1985 and 1990). He sought to crush dissent by any means, including extra-judicial killings, unlawful acts and prolonged illegal detention by secret security forces. (Ikpe 2000:157, 158). Like Babangida, Abacha was a keen believer in northern dominance and continually used the threat of instability and promises of transition to civilian rule to maintain obedience to his regime. In 1998, Abacha announced that there would be elections later in the year, but he was set to be the sole candidate in the presidential race backed by the parties which needed his express permission to operate. However, before the foregone election took place, Abacha died in June 1998 from a sudden heart attack. Rumours remain to this day as to whether it was an assassination or simple heart failure: he was said to be spending the night with foreign prostitutes.

Two days after Abacha's death, General Abubakar Abdulsalam assumed leadership of the country. He set a new economic course to address the troubling state of the economy (and especially addressing the issue of sanctions brought against Nigeria during the Abacha rule due to gross human rights abuses) and most importantly, finally started a sincere process of transition into civilian rule. Abubakar dissolved all political parties founded during the Abacha regime, seizing their assets (Momoh & Thovoethinm 2001:5). He restored various official bodies that had been decommissioned by Abacha so that elections could be held and power transferred. Between December 1998 and February 1999, there were four rounds of elections: local government councils, state Houses of Assembly, the National Assembly and finally for the presidency (Omotola 2010:543). The three political parties that ran in the elections all had clear dominance in particular geographical and ethnic areas. The overall winner was General Olusegun Obasanjo, who had previously served as the country's military ruler between 1976 and 1979. He remained in power as the democratically elected president of Nigeria from 1999 to 2007. Although fraud and irregularities marred the election, Obasanjo not only had the support of the northern elite but also military officials, who bankrolled his well-funded campaign (Ihonvbere 1999:58,59). With Obasanjo's victory in 1999, the current Fourth Republic was born. Nigeria saw three further presidential elections, one in 2007, 2011 and 2015. The 2007 and 2011 elections, in particular, saw widespread violence and allegations of electoral fraud. The 2015 elections brought General Muhammadu Buhari back into power as the president of Nigeria, once again on the appeal of his stand against corruption. The cycles do in fact repeat, and indeed 'very little' but also 'a very great deal' changed in Nigeria.

The Nature of the Nigerian State

Some fifty years have passed since the independence of Nigeria from colonial rule, and as explained above, the country has seen a cycle of civilian politics, followed by military coups and an ever-more central-ized economy in the hands of a strengthened federal state. Yet, funda-mental questions about the nature of that state, and most importantly the 'nation' of Nigeria as whole, remain from its creation as a geo-graphical zone during the colonial era. Renan, in his often quoted lecture titled 'What is a Nation', delivered in Paris in 1882, noted a key dynamic in the formation of a nation:

A nation is a soul, a spiritual principle. Two things, which are in truth the same, constitute this soul, this spiritual principle. One is situated in the past, the other in the present. One consists of the common possessions of a rich heritage of memories; the other of present consent, the desire to live together, the will to continue to accredit the heritage that one has received undivided. (Quoted in Barash 1999:40)

Nigeria has neither a common possession of a heritage of memories shared by all its peoples that can bring a wide topography of ethno-linguistic communities together, nor a shared desire to live together and a will to accredit an undivided heritage. As Adenbanwi and Obadare point out, in the 50 years since Nigeria's independence, 'the secret is out', that there is no nation called Nigeria (Adebanwi & Obadare 2010:399). Novelist Chinua Achebe observes that 'in spite of the tendency of people in power to speak about this great nation of ours there is no doubt that Nigerians are among the world's most unpatriotic people' (Achebe 1984:15). It is, therefore, no surprise that the question of whether Nigeria can stay together as a country frequently emerges in arguments, articles and intelligence documents.[2]

The answer to how it survived a bitter civil war and in spite of intense ethnic and territorial politics remains intact as a country most probably lies with the very 'curse', oil revenues, that is said to be causing corruption and bad governance in Nigeria. As Naanen and Nyiayaana put it, 'the indications are that as long as the oil continues to flow, it is unlikely for any part of the country to willingly assert a sovereign nationhood and deprive itself of the enormous financial benefits of that vital natural resource' (Naanen & Nyiayaana 2013:113). Hill observes the same interdependency that keeps conflicting sides together: 'the development and entrenchment of Nigeria's rentier economy mean that the thirty non-oil producing states depend on the Niger Delta and Abuja for much of their income. Quite clearly, they will only continue to receive this revenue so long as the country remains intact' (Hill 2012:91).

Richard A. Joseph offers a helpful way of conceptualizing this with 'prebendalism' and 'clientelism' in Nigeria in his 1987 study, *Democracy and Prebendal Politics in Nigeria*, still widely cited today. Drawing the concept of prebendalism from Max Weber's study of feudal societies in Asia and Europe, Joseph demonstrates a complex dynamic of how offices of the state have become centres of distribution of lucrative state revenues. This not only increases the competition for those offices but also the personal appropriation of such public offices for personal interests and social expectations of the holders of these offices to uphold the interests of their constituencies who have enabled them to reach the office and to share benefits. These form a basis of patron-cliental relationship that can be seen from the top of the state structures to federal level politics, business contracts and the day-to-day experiences of individuals (Joseph 2014:55–56). In the absence of a state structure that can offer a fair distribution of state resources and equal opportunities, such clientelism in a prebendal state becomes a safety net and a means for individuals at all socioeconomic and political levels to advance and protect their opportunities (Joseph 2014:57–63). Joseph points out that even though the 1966 to 1979 military rule used the discourse of ridding Nigeria of corrupt officials and their relationship with businesses, prebendalism also affected the structures of the military and the political performance of military governors of states, and most importantly, by centralizing power and economy, it has paradoxically fuelled prebendalism (Joseph 2014:69). This, Joseph, argues has also been the reason behind demands for and maintenance of electoral politics and a democratic federal structure, since only within such a system can all communities compete for or seek to hold the prebendal offices of the state (Joseph 2014:57).

Similar observations can regularly be seen in writings of experts on Nigeria. In his 2011 study, Ejiogu observes that 'patronage-clientage has become a normative instrument central in the conduct of state affairs at every level' and that 'it bred the corruption and the abuse of public office that are now staples of politics and economy in Nigeria' (Ejiogu 2011:6). The impact of this on the electoral process and party politics in contemporary Nigeria is highlighted by Darren Kew who notes that over the five decades since Nigeria's independence, the nation's elites have shown a declining interest in clean elections. Kew argues that immediately after the independence of Nigeria, 'ethnicity became the primary social category for political mobilisation and ethnic-based political parties came to dominate the regions' (Kew 2010:501). Kew observes that this led to an *ethnic security dilemma*, in which ethnic groups perceived an increasing threat from others as they sought to control the state and protect their group's interests, thus creating insecurity for others (Kew 2010:501–502). However, Kew saw a shift in the Second Republic following the oil boom 'from traditional ethnic sources of political loyalty and organisation to a more personalised politics known as neopatrimonialism, the 'big man' or 'godfather' structure of patronage politics' (Kew 2010:500). While ethnicity remained a primary channel for political mobilization and appeal, 'by the fall of the Second Republic, personal interests began to take on far more importance to elites than ethnic interests, with complex multi-ethnic relationships possible, greased with the vast oil wealth available' (Kew 2010:504).

The shift from ethnic interests to a more complex web of personal interests and clientelism that might or might not be pursued through ethnic politics is a wider trend that can be seen across Africa. This is an important indication of how ethnic identities and solidarities are constructed, maintained and transformed in a given context. This is captured effectively by Bruce Berman who observed the evolving nature of ethnicities and neopatrimonialism across postcolonial African states. He argued that the pattern of state-society relations, patronage systems, ethnic communities and identities have created an 'uncivil nationalism', a process which has denied 'communities of cultural identity and social responsibility' while at the same time creating a 'competitive political tribalism defined by purely materialistic and opportunistic relationships to the state through the control of patronage' (Berman 1998:339). Berman has pointed out that 'while the patronage networks of colonialism were often built on the base of the complex relations of clientage and dependence that existed in many pre-colonial societies, in the context of a political economy based on money and markets the relationships became increasingly focused on access to short-run material benefits rather than the establishment of long-term ties of mutual support' (Berman 1998:330). The significance of such an understanding of ethnic solidarities and how other forms of identification and alliances impacted social and political relations is an important point, as we try to understand how religion became an increasingly visible and dominant aspect of the same social and political outcomes of a prebendal state.

Religion and Politics in Nigeria

In their essay, 'Religion, Politics and Democracy in Nigeria', Akwara and Ojomah argue that 'the conflict between religion and politics in Nigeria is older than the Nigerian state. Religion formed the basis upon which the Fulanis invaded the Hausa homelands and established the Sokoto Caliphate. It also served as a forerunner of colonialism from the coast as it paved the way for the British to overrun the southern coastlands, exploit its economic resources, abolished the peoples' traditions and socio-cultural practices, and implanted Christianity. Nigerians therefore became religious before their unification into the modern Nigerian state in 1914 by the British' (Akwara & Ojomah 2013:65). Leaving aside the problems with their historic claims, the authors use their brief argument of an intrinsic clash between religion and politics as a basis to conclude that 'the failure of democracy in Nigeria cannot be attributed to the failure of the nation to develop economically alone; or to the artificiality of western democracy itself with its sets of institutions and practices; or to the absence of supporting values for democracy, and or, the relationship between the developed western nations and Nigeria, especially the effects of colonialism and neo-colonialism on the country; but on the negative effects of religious practices on the nation's political processes; engaging in the political process from a religious perspective, and turning political differences into ethno-religious conflicts' (Akwara & Ojomah 2013:66). It is a tempting but problematic conclusion. Religion, like ethnicity, has deep roots in the history of peoples of Nigeria as can be seen in the brief description of pre-colonial social and political dynamics set out in the sections above. However, like the definitions of ethnic boundaries and the contextual significance they acquire, religious allegiances, issues and politics too have shown a fluid nature in Nigerian history. As explained above, in the phase immediately after Nigeria's independence, ethnicity played a major role in the political process, gradually giving way to looser allegiances in pursuit of interests. From the 1970s onwards, particularly in the lead up to and during the Second Republic we start seeing an increasingly religious polarization, the emergence of religious tensions between Muslims and Christians, and the framing of Nigeria's chronic problems through a religious language (Gbasha 1995:304). The reasons behind this are a complex web of three major layers: domestic politics; the impact of socioeconomic and political changes on religious communities; and the international trends which interact with and impact each of these.

Layer I

At the domestic political level, particularly in northern Nigeria, the advancement of religion has shown itself both as an ideological vision and as a way of forming political allegiances, establishing constituency support and achieving political mobilization. We can demonstrate this through three examples. The first example is Northern Premier Ahmadu Bello's Islamization campaign following Nigerian independence. As explained above, Islamic structures were a key part of the control of northern Nigeria before and during the colonial era. Thus, it is not surprising that there were attempts to enable their continuation. John Paden notes that political leadership in the North initially consisted of 'younger educated elements, who start the formation of parties' but after 1960, they 'see their party "hijacked" by more traditional elements' and Ahmadu Bello emerged as the political leader of the North, embodying a united front, and assumed the honourable title of Sardauna, and the official role of the Premier of the Northern Region' (Paden 1986:177). His political vision of a united northern Nigeria was intrinsically linked with the campaign he launched for the official promotion of Islam. After independence, northern Nigeria was indeed home to the vast majority of Muslims in Nigeria, but by no means were all parts of northern Nigeria homogeneously Muslim. Hunwick notes that the Muslim population of the North was not distributed evenly and that while seven provinces were Muslim-majority, five were not, which meant that some 30 per cent of the northern population were non-Muslims (Hunwick 1992:146, 147). That is why, while the Northern People's Congress (NPC) campaigned with the slogan of 'One North, One People', the proselytism campaign by Ahmadu Bello was central to the political vision of a purely Islamic North (Hunwick 1992:146, 148). It is, therefore, no surprise that Ahmadu Bello regularly referred to the Great Jihad of Othman Dan Fodio and that his movement for the renewal of Muslims, promotion of Islam and advancement of Islamic rule was named 'Usmanniya' (Paden 1986:552, 553).

Ahmedu Bello's campaigns for the Islamization of Nigeria overlapped with and were enabled by his attempts to gather international support. The Sardauna's first pilgrimage to Saudi Arabia in 1955 was a key turning point and the beginning of his frequent visits to the country. In the process, he developed links with the Saudi royal family and received a formal state welcome to the country. In 1963 'the Saudi monarch King Saud gave him a plot of land in Medina where he built a house' (Williams & Falola 1995:213). His networking and close relations with key Muslim countries also included Jordan,

Egypt and Morocco, which all granted him financial aid as well as honorary degrees and close working relationships (Williams & Falola 1995:212–213). In fact, Pakistan and Sudan contributed legal experts to help the formation of new penal codes in northern Nigeria (Williams & Falola 1995:214).

Bello made no secret of his attempts to convert the rest of Nigeria and to bring the country under Islamic control. In 1965, he spoke at the World Muslim Congress, claiming that 'within a period of five months he was able to convert 60,000 non-Muslims' and appealed 'to his fellow Muslim brothers to come together and form an inter- national organization (which helped in the propagation of their reli- gion) that would rival that of Christians. He also pointed out that the Jews were making inroads into Nigeria through their financial assist- ance to the federal and southern regional government' (Williams & Falola 1995:215). As a result of his appeals 'Saudi Arabia donated £160,000 towards the continued propagation of Islam in northern Nigeria while Kuwait donated millions of pounds' (Williams & Falola 1995:215).[3] Ahmedu Bello's Islamization campaign and its successes were not simply about winning hearts and souls for Islam. As Gbasha argues 'for many non-Muslims in Northern Nigeria, conversion became the necessary compromise they had to make for them to obtain little crumbs from the powers that be in Kaduna. Thus, the government in Northern Nigeria was directly involved in spreading Islam. In fact, during the time of the Sardauna, Islam was virtually returning to the status of an undeclared state religion in Northern Nigeria' (Gbasha 1995:31).

The second example of the politics of religion in northern Nigeria is the fierce tensions over the Shari'a law that took place between 1976 and 1979 in the process of writing the constitution of the Second Republic. The tensions were sparked by proposals for a Federal Shari'a Court of Appeal. For Christians, this was seen as creation of a parallel legal system and a parallel supreme court, and would have expanded Shari'a law from Muslim-majority states to the entire country (Hunwick 1992:149). As Clarke points out, 'the contentious issue of the establishment of a federal Sharia court system goes back a long way and was even raised in the pre-independence period' and 'Ahmadu Bello made a demand for such a court in the early 1960s' (Clarke

2007:528). However, the shift from the military regime following the collapse of the First Republic with its strong ethnic clashes galvanized an old debate and turned into the main point of contention as the door for civilian politics once more opened. Ukiwo makes an important observation that the possibility of democratization in political systems with no rules and boundaries having been institutionalized results in 'political gladiators who prefer efficiency norms to legitimacy norms', and thus deploy ethnicity and religion as tools of political power, which can be named as not so much as an ethnic conflict but 'democratic conflict' (Ukiwo 2003:119). Such a 'democratic conflict' was reduced to a South-North and Christian-Muslim dichotomy during the Babangida regime, which created a system with two parties with almost identical political outlooks (Falola 1999:226). The experiences of the First Republic had shaken the confidence of the electorate in secular ethnic politics; political actors were regularly using religious verses as political songs and promising the inclusion of Shari'a or protection of secularism in the constitution (Falola 1999:168). In fact, some religious leaders 'began to reject the constitution, calling instead for a theocratic state with moral leaders. Colonel Ghaddafi of Libya and the Ayatollah Khomeini of Iran provided alternative models of leadership, both widely believed to be strong, popular, honest, moral, and committed to their people' (Falola 1999:169). Influential Shiite preacher Sheikh Ibrahim El-Zakzaky openly demanded the creation of an Islamic Republic of Nigeria (Falola 1999:187). Proposals for a secular constitution by Christians and southerners were widely rejected. Influential Muslim leader Chief Adegbite declared: Secularism has no place in Islam since Islam is a religion as well as system of life and government. You cannot separate religion and politics in Islam for religion must exert the correct influence on politics (quoted in Williams & Falola 1995:21).

When the debates threatened to split Nigeria into two, the military regime intervened. The outcome was not what northern leaders had hoped, but the 1979 constitution ended up containing 'more far-reaching provisions on religion than all of the previous ones. For the first time, a pronouncement was made that the country was secular. State religion was prohibited'. (Williams & Falola 1995:136). It required the state to be impartial to any religion and to uphold fundamental human rights including freedom of religion. It banned formation of political parties along religious lines and provided that no party could restrict membership to members to a particular religion (Williams & Falola 1995:137). As Williams and Falola conclude:

It may in fact be argued that the Shari'a debate was less about religion, but more about power. In the Assembly and the pages of the newspapers, most of the polemics revolved around religion. However, in private and in the corridors of the Assembly, discussions reveal that participants were trying to use the debate to position themselves appropriately for the Second Republic. (Williams & Falola 1995:139)

The political debate subdued for the time being, only to show itself once again in later elections. The question of how the Federal state related to religion or secularism remained as a point of contention and an area which politicians could exploit. Following the military coup that brought the Second Republic to an end, Babangida continually and brutally exploited the tensions in the country. In 1986, without even informing the members of his own cabinet or opening it to larger political discussion, he officially entered Nigeria into the membership process to the Organization of Islamic Conference. The step caused unrest across the country, fuelling riots and clashes. Christians saw this just another step in the secret agenda of the North to turn Nigeria into an Islamic country and subjugate them. Babangida' s rule saw violent outburst of clashes between Christians and Muslims, and the emergence of militant religious fundamentalists. In response 'Babangida underplayed the consequences of religious riots, seeing only those aspects that threatened his own power. He set up fact-finding missions but was quick to disregard their findings ... He set up well-piled clientelism that sucked into its patronage religious leaders seeking money and positions' (Williams & Falola 1995:108). The issue of Shari'a law, which had not been solved and been only pushed aside, returned to the limelight once again in 1999, when the governor of northern Zamfara State unilaterally introduced Shari'a penal code, and within the following three years twelve other northern states had adopted it too (Aloa 2013:134).[4] The outcome was serious human rights abuses and violent clashes across middle and northern Nigeria (Ukiwo 2003:125).

The third example of the politics of religion in Nigeria is the impact of Islamic politics on Christians and Christian activism. The relationships between Christians and other non-Muslims and Muslims have in no way been as tense elsewhere in Nigeria as they have been in the North. While hegemonic visions of Islamic rule dominated the North, in Western Nigeria, for example, among the Yoruba, Muslims and Christians remained in good relations, with many families having members from both religions. For them, their ethnic identity as Yoruba and the traditional power structures that emphasized it provided a unifying framework beyond a particular religion (Kukah & Falola 1996:1). However, the strong presence of religious agendas from northern politicians at the federal level and the forcing of Islamic expansion in the North affirmed the fears of the dominantly Christian South and other non-Muslims that northern Nigeria not only wanted to seize control of the Federal Government and to push out non-Muslims from the North but also to turn Nigeria into an Islamic state. The outcome of this has been threefold: immense mistrust, parallel religious demands and religious mobilization. Williams and Falola note that previously, while Muslims complained that southern Christians had far too much foothold in the central government and economy due to southern regions having had longer engagement with Western style education, as 'Muslims become more assertive and more influential in the executive centre, Christians become worried and complain of deprivations and an impending Islamic takeover of the state' (Williams & Falola 1995:306).

This was to mark a turning point for Christians in Nigeria. As Komolafe argues, 'one of the features of Nigerian Christians, at least until early 1980s, had been their lack of interest in politics' (Komolafe 2013:185). Christian churches and organizations were too diverse with no unifying political cause or agenda, except in the emerging response to Islamic dominance of Nigeria. In 1976, a nationwide ecumenical umbrella organization named the Christian Association of Nigeria (CAN) was established, with the aim of providing a unified voice for Christians. Komolafe notes that CAN 'launched itself fully into a confrontation with what was perceived as a systematic Islamization of Nigeria through the Muslims' constant efforts to implement Sharia law system of governance for all of Nigeria. It is fair to say, then, that the Muslim agenda, more than any other single factor, has provided legitimacy for the continued existence of CAN and explains its orientation to political activism and religious ecumenism' (Komolafe 2013:185). Given that Christian traditions did not have an equal to a political Islam and Christian politicians and public voices continually demanded upholding a secular system of governance, Christians found themselves mimicking requests by Muslim groups. For example, CAN has requested 'ecclesiastical courts for Christians, restoration of full diplomatic relations with Israel, and the setting up of pilgrim welfare boards for Christians' (Komolafe 2013:188). While Muslims had guaranteed funds from the central government to attend pilgrimage in Saudi Arabia, which is a requirement among the basic tenets of Islam, Christians argued that they should also be sent to pilgrimage to Israel or Rome, which is not a clearly expressed religious obligation in Christian traditions.

The political mobilization of Christians along religious lines became visible in the 1987 local government elections. Christian political candidates had now begun appealing to CAN and other Christian networks for support to their campaigns. Williams and Falola note that in the Middle Belt, many Christian politicians won the elections with the political mobilization and support of CAN, and in fact, Kaduna Municipal Council was won by a reverend (Williams & Falola 1995:109). Williams and Falola note an important outcome of the 1987 elections: 'to a number of Christian politicians, one lesson was that if they could unite on the basis of religion, they would achieve victory. In the subsequent years, the game became similar, up to a point that religion attained the importance of ethnicity in the calculation of power' (Williams & Falola 1995:109). At the national level, the perception of northern and Islamic dominance continues to fuel political mobilization and alliances. A leading Christian pastor with a large congregation in Lagos told me in an interview that unless Christians unite with other non-Muslim groups, it will be inevitable that northern politicians would turn Nigeria into an Islamic state. The pastor spoke of his plans to bring a unified political pressure against emerging talks of Shari'a-based banking structures to be created nationally, which he saw to be yet another attempt.

Layer II

While Layer I explains how religious beliefs and religious organizations and religious demands have effectively become powerful political realities, it does not necessarily explain why they have had such a hold on and appeal to the public and thus were utilized easily by political

entrepreneurs. The reasons behind that lie in two major social developments: socioeconomic relations and the reemerging social significance of Christian and Muslim clergy, organizations and places of
worship. Falola points out that the oil boom in the 1970s initially
created good outcomes such as an emerging middle class, free universal
primary education and increases in pay and development projects, but
from 1975 onwards it started showing its dark side with millionaires
emerging, the number of poor increasing and other economies besides
oil production and sale ignored due to easy money (Falola 1999:14).
Decreasing oil prices pushed Nigeria to undertake foreign debt to
sustain its spending, increasing anger in the country towards the
sudden shift from the hope of economic flourishing to an increasing
divide between economic classes with political links and average citizen
was a factor encouraging the military to seize power once again from
the civilians with promises of ending corruption and bringing equality
(Falola 1999:14, 15). However, as explained above in the overview of
Nigeria's never-ending cycles of corrupt civilian rule were followed by
equally corrupt and brutal military governments. Military governments banned any possibility of civilian politics and public spaces for
expression of discontent and civil organization, so religious establish-
ments became the only networks and public arenas which could be
shielded from government control (Williams & Falola 1995:107).

Adogame argues that the deterioration in trust of government
bodies, trade unions and cultural associations meant religious institutions played a distinctive role, providing networks but also influ-
encing individuals to partake in civil and religious voluntarism
(Adogame 2010:493). According to Ibrahim, religious organizations
offered a chance for zealous clergy to reach money, power and
a comfortable life, a safety net for poor, widows, and those who
seek jobs and support, and an arena for political struggle (Ibrahim
1991:125, 126). All across Nigeria, new churches, brotherhoods and
religious movements emerged, offering quick answers and spiritual
help to those looking for answer and support to survive in a Nigeria
in flux, but also a chance for the personal financial and social advancement of clergymen. Adogame rightfully notes that 'the coterie of charismatic leaders and celebrities, religious icons, spiritual entrepreneurs
and charlatans … has invented religious empires endeared to the
personality of the founder/leader, sometimes leading to their being
dubbed as "family businesses" or "private enterprises"' (Adogame

2010:496). All across southern Nigeria, mega churches with Pentecostal preachers and thousands of members have emerged since the 1970s
(Diara & Onah 2014:396). With self-claimed prophets and entertain-
ing church services, preaching a prosperity gospel – that if you believe
and support their churches, God will bless you in return financially
and heal sicknesses and empower you to live a successful life – they
formulated a winning product to cater to a population facing dire
challenges. As Adogame puts it, 'religion or spirituality has served as
a significant source through which many Nigerians seek understanding
of their complex reality and existence, and it serves as a panacea for
their various existential problems of day-to-day living' (Adogame
2010:480).

While traditional Muslim and Christian denominations might not
have benefitted from the same financially rewarding outcomes enjoyed
by Pentecostal churches, they too increasingly enjoyed prominent roles
and privileges at state functions and in state provisions in states where
their religious community enjoys a majority (Sampson 2012:123).
Thus, political and socioeconomic developments have resulted in the
increasing significance of religious institutions since the late 1970s.
Religious and political entrepreneurs have effectively blurred the lines
between personal interest, political mobilization and spiritual performance in an increasingly open-market competition among religious
groups to increase their number of adherents.

Layer III

However, it was not only the developments in Nigeria that enabled
such a renewed importance of religion in Nigerian political and public
space in the late 1970s and particularly the 1980s. Both the domestic
political and socioeconomic changes in the country have overlapped
and interacted significantly with international developments. Traces of
this have already been mentioned above in that both Muslim and
Christian networks brought aid, relief and financial support for religious activities from their co-religionists abroad. At the structural level,
such networks and exchanges have increased in Nigeria, and globally,
since the 1970s due to tangible factors such as the ease of international
travel, communication, media and increasing international bodies,
organizations and activism in the world. These factors not only
enabled chances for Nigerian elites to develop connections with the

world, but they also opened spaces for international trends to impact domestic developments. Saudi financing might have provided a particular version of conservative Islam to advance in Nigeria, but the Iranian revolution of 1979 had a direct impact on political visions of an Islamic state of Nigeria. Various Muslim groups have emerged in Nigeria, demanding a central role for Islam in politics and structures, such as the Muslim Brothers with Sheikh El-Zakzaky as their leader. His early views had followed the Egyptian Sayyid Qutb, but he was deeply influenced by the 1979 revolution, including the conversion of the Sheikh to Shiism (Aloa 2013:133). Thus the politics of religion in Nigeria was both enabled by realities of increasing internationalism in the world but also shaped by the ideas and visions that were transmitted through them from the 1960s and 1970s.

A similar wave of international developments have impacted Nigeria since the 1990s in the form of increasing Islamist militancy across the world, particularly since the September 2001 terror attacks on the United States and the subsequent 'war on terror' that has been unleashed. The effect of this shows itself in three areas. Firstly, the 9/11 attacks and their aftermath attracted support and condemnation among Muslims and Christians. Following the 9/11 attacks on the World Trade Center in New York, there were celebrations of the event by Muslim youth. Later, widespread protests against the US invasion of Afghanistan triggered clashes with Christians, taking some 200 lives (Ukiwo 2003:125). In response, Christian groups were seen in a celebratory tone and supportive of the US campaign and Nigeria's support for the United States' 'war on terror'. Secondly, both Christians and Muslims increasingly began reading their own conditions in Nigeria in terms of the global language of 'us versus them' that emerged after the 9/11 attacks. Aloa notes that 'Christians began citing violence of Muslims against non-Muslims in Sudan, Yugoslavia, Cyprus, Kashmir, Indonesia, Egypt and others, while Muslims have cited places like Iraq and Afghanistan as evidences of a global Christian assault against Muslims. In a bizarre way, neighbourhoods in some of the key cities in northern Nigeria were renamed to suit global Christian/Muslim conflicts, with names like Kandahar, Jalalabad and New Jerusalem being used to depict whether they were held by Muslim or Christian armed gangs' (Aloa 2013:142). In fact, this domestication of an imagined global battle between Islam and Christianity was visible in all of the interviews I conducted in Nigeria. For example, a Christian seminary professor interviewed said 'the fight between Islam and West spills over to here'. Thirdly, as will be demonstrated further in a later section, the post-2001 period saw increasing mobility between international militant organizations. In other words, many of Nigeria's jihadist groups gradually moved on from being local insurgencies and underground networks into receiving more weapons, training and fighters from outside Nigeria. The latest phase of this in Nigeria and Western Africa has been the links developed between local groups and the Al Qaida in the Magreb that focuses on the West of North Africa and mercenaries and weapons flowing into the area after the collapse of the Qaddafi regime in Libya. In fact, Nigeria was 'one of the two African countries specifically mentioned by Osama Bin Laden in one of his video releases in 2002 as places where Muslims should rise in rebellion' (Gow et al. 2013:242).

These three layers have contributed to the building of tensions between Muslims and Christians in Nigeria. A complex history of both domestic and international developments have directly impacted relations between the adherents of both religions and shaped their political and religious visions and responses. Therefore, the context that enables ethno-religious violence in the country cannot simply be reduced to arguments that promote religion as the cause of high levels of violence in the country.

Religious Violence in Nigeria

The history of ethno-religious violence in Nigeria dates back to the early nineteenth century, as we see in the case of the 'jihad' unleashed by Uthman Dan Fadio that created the Sokoto Caliphate. However, the roots of current ethno-religious tensions in the country start to appear in the so-called Sharia debates of the late 1970s, which were followed by increasing violence along ethno-religious lines in the 1980s. This decade began with violent attacks by the Muslim Maitatsine sect on Muslims and Christians alike and numerous riots in Kaduna state. Clashes escalated into large-scale violence in Kaduna, Zaira, Kafanchan and Katsina during the late 1980s, which took thousands of lives. Most scholars agree that the specific incident that marked the start of contemporary ethno-religious violence in the country was on 6 March 1987, 'the first most brutal confrontation between Christians and Muslims' that lasted for ten days (Falola 1998:179).

The violence began at the Advanced Teachers College at Kafanchan as a clash between Muslim and Christian students. Christians had organized a week-long Missions week on the campus, with seminars, movies and teachings. According to Falola, while the university authorities granted permission for the events, Muslim students were disturbed particularly about the large banner hung on the school's main entrance that read 'Welcome to Mission 87 on Jesus' Campus' (Falola 1998:180). However, it was the presence of an ex-Muslim who became a Christian as one of the speakers that most infuriated the Muslim students. When rumours spread that the ex-Muslim was insulting the Qur'an and Prophet in his talk, large numbers of Muslims turned up at the event. Falola notes that what happened next is not clear; Christians claimed the Muslims rushed to attack them and they fought back in self-defence, Muslims said they asked for clarification from the speaker and a Christian student slapped a Muslim student, which caused a small fight, both sides claiming to be fighting in self-defence (Falola 1998:180. Yet the fights did not stop there. Ibrahim notes that the clash lead to 'outbreaks of violence not only in the local town, but also in Funtua, Zaria, Kankia, Daura and Kaduna. As many as 19 were killed, while 5 mosques, 152 churches, 152 private buildings, 169 hotels and beer parlours and 95 vehicles were reportedly burnt and/or otherwise damaged' (Ibrahim 1991:123). In the early 1990s, there were increasingly violent incidents in Bauchi as well as Kano, Katsina and Kaduna. Some estimates cited 10,000 people being killed in Muslim-Christian clashes between 1999–2003 (Mahmud 2013:5). A leading scholar of Nigeria, John Paden cites a government report from October 2004, which estimated nearly 54,000 dead between 1999 and 2004 in Plateau State alone (Paden 2005:52). Al Jazeera reported that at least 1,000 people were killed in the Jos area in 2010 (Al Jazeera 2011). During 2011 alone, the number of people reported dead by international media and local groups points to more than 1,500 people across the Middle Belt and Northern Nigeria. Many more have been displaced and suffered serious physical and material damage.

The sheer size and complexity of violent incidents are simply overwhelming. In fact, Nigerians often express feeling numb about the ongoing violence in their country. A *Sahara Reporters* opinion editorial, 28 April 2014, on the school children kidnapped by Boko Haram says: 'It is a story that captures everything bad about Nigeria and paints a graphic of a helpless Nation, serially served by terror, by a terror group that has abandoned any human conscience until the country became numb to violence' (Aniedobe 2014). Similarly, Lola Shoneyin notes that 'the constant onslaught of violence and murder from the north may bring about numbness in some quarters' (Shoneyin 2014). In his article, 'Why are Nigerians Numb to Slaughter', Terya Tilley-Gyado says that 'in Nigeria, nobody speaks of terrible things. Where some unimaginable atrocity has been committed the news is often met with pursed lips, a double snap of the fingers and a swift motion over one's head to invoke a purge against evil. To speak of terror is to welcome it into one's life' (Tilley-Gyado 2012).

What is equally overwhelming is the ease in which violence is deployed and quickly loses proportion. During one of my research visits to Jos, Nigeria, I got trapped between Muslim and Christian youths wreaking havoc, burning cars and attacking anyone who looked like they belonged to another religion. The anger and non-discriminatory nature of violence towards everything and everyone meant that I eventually had to hide in a shop with shutters closed down till the army arrived and put an end to the clashes with similarly indiscriminate use of force including live rounds fired into the air and into the crowds. Throughout the day, Muslim and Christian contacts in the city reported different accounts of why and how the violence started and who were the victims and perpetrators. With at least six people dead, ten injured and serious material damage caused, it later emerged that the incident was triggered because of a dispute between a Christian customer and a Muslim tradesman at the local market. When the news of the fight between the two men reached fellow believers, the story evolved into one of Muslims and Christians attacking the other party, which caused Christian and Muslim youth to walk towards the market area and violently attack anything and anyone on their way.

This ease of violent episodes emerging from simple interactions and large numbers of fatalities and histories of such incidents across Nigeria call for an analysis that can place ethno-religious violence within its historic and overall context. Most discussions on ethno-religious violence in Nigeria have focused on Plateau State, particularly Jos. While it is true that ethno-religious violence shows itself most visibly in the Middle Belt with its mixed Muslim and Christian populations sandwiched between a dominantly Muslim North and dominantly Christian South, any analysis of ethno-religious violence in

Nigeria that exclusively focuses on this troubled state and most particularly the city of Jos, will be limiting. Therefore, this section has offered a wider context of violence in Nigeria. Next, I will break the large number of violent incidents into particular types to reach an initial conclusion about the complex dynamics behind ethno-religious violence.

Political Violence in Nigeria

The link between politics and violence has been a common thread in the politics of Nigeria since its creation under colonial rule and its independence and throughout subsequent military coups. In fact, Adebanwi and Obadare note that since the 1966 coup and state of emergency that was declared in the Western region, it became impossible 'for the relations of *(ex)change* of political power to be carried out or facilitated without manifest or latent *violence* in Nigeria' and point to the perpetual state of emergency this has created:

Whether that violence consolidates, re-establishes or attempts to break existing violence; whether it is practiced as a military coup or counter-coup, a civil uprising or ethno-regional, inter-ethnic, inter-faith or political violent clashes, hegemonic or counter-hegemonic suppression, oppression or revolt, pro-democratic, student and workers' riots or election violence, police killings, pogrom, rebellion or civil war, Nigeria has become a permanent *state of emergencies* – with hardly any means, method, or institutions for efficiently addressing emergencies beyond more violence. (Adebanwi & Obadare 2010:391)

Thus, it is no surprise that post-1990s civilian party politics in Nigeria has seen violent outbursts, fragmented large-scale violence for and against independence, top-to-bottom use of force to exercise national sovereignty and local political mobilization in pursuit of local political and personal aims. Given that at the local level political stakes are high and the electoral system is often fraudulent, political actors often utilize multiple means to garner support, form alliances and ensure certain political outcomes, as they cannot simply count on mainstream constituency politics and vote gathering. Charles Tilly offers a helpful conceptualization of such actors in his discussion of "political entrepreneurs" (Tilly 2003:34). According to Tilly, political entrepreneurs engage in the activation of boundaries and relations, connecting and disconnecting distinct groups and networks, coordinating organized action on part of coalitions of interest and representation of people they claim to be speaking on behalf. Tilly captures the role played by political entrepreneurs in political violence well:

> Political entrepreneurs wield significant influence over the presence, absence, form, loci and intensity of collective violence. When they promote violence, they do so by activating boundaries, stories, and relations that have already accumulated histories; by connecting already violent actors with previously nonviolent allies; by coordinating destructive campaigns; and by representing their constituencies through threats of violence. After the fact, both participants and observers speak of deeply felt identities and age-old hatreds. (Tilly 2003:35)

They do so for personal aims, seeking to hoard, exploit and maximize their interests. Within that context, violence and most importantly threat of violence becomes an effective tool. They seek to achieve this through another group of political actors which Tilly names *violent specialists* (Tilly 2003:35). "Violent specialists" can be working both within the state, as police, secret service or regular soldiers whose work is to deploy and control means of violence, or outside of the state, incorporating a wide range of trades, from gangs, to mafia, experts in martial arts, bodybuilders or mere unemployed groups of youth willing to take physical risk as part of a day's work. Both of these groups, political entrepreneurs and violent specialists show themselves clearly and strongly at all levels of Nigerian politics, particularly in local politics. Local political figures have strong links to groups and individuals that can be used for threats of personal and communal violence. This is seen at a purely economic level in Lagos with the notorious 'Area Boys', street gangs used for extortion and control within a mafi-style patron-cliental relation. A more political example of violent specialists are the 'Bakassi Boys' in Igbo-dominated areas. International Crisis Group notes that they

> have at various times been recognised as state vigilantes and sponsored by governors. Legitimized as the Anambra Vigilante Service (AVS) between 1999 and 2003, they were suspected of involvement in several political muggings, abductions and assassinations, and widely perceived as the thuggish instrument of the then governor, Chinwoke Mbadinuju. From 2004 to 2005, Mbadinuju's successor, Chris Ngige, used the Bakassi Boys to guard himself and key officials at the Government House in Awka, following the

federal government's withdrawal of his police guards and other security privileges. (ICG 2006:17)

The wide demand for violent specialists shows itself in how militants from Niger Delta have been headhunted and offered jobs in other parts of the country as military and security 'advisers'. There are also religious violent specialists, who have been used in a similar fashion to advance political aims and enforce religious values, as can be seen in *hisba* groups that caused havoc in northern Nigeria after the introduction of Shari'a. In an interview with the *Economist,* Saidu Ahmad Dukawa, director-general of Kano's *hisba* states that 'the role of the *hisba* is to command people to do what is good and prevent what is evil' and 'we have seen an increase in good morals since we started, such as a fall in prostitution and more women voluntarily wearing the hijab' (*Economist* 2010). While the notion of *hisba* has roots in the Qur'an as adherence to rules of Shari'a and public and personal accountability, its use in Nigeria is intrinsically linked with politics, both that of the introduction of Shari'a but also the sustaining of local level political control. ICG notes that

in states such as Kano and Zamfara, the Hisbah groups, operating under the governors, began widespread campaigns of harassment against ordinary citizens. They have seized thousands of motorbikes ("okadas") from male taxi drivers who, they claimed, transport female passengers in violation of the dictate that non-related men and women should not travel together. The same governors who supported the Hisbah harassment have failed to establish ombudsmen to monitor the actions of public officials, a customary mandate of Sharia. The Hisbah have continually clashed with civilians who have resisted their intrusions and with the federally-controlled police, who accuse them of attempting to usurp their role. (ICG 2006:17)

National-level disputes over elections and about the ethnicity and religion of the president are perceived as direct opportunities or threats by local politicians and communities in a prebendal state since the personal ethnic and religious affiliation of national rulers are seen as links to maximize access to central revenues. Yet, the fierce competition for local political posts, which has direct outcomes for control of state revenues and services and opportunities received by individuals, often aggravate economic and social grievances, ethno-religious fault lines and the regular use of threats and actual use of violence by violent specialists, paid and supported by local political and business elite, trigger wider ethno-religious violence beyond their initial scope. This can be seen in the build up to and aftermath of the April 2011 elections in the country.

Even though the elections were hailed as one of the most transparent and reliable in the country's turbulent history, various political groups applied bullying tactics in the lead up to the election and unleashed violence which took an estimated 1,000 lives across northern Nigeria after the elections. The primary source of incitement and actual violence were supporters of the Congress for Progressive Change (CPC), whose Muslim presidential candidate Muhammadu Buhari lost elections to the People's Democratic Party's (PDP) Christian candidate Goodluck Jonathan. Before and throughout the elections, the CPC regularly warned of retaliation if the presidency and local governorates in particular locations shifted to Christian candidates. Christians interviewed during research in northern Nigeria reported bullying and limitations faced during the registration process as well as the actual voting day from CPC supporters. When the election results indeed did not turn out according to the CPC's anticipations, CPC youth began attacking not only PDP supporters and offices, but also Christians, their properties and churches. This triggered equally destructive attacks by Christians on Muslims in towns where Muslims are minorities.

This was the case in Kaduna state. I visited Kaduna state before and after the 2011 elections and interviewed Muslim and Christian leaders, as well as victims of violence. Kaduna was seen as a 'success' story of how brutal violence in the early 2000s calmed down and Kaduna city itself was seen as a promising model of how Nigeria can overcome decades-long ethno-religious violence. This was largely due to the praiseworthy efforts of the then Muslim governor. Tangible expressions of political will, such as the creation of Operation Yaki, which set up security personnel to address signs of ethno-religious violence, and creation of official structures that bring Muslim and Christian leaders to raise concerns and grievances and incorporate them into state structures, has indeed achieved an important progress towards peace. However, Muslims and Christians interviewed in Kaduna all pointed out that the peace was deceptive and it was fragile, as all of the root causes of grievances were still there. Muslims and Christians did not trust one another; rumours of the other group pursuing sinister projects to harm the other such as spreading HIV and piling weapons in secret locations were too common. Christians and Muslims were forced to move out of each other's neighbourhoods. Muslims and Christians interviewed were all confident that they were in fact the majority in the state and they were 'indigenes' or had settled in the area for three or four generations, thus were entitled to indigene rights. In 2011, however, both the outcome of national elections that brought a Christian president into the office as well as the outcome of local elections, which for the first time in thirty-five years placed a Christian into Kaduna's governorate, triggered an outbreak in violence and evocation of underlying issues. The CPC not only declared the election results to be rigged, but also used its thugs to unleash attacks. All across Kaduna State, CPC supporters began attacking not only PDP supporting Muslims and PDP facilities, but events quickly turned towards burning churches and attacking Christians en masse. News of Christians being attacked and killed in other towns quickly triggered Christian youth confronting and indiscriminately attacking Muslim looking individuals and mosques. During the few days in which the violence lasted, entire sections of towns were burnt and destroyed and hundreds of Muslims and Christians were killed brutally. During my post-election visit to the city, towns in Kaduna State that had seen violence were still tense and the destruction of properties and places of worship, especially churches, were at inconceivable levels. On various occasions, I was even advised not to travel to certain towns nor to talk about the events.

The common occurrence of political violence in Nigeria demonstrate the almost normalized, if not routinized, place of violence as a possible form of political expression, but also how the calculated politics of elites can trigger wider ethno-religious conflict. However, the presence of political elites that seek to maximize interest by deployment of violence does not explain why the violence is there in the first place and why political and violence entrepreneurs succeed in creating larger violence. Possible answers to this question can be found in the very nature of the Nigerian state, its prebendalism and its effects on common citizens.

Violent Outcomes of a Prebendal State

There is an intrinsic link between on one hand the evolution of Nigeria's rentier economy, its prebendalism in a geography that is seeing intense deforestation, mass increase in population and lucrative revenues gained form oil and on the other hand the high levels of ongoing violence. Gore and Pratten rightfully note that 'since 1999 and a return to multi-party democracy, Nigeria has witnessed intensified contests concerning rights over economic re-distribution and judicial authority, and the privileges of representation and patrimony' (Gore & Pratten 2003:213). Given the normalized presence of political violence, it is no surprise that such an intensified contest fuels and drives violent outcomes. This can be seen in three different types of violence in Nigeria: (i) violence triggered by a central government monopoly of resources; (ii) violence triggered by allocation of revenues in a federal structure that demarcates 'indigenes' from 'settlers'; and (iii) violence that is primarily an expression of opportunism.

The Niger Delta crisis is a perfect example of (i), how politics of a prebendal federal government can trigger cycles of violence as well as organized crime with deep roots in underprivileged communities. Some 95 per cent of Nigeria's export revenues and 85 per cent of government revenues depend on the oil and gas sector (Francis, Lapin & Rossaiasco 2011:5). The vast majority of these natural resources are found in southern Nigeria in a large area referred to as Niger Delta, which includes nine oil-producing states: Abia, Akwa Ibom, Bayelsa, Cross River, Delta, Edo, Imo, Ondo and Rivers. With its population of 32 million and over 40 ethnic groups with 120 distinct languages and dialects it is one of the most densely populated areas of the country. Hill points out that thirty non-oil producing states depend on the Niger Delta and Abuja, the capital city, for much of their income (Hill 2012:91). While the Niger Delta plays the role of funding the central government in Abuja which in return maintains the rentier economy that sustains other states, since the independence of Nigeria, the people of the Delta have not reaped the benefits. The International Crisis Group cites the findings of a Nigerian federal government ministerial fact-finding visit to the region in 1994, which has stated the following: 'basic facilities like roads, potable water, electricity, health care and education are completely absent in many communities and nonfunctioning in others where they exist . . . On the whole, the scale of physical neglect of the oil producing areas is enormous' (ICG 2006:6).

The people of the region have long expressed reactions against the domination of the state by the Hausa, Igbo and Yoruba. While as early as 1966, before the Biafran War, there were attempts by Niger Delta groups to gain independence, it was not until the late 1990s that we saw the emergence of violent ethnic clashes, militant and criminal groups, attacks and kidnapping of oil workers and fierce and violent political clashes (Naanen & Nyiayaana 2013:120). This is largely attributed to the complete loss of belief in the region that peaceful politics and political demands would move the central government to hear their grievances (Naanen & Nyiayaana 2013:116). In fact, even though elections took place, their results were often manipulated by the national political elite. Suberu points out that 'although his policies on the Niger Delta during the 1999–2003 period were extremely unpopular in the region, President Obasanjo was still credited with landslide victories in the Niger Delta states in the 2003 elections' (Suberu 2010:470). If the outcome of elections can be fixed, then there is little incentive for grass-root empowerment. A prebendal state can act in its usual structure of deals cut with local powerful elites. So, even though there have been initiatives since 2009 that offered amnesty to militants, which more than 20,000 militants took[5] and agreements to increase the Niger Delta's share of oil revenues, not much has changed in the day-to-day experiences of people of the region. Mass unemployment and underdevelopment in the region continues as the oil industry is notoriously high in the monies it generates, but low in employment and development of its production areas, along with the environmental damage it can cause (See Amnesty International 2013b).

Type (ii) violence emerges from the clash of 'indigenes' and 'settlers' due to the same root causes of nature of Nigerian state structure and the lack of access to state revenues. While most people in Nigeria see classifications of 'indigene' versus 'settlers' as giving clear legal rights, the 1999 Nigerian constitution provides no clear basis for entitlements. However, the so-called Federal Character Principle in Article 147(3) obliges the president to appoint a minister from each state, 'who shall be an indigene to that state'. The article does not provide any further elaboration on what an indigene is. The only insight into the elusive phrase comes in Article 318(1), which states that when the words 'belong to' or 'its grammatical expression when used with reference to a person in a state refers to a person either or whose parents or any of whose grandparents was a member of a community indigenous to that state'. In contrast, the constitution includes strong and clear provisions that ban discrimination on the basis of ethnicity and religion.

No matter how feeble it is legally, the definition of certain groups as indigenes and others as settlers is not simply a matter of identity satisfaction granted to those who can trace a historical heritage linked to the towns in which they live. The 700 Local Government Area (LGA) authorities that govern the country establish the status of indigenes. The LGA issues certificates for people who can 'prove' that they are indigenes to the area. The certificates enable access to jobs, federal government funds, scholarships and the right to run for political offices. Some people are denied certificates altogether, even though they are indigenes, making them stateless within Nigeria with no access to any opportunities provided through local governments. Thus, exclusion of certain groups and privileging of others are enabled by the structures of the country, which has triggered fierce competition over local political posts and inevitably, violent expressions of grievances and desire to protect communal interests. This is amplified by the fact that Nigeria has seen tremendous levels of in-country migration since independence, thus the territorial ownership have been increasingly contested. Nnoli states that

between 1952 and 1963, an estimated 644,000 migrants poured into Lagos at a yearly rate of nearly 59,000 ... Between 1952 and 1963, a total of 124,989 Southerners migrated to the North. Out of these, 54 per cent went to the central core area of Kano, Zaria and Jos divisions and Kaduna regional capital territory ... From the North, some 167,689 migrants came to the three main cities of Kano, Zaria and Kaduna.' (Nnoli 1995:30) As Nnoli draws our attention to, 'major cases of inter-ethnic conflict tension and violence in the history of Nigeria have occurred in these towns or originated from them' (Nnoli 1995:30).

Throughout 2011, there were raids by large number of Hausa-Fulanis in Bauchi and Borno states that forced more than 4,500 villagers to be Internally Displaced Persons (IDPs) and to flee for their lives (CSW 2011a). In the Middle Belt, since no community can declare a clear-cut majority, the issue of who has the 'rights' over the land has become explosive. While in northern Nigeria indigene status is not a point of contention, as the power structures are clear, in places such Plateau State, especially in the city of Jos, regular incidents of violence occur especially before and after local government elections (Okereke 2013:150). This relationship to politics is exactly why a Christian bishop interviewed in Nigeria said 'Jos' crisis is everything but religious'. For example, in November 2008 hundreds of Christians and Muslims were killed, properties, business and places of worship burnt to ashes and more than 10,000 fled their homes following disputes over a local government election (BBC News 2008). The violence began by Hausa-Fulanis protesting against the victory of the Christian candidate and quickly turned into a full-blown conflict where Christians and Muslims were attacked randomly and indiscriminately. In response to the violence, the military used disproportionate force and enforced a curfew, killing scores of people in the process.

I visited the areas damaged during the 2008 riots and met with representatives of various Christian-majority indigene communities, such as Birom, Afizere and Anaguta, as well as Hausa-Fulanis, Muslim and Christian clerics, and representatives of civil society groups. Indigene groups feel that Hausa-Fulani politicians issue indigene certificates to their own tribes and Muslims even though they might be new settlers and deny certificates to the rightful indigenes of the area. Hausa-Fulanis feel that they should not be seen as settlers as their families have been in the city for two or three generations. Given the acute unemployment among the youth and the economic opportunities provided by political offices and power gained by patronage systems based on issuing of certificates, violence is triggered easily and automatically takes on a form of religious clash between Christians and Muslims. This is because it is the religious boundaries that mark differences between ethnic groups, such as the Muslim-majority Hasua-Fulanis and other ethnic communities of the Middle Belt, mostly Christian with a smaller portion of traditional Nigerian religions.[6] The outcome of this is truly staggering: according to a report of the Plateau State Committee for the Rehabilitation and Reconciliation of Internally Displaced Persons, between 2001 and 2004, there were 53,787 recorded deaths in the conflicts in the state, 280,000 people were displaced, 1,300 cattle slaughtered and about 25,000 homes destroyed in the clashes (Okereke 2013:174).

The gradual transformation of indigene versus settler conflict into an ethno-religious conflict escalates the initial cause of violence to a much larger religious framework that moves beyond the politics of the Middle Belt to all of Nigeria and turns the local tension into a continuation of global developments involving apparently Christian and Muslim-majority nations. Ukiwo captures this dynamic while commenting on the September 2001 clashes that saw more than 1,000

fatalities in Jos alone (Ukiwo 2003). He notes that while 'the immediate cause of the riot was a dispute between a Christian woman and a
Muslim outside a mosque, the riots have been linked to the appointment of a Muslim as head of the lucrative post of coordinator of
the federal government's Poverty Alleviation Programme (PAP)'. The
Muslim Hausa-Fulani appointee eventually resigned from the post due
to the opposition of Christians and other indigenes, which charged
feelings of injustice among Muslims. Ukiwo says that the crisis in town
deepened

when Muslim youths took to the streets to celebrate the terrorist attack on
the United States three days later. When the United States began retaliatory
attacks on Afghanistan a month later, demonstrations by Muslims youths in
Kano degenerated into a riot in which 200 lives were lost. The youths were
protesting not just at the attack on Afghanistan but at the fact that the
Nigerian government supported US efforts to apprehend the masterminds
of the 11 September tragedy. (Ukiwo 2003:125)

A prebendal state with weak rule of law also turns violence into a
low risk opportunity for personal and communal gain, which is type
(iii) mentioned at the start of this section. A more organized and
regular expression of this is the raids by Hausa-Fulani tribesmen and
cattle herders across Plateau State. There are numerous ongoing cases
of Christian villages and cattle owners being attacked in rural areas,
their properties and stocks looted, houses burnt and many left dead.
Poor villagers often find themselves in further difficulties if they report
their stolen cattle and file complaints. A nineteen-year-old boy interviewed at the outskirts of Jos still had fresh wounds from the attack
on his house and farms two days earlier, which left his father dead,
destroyed all of their property and took away more than 100 cattle.
This last attack which completely destroyed the future of his family
and caused the young man to be relocated continually with the fear of
being hunted down was in response to an earlier raid by Hausa-Fulanis
which the family reported to the police and pursued their case at the
courts. They were verbally warned to withdraw their complaints by
Hausas. If not, they would face the outcomes. The family did not back
down. Their attackers, who are known by authorities and local communities, were not brought to justice. Christian Solidarity Worldwide
recorded 50 dead, mostly women and children, in fourteen attacks on

villages in Plateau State by Hausa-Fulani tribesmen during the first three months of 2011 alone (CSW 2011b).

Such raids are clearly organized against particular villages that are weaker and from different ethnic groups than those of the attackers, most of the time Christian, with a clear aim of stealing livestock. A pastor told me in an interview that this was not a religious issue, that 'there are economic undertones, but religion gives them a reason', thus they attack non-Muslims and see their looting as jihad and the legitimate spoils of war. The Hausa-Fulani tribesmen's raids trigger retaliation from Christians, who attack Muslim villagers. A Muslim woman activist interviewed in Jos told that in 2010, a group of Christians took 264 cows and eleven members of her family were killed, alongside seventy-two other people who died in her village. She said 'Nobody did anything, even though some of the attackers are known'. There are also wider cases of opportunism provided by outbursts of violence for a wide range of actors. Almost every incident of ethno-religious violence in Middle Belt Nigeria includes looting of houses and shops. Whatever the initial reasons or the multiple motivations and reasons behind the attacks, opportunities provided by overall chaos and clashes provide ample opportunities for criminal acts. During a group interview, a village elder in Kaduna area mentioned without giving an example that sexual violence also happens within such contexts, but it is almost never reported for cultural reasons.

All of these expressions of violence – whether over the issuing of LGA 'indigene certificates', criminal networks in Niger Delta, Hausa-Fulani raiders, individual momentary opportunism or overall crime rates across the country – are outcomes of the lack of a fair system and rule of law that can guarantee and protect each and every individual and an economic system that is geared for the betterment of the entire country. It starts at the macro-level of national politics and the sharing of central government revenues by high-level political elite interests found alongside competition between states and regions. Individuals who have no political and economic access often have no other way than to use physical force to protect or maximize their interests. It creates conditions for incentives for personal participation in violence for personal gains, such as stealing, taking revenge against a known neighbour, partaking in a thrilling mass violent episode and expressing sexual aggression.

Violence in the Name of Religion

If violent political competition and the asserting of communal and personal interests in a prebendal state can be said to be the inevitable outcomes of those political and economic structures, there are also types of violence that emerge as a reaction to those structures. Secular politics has failed to provide a fair society that could create a united Nigeria with a strong sense of equal citizenship and a state that upholds the rights and interests of all. As argued in previous sections, the disillusionment of majority of the population and attempts and strategies to survive a prebendal state highlighted ethnic politics and strengthened ethnic identities and solidarities. Yet, since the 1970s, the ethnic political visions and elites too have failed to address the injustices of the system. The increasing importance of religious figures, organizations and sentiments since then were clear expressions of demands for a fairer and purer society and a longed-for hope and promised vision for the future. While such sentiments were open to manipulation by the political elite, as we saw in the politics of the introduction of Shari'a in the northern states, for many these did not go far enough and the political and religious elite too were seen to be part of the problem. This resulted in widespread demands for more public morality, the protection of the society from religious impurity and advancement of the 'right type' of religion. Within the context of widespread violence in Nigeria, the competition for purity of society and protection of religious values has created three distinct but interrelated types of violence that moves beyond mere ethno-religious demarcations and politics of indigenes versus settlers: *ideological violence, prophetic violence* and *cultic violence.*

The strong presence of the use of violence for ideological ends can be seen particularly in northern Nigeria and the Middle Belt region, especially among the myriad of Islamist elites, local networks and clerics. Glorified memories of the Sokoto Caliphate and the Great Jihad which had been launched to expand Islam to the rest of West Africa and Nigeria are still widely alluded to by Muslims, particularly in northern Nigeria. Far from being melancholic about a long lost kingdom that now seems too far away to restore, Muslims interviewed particularly in northern Nigeria held passionate beliefs that not only Muslim-majority states but the whole of Nigeria should be based upon Islam and the place of non-Muslims in Muslim-majority societies should be subjugated to provisions of Shari'a. These beliefs that refer to traditional Islamic jurisprudence about the place of minorities in a Muslim society and the place of Islam in governance for all provide strong frameworks for the use of violence, not simply legitimized by the outcomes of a prebendal state, but allowed, rewarded and at times demanded by God. Divinely-sanctioned mistreatment of minorities, as enshrined by Shari'a laws, results in socioeconomic exclusion and ultimately violence against vulnerable minorities in the North. In Katsina, a leading Muslim academic and community activist told me that whoever does not obey Shari'a, including non-Muslims, should be punished severely. Consequently Muslims who decide to leave Islam for Christianity are killed and severely punished across northern Nigeria. Non-Muslims find themselves at the mercy of local authorities and religious figures and vulnerable to attacks by Muslim youth. A group of Christian university students in the same area reported to me numerous incidents of being called derogatory names, thrown stones at and arbitrarily beaten simply because they are Christians. Christian girls reported incidents where they were forced to wear Islamic outfits and assaulted by Muslim men who called them prostitutes. There are also worrying accounts of modern day slavery in northern Nigeria, which can be taken as another sign of an ordering of the society and hierarchical levels of entitlement and exclusion.

These issues ultimately lie at the heart of why Christians living in the Middle Belt and northern Nigeria protested widely against the implementation of Shari'a in those states and also why their protests have attracted violent response. Akwara notes that the peaceful protests of Christians in the North against introduction of Shari'a Law in early 2000s which they saw as dividing Nigeria and ultimately aimed at them was met with violent responses, leading to 'organized killings of Christians in northern cities and the burning down of churches and other places where Christians are found especially their homes and shops across the northern region', which triggered 'reprisal killings of Moslems [*sic*] in the eastern towns of Aba, Owerri, Port-Harcourt Onitsha and Asaba' (Akwara et al. 2013:71). The desire for a religious moral ordering based on a clear Islamist ideology also show itself in violence against non-mainstream Muslim groups and between various Islamic sects. Sufi brotherhoods (*tariqa*) have both been victims to attacks and campaign by mainstream Sunni Muslims as well as clashing with each other out of theological differences and for spheres of influence. Mainstream Sunnis see Sufi mysticism, the veneration of spiritual leaders and importance of shrines as heresy, but still closer to each other than to Shia Islam. Meanwhile Sufi orders, such as the Qadiriyya and Tijanniya brotherhoods are locked into decades-long fierce competition with each other with sporadic episodes of violent clashes (Falola 1998:225–246).

In localities where Muslims and Christians share close to even numerical presence, religious violence often turns into larger clashes, moving beyond the scope of its initial perpetrators and indiscriminately turning both Muslims and Christians into victims. This is all the more so in the *prophetic violence* which is often deployed for demanding public morality, respect to religious values and proper conduct. Prophetic violence can be seen in the disproportionate response given to activities of other religious communities that are perceived to be shaking, harming or polluting the sacred space of a religious community. For example, in October 1991, a religious conflict erupted in Kano, after Muslim groups led by the Izala sect began protests against the news that a German Christian evangelist would be preaching in the town, leashing attacks on Christians and destruction or properties, murdering 'scores of people, mainly Christians. The violence was eventually brought to an end by a vigorous and determined counter-attack mounted by the Igbo Christian residents of the city' (Nnoli 1995:207). Similarly, widespread violence erupted in Tafawa Balew in Bauchi State in 1991. Adebayo notes that the initial cause of the incident is not clear, however 'while some believed that erupted following an attempt of a Christian to slaughter pigs in the Muslim section of the town's only abattoir, some said it was ignited consequent upon roasted meat (suya) made of pork and sold to a Muslim' (Adebayo 2010:216). Given that pork is *haram* in Islam and pigs are seen as dirty animals, their blood and meat are seen as an abomination of the sacred and as defiling to Muslims. Two further examples demonstrating this type of violence well are the Miss World Crisis in 2002 and the Danish Cartoons Crisis in 2006. In 2002, when it was announced that the Miss World pageant contest would be held in Nigeria, Muslim voices increasingly protested against such an 'immoral' event to be held in the country, especially during Ramadan (Sampson 2012:118). When the issue turned into a stand against Shari'a from the First Lady of the country and Christians of the South, the issue became explosive. Riots broke out in Kaduna and Abuja, taking lives and causing serious damage. Sampson notes an interesting dynamic of Muslim groups transferring their anger over 'immorality' to Christians:

Whereas nudity is strongly abhorred by moderate Muslims and Christians, their disposition to accommodating changing societal values under temporal authority, in spite of their offensive characteristics, restrained them from actively protesting against the event, while choosing to condemn it in their Mosques, Churches and other gatherings. On the other hand, it was the exhibition of Islamic fundamentalism that resulted in the violent attacks on Christians by Muslim extremists, who associated the event with Christianity. This also demonstrates the pervasive ignorance amongst some Islamic faithful, who often associate Christianity with profanity, on account of its accommodation of social, economic and cultural activities that are seemingly immoral or perverse. (Sampson 2012:118)

This irrational transference is key in understanding how events in another part of the world involving actors with no links to Nigeria can indeed trigger violence. In 2006, global reactions towards the cartoon depicting Prophet Muhammad published by a Danish newspaper in 2005 hit Nigeria. Protests by Muslims against the insult committed by the Danish paper turned into an attack on Christians in Nigeria, who obviously had nothing to do with the liberal Danish publication. More than 50 Christians were killed and churches were burnt in Maiduguri, Katsina and Bauchi, which then attracted retaliatory attacks by Christians on mosques in other parts of the country. It is often argued that 'indeed, more people died in Nigeria as a result of riots over the cartoon than in all of the other countries of the world put together' (Gow et al. 2013:242). Okwudiba Nnoli notes the long-term impact that increasing attacks on Christian churches had on Christians, and argues that 'the Christians have become more vigilant, self-assertive and equally willing to use violence to resist attacks. They have matched Muslim political organization with their own, and Muslim religious fundamentalism with their own' (Nnoli 1995:207). This effect of violence on Christians was also observed in almost all interviews conducted in Nigeria. One Christian pastor in Kaduna told me that 'Christians ran out of cheek to turn', in allusion to the call of Christ to turn the other cheek to those who persecute his followers. The pastor had seen brutal incidents of violence and told me that a Christian also has a responsibility to protect his family, community and the church. Members of a Christian ethnic group also told me that they were getting prepared 'to teach Muslims a lesson'. In contrast to the language of Jihad and the fight against blasphemy and immorality among Muslim perpetrators, for Christians vigilantes the rationalization process goes through a Weberian separation of ethics of conviction versus ethics of responsibility. Theological beliefs on forgiving of the enemy is temporarily suspended in order to protect one's family, church and ethnic group, and in the process freezing ethical and spiritual questions posed by strong theological convictions.

Both *ideological* and *prophetic* are reactionary in nature but still seek to reform society through enforcement of religious ideals within the established order. In contrast, *cultic violence* has no such clear aim. If certain expressions of violence can be said to be emerging from a reaction to a corrupt and secular country and its ruling classes, cultic violence not only reacts to the same ill but also to the religious establishment and mainstream religiosity as well, and completely rejects the established order. It promotes a retreat into a close-knit community at a cosmic war (a concept which we will discuss at length in later chapters). Nigeria regularly sees the emergence of cultic groups that centre around charismatic preachers with non-traditional Islamic theologies. They blend apocalyptic visions with twentieth-century discourses of political Islam with high levels of violence. Their extreme use of violence breaks all rules of traditional doctrines of jihad that bring boundaries to the use of violence, such as not harming the innocent and fellow Muslims. These often appeal back to and follow similar language and efforts to the Great Jihad of Othman Dan Fodio.[7]

A key example of this is the Maitatsine, found by the charismatic self-declared prophet and preacher Muhammadu Marwa. It was Marwa's nickname, 'the one who knows how to curse', Maitatsine, that gave the sect its name, following his fierce and angry preaching that often got him into trouble with local authorities and Muslim clerics. He eventually declared himself to be a prophet with divine powers and attracted more than 10,000 followers by 1980 (Falola 1998:143). Raymond Hickey observes that the 'urban Muslim poor were attracted to Maitatsine because he condemned the hypocrisy and ostentation of the nouveau riche and promised redemption and salvation to God's righteous people' (Hickey 1984:253). Falola points out that followers of the sect carried posters of Ayatollah Khomeini and Muammar Khaddafi, 'indicating that they accepted these two as model political reformers – the *Mujahhid* – of the very kind that Nigeria needed'

(Falola 1998:145). While such expressions might come across as mainstream, Marwa's followers shaved their heads and increasingly lived in together, secluding themselves from the world and other Islamic groups and Marwa's teachings and declaration of himself as a prophet brought him into conflict with mainstream Islam. The sect's clashing with police and others reached such levels that eventually it took the Nigerian military to clamp down and seize control of the sect's headquarters in 1980. By then, the violence unleashed by Maitatsine took the lives of more than 5,000 people and splinter groups and self-declared successors continued to unleash occasional attacks on security forces in other towns till the mid-1980s (Fasua 2013).

This takes us back to the case of Boko Haram. It is a similar cultic organization to Maitatsine that emerged in northeastern Nigeria in 2001. While the full name of the group is 'the Congregation of the People of Tradition for Proselytism and Jihad', it is often referred to by its nickname in Hausa language, Boko Haram, which literally means 'western education is sinful (*haram*)'. Biographical details of its founder, Mohammed Yusuf, remain sketchy with different accounts of his upbringing and education. However, Yusuf had exposure to a variety of Islamist movements in Nigeria, including Shiite and Sunni ones, and had exposure to both Iranian and Egyptian Islamist thought. The mosque, Ibn Taymiyya Masjid, founded by Yusuf evolved into a settlement with its own governance structures, refusal of Nigerian state governance and calls to application of strict Shari'a laws and refusal of all that was from the Colonial West. His teachings focused on establishment of an Islamic order, with the symbolism of retreat from corruption for the true believers, like in Prophet Muhammad's *hijra* from Mecca to Medina. While the sect was not initially violent, from 2004 to 2009, there were attacks attributed to Boko Haram members and subsequent arrests, including that of Yusuf (Pantucci & Jesperson 2015:5, 6). Yet, it was really in 2009 and onwards that the Nigerian state showed increased responses to the organization. Legislation passed in 2009 in Borno state that required all motorcycle drivers to wear helmets triggered the start of clashes between Boko Haram followers and security personnel. When police officers stopped a group of Boko Haram members riding their bikes without helmets during a funeral procession and they refused to comply, what followed was a confrontation leaving scores of injured behind (Comolli 2015:53). Police raids on Boko Haram facilities following the incident triggered

attacks by Boko Haram against police stations and government buildings in Borno, Kano, Katsina and Yobe. Government gave the green
light to seize Boko Haram's headquarters and taking control of towns
under Boko Haram's control. Following three days of clashes with
the security forces, Yusuf was captured and killed, along with some
800 sect members. His compound was destroyed and many followers
fled Nigeria to neighbouring countries or went into hiding (Comolli
2015:54).

In 2010, the group reemerged in Maiduguri under the leadership
of Abubakar Shekau, a student and high-ranking officer of Yusuf, with
a much harsher preaching of militant jihad rather than a purifying
hijra. 'Shekau has translated Yusuf's theological positions into simple
slogans that present audiences with an all-or-nothing choice between
Islam and democracy' (Thurston 2016:11). Shekau ushered in a violent
phase with increased militancy. He also attracted foreign fighters and
developed links with other militant groups in northwest Africa. He has
been behind attacks to Christians and Muslims alike, schools, churches
and increasingly government targets and state buildings. Aloa notes
that 'the Boko Haram phenomenon is undoubtedly the most complex
and most extensive manifestation of Islamic radicalization in Nigeria's
history. Between 2009 and January 2012, about a thousand people
died as a result of the group's activities' (Aloa 2013:136). In 2013,
violent attacks by Boko Haram increased, showing a greater level
military sophistication and raising suspicion of increased engagement
with international jihadist groups. Al Jazeera news reported that
between May and December 2013 alone the group killed some 1,200
people (Al Jazeera 2014). Femi Fani-Kayode, a former minister, stated
that 'all in all Nigeria has lost almost 8,000 innocent civilians to Boko
Haram in the last three years and that includes women and children'
(Fani-Kayode 2014). Heavy-handed counter-operations by Nigerian
security forces, including aerial bombings of towns, have also taken
thousands of lives, particularly since 2009, though no exact figure is
publicly available. A statistical analysis of event data relating to Boko
Haram attacks and Nigerian state responses between 2009 and 2013
have revealed that 'military operations increased risk in Nigeria by
increasing the frequency of terrorists events, as well as the probability
that an attack will happen in the following month. The more military
operations there are, the more that probability of a terrorist attack in
the following month increase' (Stevenson 2015:18). In fact, the same

study showed that responses given by the police and local vigilantes had not only been more effective than responses of the Nigerian military, but also were more likely to prevent future attacks (Stevenson 2015:18). Thus, the link between brutal and indiscriminate use by the military in fuelling violence by groups like Boko Haram can be asserted in confidence.

All of these three types of violence – ideological, prophetic and cultic – cause much wider violence across the country. The spread of violence beyond its immediate context is enabled by two important carriers: media and religious professionals. The role of media in mass violence is a common phenomenon. Sampson cites the example of the 1987 violence at Kafanchan, when radio broadcasts included allegations that 'Christians were killing Muslims indiscriminately, burning their Mosques and copies of the Holy Qur'an, and banishing them from the town' and 'that an itinerant preacher had misquoted the Qur'an and blasphemed the name of Prophet Mohammed, urging Christians to kill Muslims and burn their Mosques' (Sampson 2012:123–124). The outcome was attacks on Christians across Kaduna state. Religious professionals, whether Islamic or Christian preachers and clergy, play an important role in the maintenance of mistrust and emotive and, at times violent responses given to other religious groups. A Christian pastor interviewed in Kaduna told how he was in the market place buying fruits, and the mosque next door was broadcasting the sermon of the imam from loudspeakers. The Imam was urging Muslims not to allow Christians to build churches, because it would attract God's wrath on their lives and that voting for any Christian political candidate was akin to apostasy. Omotosho documents how Muslim and Christian clerics represent one another, dehumanizing, and at times preaching dangerous incitement. He notes that the 'inter-religious violence is encouraged by the failure of religious leaders or intellectuals to imbibe the spirit of "live and let live" by accepting the existence of other religions alongside their own and through demonstrating this acceptance by recognising all necessary rights to which others are entitled' (Omotosho 2003:29). This is also argued by Sampson, who notes that 'the mockery of opposing faiths is also compounded by the pervasive stereotyping of religious adherents. For instance, Muslims, especially those from the northern part of Nigeria, are in the habit of referring to all non-Muslims as *Arna* or *Kafir*: Arabic words for 'heathen' or unbelievers; while it is fashionable

for Christians to refer to all Muslims as terrorists and violence-
mongers' (Sampson 2012:121). Such representations only fuels the
dehumanization of the 'other', which is a key mechanism in violence.

Conclusion

This chapter demonstrated the complex background to violent episodes of ethno-religious violence in Nigeria. It showed that both Islam
and Christianity were latecomers to Nigeria, following trade routes
and missionary zeal of expansion. It noted the important historic
processes that have formed the close relationship of religion with tribal
identities and political solidarities during pre-colonial and colonial
times. It demonstrated that while by the time of independence, ethnic
themes and solidarities had dominated federal level politics as dominant ethnic groups sought to secure their interests and regional superiority, and minority ethnic communities increasingly felt marginalized and
excluded. Subsequent military regimes, alongside corrupt civilian politics formed a fierce political competition for resources, national and
domestic political power and access to revenues. As the oil boom
overlapped with increasing deforestation and rapid movements of
people across the country, the gap between those who could access
power, business and money and those that depend on the patronage of
those who can increased. Within this context, religion saw a powerful
resurgence in politics at the national level. Public demands for a fair
society and calls for implementation of public morality opened a new
chapter for political significance of religious figures and places of
worship which emerged as one of the few venues of civil society,
support and mobilization.

Increasingly, Nigerian national politics included religious concerns
and themes, and the North-South divide became framed through the
language of Islam versus Christianity. This was fuelled further by
the international developments since the 1979 Islamic Revolution in
Iran, triggering political Islamic groups to push forward visions of
an Islamic Nigeria, which caused anxiety and political mobilization among Christian religious organizations aiming to counter it.
Since the 1980s, Nigeria has seen direct clashes between Muslims
and Christians triggered by religious sensitivities, rumours of attacks
on co-religionists elsewhere and wider violent episodes triggered by
local election results and sudden political changes. These were within

the context of legacies of brutal military regimes and the Biafran War as well as the increasing use of organized crime and mobilized political violence across the country and local rebellions by minority ethnic groups demanding fair access to state revenues as the country shifted into civilian rule.

Violence has become all too common and frequent. Trust in security forces has been low and often they themselves have been the source of disproportionate use of force, State structures have not upheld the rule of law or ever brought perpetrators of violence to justice. Violence continued unchecked in Nigeria, only increasing in size and scope. An officer with the Jamaat Nasurat al Islam said in an interview that 'even though governments were aware, they failed to take action against violence, and violence escalated'. A Christian pastor I interviewed in Jos also pointed to the lack of response by governments as key to why clashes continued to happen. He said that attackers who are arrested get released. Some killers have been guilty of few attacks but keep getting released, so the attackers think nothing will happen to them. A high ranking judicial figure in Plateau State told me at a small meeting that the culture of impunity was the problem; prosecutions were limited and political pressure real. The sense of helplessness, frequent violent incidents and no sense of rule of law and justice is the reason why many Nigerians speak about feeling numb over witnessing levels of violence unparalleled in most parts of the world. Within such a context, resorting to violence to protect one's self and community and assert interests and grievances become low risk, a normal possibility and sometimes the only chance for the disadvantaged. During an interview, a Muslim female activist said that there were three reasons behind the conflicts: envy due to some tribes looking at others and seeing their economic and political advances; fear because each group becomes afraid of the other; and threat since each group sees another one as a danger. It is these three powerful emotions – envy, fear and threat – that continues to fuel zero-sum social, political and religious contentions in Nigeria. In the process, Nigeria has not only produced dangerous cults and terror organizations with deep religious apocalyptic visions, retreating from the society and deploying violence in visions of reform and purification, but it has also seen the accommodation of violence as the only option left even among religious communities with strong religious teaching of 'turning the other cheek'.

Since the 1990s and particularly since the 2001 attack on the World Trade Center, Nigerians have verbalized their own local experiences through the emerging global fault lines of 'Islam' vs. 'Christian West'. This language not only grants a cosmic meaning to very local and tangible issues, but also results in developments in Nigeria being picked up by global actors promoting an imagined global clash between Islam and Christianity, International attention given by global Christian and Muslim networks, ranging from mainstream non-governmental organizations through faith-based aid and relief groups to more dangerous religious political agendas funded by foreign countries and foreign religious militants building bridges with Nigerian groups have only fuelled deep historic misperceptions between Christian and Muslim groups and amplified local problems. As a result, many Nigerians themselves have come to see inherent distances and animosities between themselves and members of the other religion. Some of these perceptions reach implausible levels. During my interviews in Nigeria, there were Christians who described how Muslim men were sent with syringes to inflict Christians with HIV in marketplaces and that mosques are used to hide mass stocks of weapons. A Muslim officer with JNI cited previously said he heard stories of some Christian tribes eating human flesh. Interestingly, most people interviewed in Nigeria still expressed that they actually have good friends and neighbours from the other religion and in many violent incidents, people from other religions have protected each other. Yet, familiarity does not diminish the perceived threat of the other. A Christian pastor made this point by citing an old traditional saying in an interview in Kaduna: just because you are familiar with the chicken, it does not mean you don't slaughter it.

3 | *Religious Violence in Egypt*

The sparkle in his eyes and warm tone of voice almost distracted me from the gravity of the events he was describing. A group of villagers attacked his monastery on the borders of a desert town in Upper Egypt; the group beat the monks, looted their agricultural tools, and destroyed some of their facilities. Sitting in his long black robe, his arm in bondage, face still full of bruises, he was adamant to tell of not only the attack itself but the human stories and miracles as he saw them. He described how one of his fellow monks is so short that he could not run away fast enough from the attackers in the fields. He fell to the ground. As the attacker raised the back of a shotgun to beat him, out of nowhere bees came to sting the assailant, causing him to run away and leave the monk alone. He smiled widely while telling me the story and describing the short monk, adding that it was a miracle that the Lord protected him. Yet, neither the miracle nor smiles took away the images of wounds suffered by other monks he moved on to show me. While we walked around the compound to see some of the damage, police officers in civilian clothes came to stop the tour and forced me to leave abruptly.

The violence against Christians in Egypt particularly attracted global attention during the summer of 2013, which saw an unprecedented level of violence in Egypt's history. On August 14, protests by supporters of the Muslim Brotherhood and President Morsi, who had been ousted and arrested in a widely backed military coup in July, were brutally dispersed by the Egyptian security forces, killing more than one thousand people in a single day (HRW 2014b). The incident caused widespread unrest across the country as thousands of Muslim Brotherhood supporters and other Islamist groups launched protests. Within a matter of days, angry crowds rioting against the clampdown by the military attacked 'more than 200 Christian owned properties' and '43 churches were seriously damaged across the country' (Amnesty

International 2013a). The Copts had no responsibility for the fate of the Muslim Brotherhood government, nor the brutal murders by the Egyptian Army, except that the head of the Coptic Orthodox Church, Pope Tawadros, had backed the military takeover of the country along with the head of Egypt's Al-Azhar University. Attacks on Copts drew condemnation globally. They were often referred to as a reminder of the risks posed by Islamists to Christians, the West and Israel. Thus, the protection of Copts has often been part of the argument for seeing the backing of President Sisi and his clampdown on Islamists as a key aspect of addressing threats caused by Islamists globally.[1] Waves of attacks on Copts by Islamists in Egypt came amidst regional turbulence across the Middle East and North Africa and serious worries over the future of non-Muslim, particularly Christian, minorities in the region. It is not uncommon to see articles with titles such as 'Is This the End of Christianity in the Middle East?'[2]

Copts are the largest Christian community across Middle East and North Africa, and thus their worsening conditions have wider implications for religious minorities in the region. Copts date their origins back to the very start of Christianity, in fact to Apostle Mark's preaching of the Gospel in Alexandria. Their unique liturgical language carries a rich historical heritage. As Anthony O'Mahony points out, 'the word Copt derives from the Greek for an inhabitant of Egypt, Arabized into "Qibt" and thence into "Copt", and has been used in modern times, especially since the sixteenth century, to designate the Christian inhabitants of Egypt and the language used by them in their liturgy' (O'Mahony 2008:488). It is difficult to establish the numbers of Copts in today's Egypt. Zeidan states that Copts constitute some 10–16 per cent of the population, but that Copts are 'concentrated in the Upper Egyptian governorates of Assyut, Sohag and Minya, where some 60 per cent of all Copts live. Some 25 per cent of all Copts live in Cairo and 6 per cent in Alexandria. Although they are a minority in all Egyptian provinces, in the Upper Egyptian governorates they reach at least 20 per cent of the local population. In addition, there are over 500,000 emigrant Copts living abroad' (Zeidan 1999:54). The numbers of Copts who live outside of Egypt are substantially higher than that now, though no official number exists.

Persecution has been an integral aspect of the history of the Copts, starting from the era of Emperor Diocletian, 'in which hundreds of thousands are said to have died' (Pennington 1982:158). The Arab invasion of Egypt in the seventh century triggered revolts by Copts which were suppressed with severity. According to Henderson, 'at the time of invasion, Coptic Christians satiated roughly 80 per cent of the Egyptian population' (Henderson 2005:156). The invasion was the beginning of the decline of Christians in Egypt from a majority to an increasingly small proportion of the population from the twelfth to the nineteenth centuries (O'Mahony 2008:488). Until the French took control of Egypt from 1798, Copts were required to pay heavy special taxes, known as *jizya* and the *kharaj,* and they were subjected to discrimination as second-class citizens with the status of *dhimmis* (Emon 2012). However, Copts and Muslims were given equal electoral rights with the establishment of Egyptian consultative assembly in 1866 (Pennington 1982:160). Throughout this period, Christians were regularly 'condemned en masse as enemies' (O'Mahony 2008:489).

It is tempting to conclude that the persecution of Copts in Egypt is a given due to Islam, or the fault lines of civilization, or the general intolerance shown by religious actors, and thus see a historical consistency in the horrendous attacks against Copts in the summer of 2013. However, a survey of major political and social changes in Egypt since the start of the twentieth century shows a complex pattern of how Copts were perceived and accommodated by the political elite as well as by wider society and how Copts sought to negotiate a relationship with their country. It shows pockets of harmony between Muslims and Christians in Egypt and eras of openness and closeness for Coptic presence in the social and political mainstream. Most importantly, it highlights how in particular contexts violence against Copts emerged, and how its frequency gradually increased from the 1990s to 2015 in line with the overall conditions in the country and regional trends. Therefore, the chapter points out that the violence against Copts is an outcome of contextual factors that enable and sustain them, and not caused by an inevitable religious or 'civilizational' reason. This chapter seeks to demonstrate this by providing an overview of developments in Egypt across the twentieth century, particularly the emergence of Islamist networks, especially the Muslim Brotherhood, and how these impacted Copts, before focusing more specifically on the attacks on Copts in modern Egypt from their emergence in the 1970s to the ousting of President Morsi in 2013.

Background

At the start of the twentieth century, Copts were enjoying a wide engagement with political life in Egypt, especially after the Revolution of 1919 against the British who had occupied Egypt in 1882. As Philipp notes, Copts were 'virtually indistinguishable from the Muslim Egyptians in terms of general culture, language, professional distribution, and geographic concentration. Religion was the only, albeit very important, mark of separation' (Philipp 1995:133). The Ottoman reform process, referred to as the *tanzimat* (Khater 2010:10), meant that many discriminatory practices were being abolished. Copts were not only joining various political parties but setting up their own. The most influential of political parties at the time, the Wafd party, not only included Copts across its leadership levels but was able to put Coptic candidates forward even in areas where Copts were not a sizeable constituency. In fact, 'the party was accused by its opponents of sheltering a "Coptic conspiracy against the Muslims" or "Coptism"' (Bowie 1977:106). This meant that Copts were able to hold more political posts than they could have had if there had been a quota based upon population estimates as suggested by the British colonial authorities. Two Copts served as Prime Minister between 1908 and 1920 (Carter 1986:177). Copts were flourishing across the cultural, social and economic spectrum in businesses, newspapers, social clubs and charities.

In 1922, Egypt achieved conditional independence from the British rule; 'independence was conditional because the British decree claimed discretion over four matters: security of British communications in Egypt, defence of Egypt if a foreign power threatened aggression, protection of foreign interests and minorities in Egypt, and the issue of the Sudan' (Makari 2007:51). British attempts to formulate a new constitution in 1923 that would enshrine 'minority rights' were condemned both by Copts and many political actors as a plan to create a sectarian divide in the country. Copts did not want to be given the status of a 'minority' and accept an alien status like the Greeks, Armenians and Italians who lived in the country. They also saw that accepting colonial protection would alienate them from their own fellow countrymen. In fact, since Copts played an important role in the Wafd party that agreed to British conditions, 'some nationalist Muslims thought that the Wafd was controlled by Copts' (Makari

2007:52). Given the milieu they were in, they saw no reason to mistrust any Muslim Egyptian who might in fact rule over them. That is why even though three Copts were part of the process of the drafting of the 1922 constitution, they did not object or see any problem in accepting the adoption of Islam as the official state religion (Hasan 2003:38). The constitution, unlike the current constitution of Egypt, did not establish Shari'a as the principal source of legislation, nor gave a particular reference to Shari'a. It protected equal rights of all Egyptians before the law, gave equal civil and political rights (Article 3), freedom of conscience (Article 12) and 'free exercise of all religions or beliefs' (Scott 2010:40). In the tradition of the Ottoman Empire's *millet system* (Stanton 2012:181–183), the constitution allowed each community to handle personal status matters through their own religious courts, even though the constitution upheld a secular vision of the state.

Thus, the Copts neither felt threatened nor were actually marginalized from the rest of the country. The primary political horizon in the country was largely dominated by the two poles of visions of an 'Egypt for Egyptians' that blended secular and European visions for nationhood with myths of Egypt's pharaonic civilization and a continuation of the privileges of the ruling elite, a limited monarchy whose interests were intermingled with colonial rule. However, the founding of the Muslim Brothers in Egypt in 1928 marked the emergence of religious politics. The organization quickly evolved into a well-organized opposition force both to the secular politics and to religious establishment (Høigilt 2011:31). The ideology behind the movement had already started showing itself in the late nineteenth century among Islamic thinkers, most importantly in the writings and works of Jamal Aldin Al-Afghani (died 1897) and Muhammad Abduh (1849–1905), which was to serve as a springboard to many of the influential Islamic clergy, thinkers and activists that gave birth to modern Islamism. Al-Afghani arrived in Egypt in the 1870s from Istanbul, where his views on reconciling science and philosophy of his day with his faith had made him infamous (Ryad 2014:133). He went on to be expelled from Egypt too in 1879 for not only continuing his teachings on trying to reconcile modernism with Islam, but also participating in Egyptian nationalist movements against European imperialism (Yohannes 2001:39). His legacy was in his attempt to show that with reason, Muslims could remain faithful to the true faith of Islam and provide Islamic-based solutions to modern-day problems. Abduh developed Al-Afghani's vision and was clear in his reading of what he saw as decay among Muslims, who had fallen under the colonial rule and lost the path of the true faith due to foreign influences. For Abduh, and for all Islamists to this day, it was clear that when 'the Islamic law is fully understood and obeyed society flourishes, and that when it is misunderstood or rejected society decays' (Høigilt 2011:30). So Islam had to be the centre of Egypt and Islamic values and its way of life had to be observed if Egyptians wanted to see an end to the corruption, immorality and unfairness of the upper-class elite and westernized secularist Egyptians. Yet, his call, just like Al-Afghani's, was not a backward-looking purist vision such as what we see in today's Salafism, but a forward-looking reformist if not revolutionary view of creation of new modern state-hood and structures based upon the unchanging core of Islam. The core of this vision is the assumption that 'the state is created in order to implement *Shari'a*. Its primary function is to enforce divine law and, by so doing, create a community of believers under the governance of Islam (*hukm al-Islam*)' (Rutherford 2006:710). Therefore, Shari'a serves as the fundamental constraint on the state power; 'if the ruler violates *Shari'a*, a citizen is free to disregard the ruler's edicts, and under certain conditions, remove him from office' (Rutherford 2006:712).

Within this interpretation of the 'problem' and the 'solution' provided, Copts were part of the problem. Simply by their presence they defiled the possibility of an Islamic Egypt. As Zeidan notes, 'in the eyes of fundamentalists and radicals, the Copts are the religious 'other', the mirror-image feared as the bearer of all negative characteristics: traitor, exploiter, collaborator, betrayer – a convenient scapegoat for all life's evils. They resent Coptic exclusivism and refusal to accept Islam as the final revelation. The wealth and high position of a few Copts arouses jealousy against the whole community' (Zeidan 1999:61). The founder of the Muslim Brotherhood, Hassan al-Banna, was clear in his views that while Muslims should accept and revere Jesus as a prophet and protect Christians, Christians should not rule over Muslims and should accept a minority position. He saw Copts to be holding too much economic and political power and social influence. (Hasan 2003:52). The appeal of the Muslim Brotherhood and Islamism particularly among poor masses increasingly became a major political force especially throughout the 1930s and 1940s, not only resulting in the loss of elections for Coptic candidates, but also igniting incidents of mob attacks on Copts and their properties. Rather than addressing the issue, the bewildered monarchy saw the emerging tide as a counterbalance to the secular nationalism that was posing a major threat against the political establishment. This caused an increasing sensitivity among the rulers to the demands of the Islamist groups and thus they began preparing for the tightening of the noose around the Copts. The 1856 Hamayouni Decree had sought to protect the rights of the Coptic minority (Tadros 2014:205). It brought inclusion in military services, guarantees on equality in employment and freedom to worship, and freedom from pressure to change religion as well as granting rights for the church to handle its own financial affairs and personal-status matters of Christians (Makari 2007:49). The Ottoman royal decree also stated that permission for church buildings must be given by the Sultan and requested by the Coptic Pope. This pragmatic Ottoman framework, which showed itself in various places across the domain of the empire, was stifled in 1934 by the interior minister Al Azabi Pasha, who added further conditions for building churches, which made building of new churches and even basic repairs and extensions almost impossible (Ibrahim 1996:9). Both the Hamayouni Decree and Al Azabi Pasha's regulations are still used in Egypt to this day.

Carter points out that by the late 1940s, Copts were increasingly being discriminated against in public and private sectors (Carter 1986:211). Together with such changing currents, there were new forms of vibrant social, religious and political efforts among the Copts. As part of the widely-referred-to Sunday School Movement, religious revival went hand in hand with a deepening appreciation of the Coptic heritage and identity (Sedra 1999:224). Political Islam was indeed causing worry, and clearly the era of the 1919 revolution and the spirit of 'Egypt for all Egyptians' were being challenged, yet Copts were still an integral part of the society from trade to public sphere. While marginal Coptic groups that went as far as demanding an independent Coptic state emerged in this period, most Copts were either in support of full Egyptian nationalism or in cautious worry over what might happen if the monarchy was to fall. The discontent towards the Egyptian monarchy that was under the de facto rule of the British colonial authority was brewing strongly from 1940s and onwards, including within the ranks of the armed forces. In 1942, the British colonial authority forced its choice of government on King Farouk by besieging his palace with British troops (Flower 1972:157). The outcome was not only the humiliation of the King and the widespread perception that the Wafd party's government was merely a colonial puppet, but also the start of the end of British rule in the country. A secret network named the Free Officers was formed in 1942 by young military officers planning a revolution. The direction of the network was given by a twelve-man revolutionary committee headed by Nasser with the aim of destroying British occupation, eliminating feudalism, ending capitalism's political power, establishing equality, forming a strong army and establishing democracy (Goldschmidt Jr 2008:144).

While Egypt enjoyed a brief economic boom during World War II, largely due to the trade and industrial opportunities that emerged from the war, the postwar period saw a tremendous economic crisis, causing huge numbers of rural farm workers to become landless and jobless and many in the cities destitute. Within this context, the Muslim Brotherhood was to envision its hallmark approach for change: providing alternative social-aid networks and enabling poor individuals (Al-Arian 2014). Thus, the Brotherhood could be seen forming trade unions as well as helping the poor and preaching its message. The movement's increasing influence brought it into direct conflict with the regime. The government's clampdown on Islamist groups in 1948 triggered a militant response and resulted in the assassination of Prime Minister Mahmud Fahmi al-Nuqrashi Pasha 'after he had declared the dissolution of the Muslim Brotherhood and had aggressively pursued the arrest of its members' (Armajani 2012:40). As a result, leading members of the Brotherhood were arrested and executed and thousands were imprisoned for lengthy times. Hasan Banna himself was assassinated in 1949. Yet, the regime was not able to hold on to its rule much longer as not only Islamists, but even Copts, leftists, socialists, European-educated secularist nationalists and most importantly a new generation of military officers too were in unanimous agreement that things simply had to change.

Under Nasser

Riots, attacks and attempted assassinations against the British and government figures continued throughout the late 1940s. However, the decisive event was the 1948 war following the creation of the State of Israel. It was the first of a series of military humiliations that played an important role in the shaping of both the secular and religious political and social actors. The war gave impetus for the Free Officers to bring an end to corrupt and self-serving politicians, the monarchy and privileged classes as well as the British influence, and they 'widened their national consciousness to Arab horizons, as they strongly identified common cause with the Palestinian Arabs' (Abou-El-Fadl 2015:293). The myth surrounding Nasser's fight to maintain his post in Faluja against all the odds during the 1948 war until he was ordered to retreat was to provide him wide popularity and admiration. Nasser's relative military success in an ill-fated campaign served as a political symbol. In his *Philosophy of the Revolution,* Nasser asked, 'is not our country another Faluja, a much greater Faluja, besieged by the enemy, a prey to the climbers and traitors and greedy?' (Flower 1972:170). It would still take a few years for the Free Officers to establish their strength and find the right opportunity. Cairo and the main headquarters of the army were seized by the Free Officers with hardly any resistance in the early hours of 23 July 1952. Egyptians had woken up to the voice of Anwar el Sadat, a member of the Free Officers who would one day be a president of Egypt, declaring: 'Egypt has just passed through the darkest period in her history ... Degraded by corruption and on the point of collapse owing to instability. These destructive factors affected even the army ... that is why it has been purged ... Egypt will welcome our movement whole-heartedly' (Flower 1972:185).

Yet, the newly-formed Revolutionary Command Council faced a momentous task of nation-building and addressing serious economic grievances. Initially, relations between the Free Officers and the Muslim Brotherhood were on good terms, as the Brotherhood had supported the revolution. The Brotherhood's leader, Al-Hubaydi, saw the political change in the country as a chance for the movement to play a much more influential role in the creation of new structures. He had hoped that the new opening might in fact finally realize the vision of an Islamic state (Zollner 2009:147). However, the visions of the Islamists and the Free Officers were inherently opposed to each other. While the former wanted the new Egypt to be based upon Islam, the latter were committed to industrialization, modernization, regional influence, national pride and social equality based upon a nation-state vision (Beinin 1989). The slogan, 'religion is for God and the nation is for all' captured the stand of Free Officers, yet the declared 'secular' vision is not to be confused with the meaning of the term in Europe or

North America as distance of the state from all religions. Religion still remained important, society still deeply conservative and laws and education carried forward a unique blend of religious input, and the Egyptian state far from keeping a neutral distance from all religions, sought to actively control and manage religion. But as Yohannes puts it, 'the message was clear enough: religion was no longer to be used as a principle of political organization which effectively put the brotherhood out of business' (Yohannes 2001:81). As riots against the junta began and different visions for Egypt among different groups became clear, the Brotherhood and other Islamist groups saw their assets being confiscated and members jailed. Following an assassination attempt on Nasser by an Islamist in 1954, the initial hopefulness turned sour as all such groups were banned, many were arrested and executed, all activities were forced underground, and the influential movement faced serious internal struggle (Zollner 2007).

As Nasser tightened his grip on power and ultimately became the first president of the new republic in 1956, it was not only Islamists who found themselves as odds with the new Egypt. He dismantled the ruling political elite and removed grandeur and royal titles. His nationalization projects and quasi-socialism caused a serious blow to Egypt's rich elite, but earned him wide respect across the vast majority of the country, which was still substantially rural. Copts, 'probably more, proportionally, than Muslims', suffered financially, as Coptic landowners and businessman lost revenues (Pennington 1982:164). Nasser's vision was clear: his economics and language mixed socialism with an Arab nationalism that extended beyond Egypt to the entire Arab world with his appeals to Arab unity and dignity (Torrey 1965:290). In his rapid nation-building programme, he abolished religious courts and brought Muslims and Christians alike under the jurisdiction of a secular legal system, thus personal-status matters that had been dealt with through Shari'a courts for Muslims and clerical courts for non-Muslims became unified under the 'civil courts'. The 1956 constitution and the provisional 1958 one had no mention of the role of Shari'a (Philipp 1995:144). With popular policies such as subsidies, caps on rent prices and creation of jobs often at the expense of suffocating the civil-service sector with overemployment, Nasser enabled the emergence of a new middle class that would have been impossible under the socioeconomic structures of the monarchy and British rule. Egypt was going through a rapid modernization process.

Nasser's charisma and strong leadership expanded his influence beyond Egypt. Both Nasser's self-confidence and anticipations of the Egyptians were boosted significantly when the treaty with Britain to withdraw troops was signed, ending the 1956 war over Suez and nationalizing the canal. Pan-Arab dreams seemed to be happening as Egypt and Syria created the United Arab Republic in 1958 (Jankowski 2002:101). As McDermott notes 'all of these developments led to a sense that there were no limits to what Egypt under Nasser could achieve' (McDermott 1988:9).

While Copts were supportive of the revolution, they did have their reservations about the Free Officers movement. Not only did there seem to be tacit cooperation between the Muslim Brotherhood and the Free Officers at least initially, the military movement did not really include any Coptic presence within its ranks, save for a single Coptic member (Scott 2010:42). However, Nasser did not have a direct discriminatory policy towards the Copts. In a true socialist fashion, he saw the church as a tool for public control and a hierarchical body that he could work with, just as he actively used the Al-Azhar University and Islamic officials to pass fatwas in support of his policies and vision, and to ostracize Islamists and control religion through mosques and religious education at the state schools (Yohannes 2001:113). As Nasser abolished political parties and the parliament and put a tight control on who could be a candidate for his Arab Socialist Union, political participation by Copts was increasingly diminishing. No Copt was elected to the National Assembly in any election from 1964 to 1976. While a new law allowed the government to appoint up to ten Copts to the Parliament, this only gave absolute power to the state to control and limit Coptic participation in politics (Philipp 1995:145). Within the process, as Philipp notes, the Coptic community 'resumed more and more the traditional stance of the depoliticized *dhimma* while the clergy was regaining a position of communal leadership' (Philipp 1988:385). In fact, the decisions in the Nasser era to abolish various lay bodies which influenced the running of the church and provided a voice for Coptic concerns and activism resulted in the strengthening of the power and scope of the church as the main focal point of Coptic life and the only legitimate channel to express concerns. Nasser allowed the construction of, and attended the opening of, a new cathedral in Cairo to serve as the Papal seat and promised that licenses for twenty-five new churches would be issued every year

(Hasan 2003:104). Nasser's autocracy did have an additional benefit
for the Copts. His clampdown on Islamists and tight control on the
society and security did minimize attacks on Copts that had become a
common sight in the 1940s. Yet, this did not stop sizeable migration
of especially wealthy and educated Copts from Egypt during the
1950s and 1960s. The same period also saw an almost complete
vanishing of non-Coptic ethno-religious minorities in Egypt (Philipp
1995:143). The start of the Coptic diaspora would eventually come to
play a significant role in Muslim-Christian and Coptic-State relations
in Egypt.

Nasser's charisma and grandeur and self-confidence became the
basis for his own unmaking. The economic difficulties of maintaining
his social vision were only amplified with his bold and ill-thought-out
Pan-Arabism and his fatal mistake in launching a 'final solution' attack
on the State of Israel in 1967. The 1967 war, often referred to as the
Six-Day War, saw Israeli forces not only skillfully winning the war
before it even began, resulting in Israel seizing more land and power
than it had before the war, but also humiliated Nasser and his allies in
the eyes of the entire world (Oren 2002). The defeat was to seal his fate
and form the contemporary map of the Middle East and most importantly bring back political Islam into the mainstream much more
strongly than before. The Muslim Brotherhood and a myriad of other
Islamist networks had remained in the shadows and suffered significantly under Nasser's iron fist. Their message, which had not gained
wide public appeal in the lead-up to and imminent aftermath of the
1952 revolution, was now seemingly proving itself: Egypt had tried
secular godless visions in the forms of nationalism and socialism, and
exchanged one yoke of colonialism for another one, as Nasser pursued
close ties with the Soviets. As McDermott notes, 'Nasser left Egypt
defeated, economically weak and unconvinced that it had been a
thawra (revolution) which had been carried out in 1952' (McDermott
1988:39). 'Islam is the solution' became a widely-heard phrase and
call. An Islamic Egypt would not only restore fairness and justice and
reach out to the poor, but would also deliver a victory against the
Zionist regime that was persecuting fellow Muslims. Nasser had tried
to curb increasing Islamist influence on the society through mass
arrests, tortures and executions throughout 1965–1966, including the
public hanging in 1966 of an influential Brotherhood leader and a
source of inspiration and theoretical basis for Islamists all around the

world, Sayyed Qutb (Yohannes 2001:91). After years of gross human-rights violations, increasingly radicalized views and wider public appeal, the demise of Nasser was also the fertile ground for a major return of a political and much more militant Islamism and unprecedented levels of attacks on and exclusion of Copts from the mainstream society. Following the swift victory of Israel in the Six-Day War in 1967, Nasser announced his resignation. There was widespread shock and 'mass scenes of public grief to see the icon humbled', which included patients being taken into hospitals suffering from trauma (Munro 2000:67). Nasser eventually revoked his resignation and remained in power for three more years, a period in which his health, Egypt's economy, and his standing in Egypt and the wider Arab world deteriorated until his death in 1970.

Under Sadat

When Nasser died on 28 September 1970, his vice president since 1969, Anwar Sadat, was appointed as an interim president and formally elected by the National Assembly a month later. President Sadat suffered from a lack of the strong charisma and public support that Nasser had enjoyed even though the latter had brought Egypt to the brink of economic, social and political collapse. He faced challenges and doubts within his own party and military cadres and continual rumours of military coups by Nasserist officers and officials. In fact, until the victory of the October 1973 war against Israel, when Egyptian troops were able to cross the Suez Canal and recapture Sinai from Israel, which had taken the area in the 1967 war, Sadat was the butt of jokes among Egyptians. A common phrase, which rhymes in Arabic, captures this well: 'Gone is the Giant, the Donkey has taken his place' (Hirst & Beeson 1981:18).

Sadat had inherited an economic crisis, unsustainable levels of employment in the state sector and subsidies and nationalized industries that were continually wasting precious resources. For Sadat, the future of Egypt lay with integration into the modern world, a liberal economy and closeness with the United States rather than with the ailing USSR. In April 1974, Sadat was to launch his own 'revolution' that represented a major break away from the Nasser era. The revolution was to be called *Infitah*, the Opening. In the October Working Paper, Sadat stated that the 'new stage in the life of this ancient people... was economic development at rates that exceeded all we have achieved up till now' (Hirst & Beeson 1981:204). This went through an economic policy that welcomed investment and trade. *Infitah* was to mean the creation of free-trade zones, the lifting of regulations on foreign direct investment, maximizing tourism, the promotion of exports and industrialization that was to bring new skills and jobs for Egyptians. The aim was 'to attract the external assistance needed to cope with an immediate economic crisis' (Weinbaum 1985:206). Sadat's policy was never meant to be full-scale economic liberalization. He kept much of the state subsidies, agricultural policies and the high rate of employment in the state. He did not pursue 'formal enactments destined to transform Egypt from a "socialist" into a "capitalist" society. At most there was to be a grafting of the one upon the other' (Hirst & Beeson 1981:206). Although the *infitah* proposal was warmly welcomed by the People's Assembly, it also attracted criticism from left-wing political voices, as well as the Nasserist elites whose interests were going to be harmed. Yet large swathes of the public burdened by the economic situation supported, if not wanted to believe in, Sadat ushering them into a better fortune. And with a change of US foreign policy towards Egypt and Sadat's efforts to raise money from rich Arab countries as well as far-flung locations such as Japan and China, Egypt seemed to be finally moving beyond its chronic economic ill-health. Within a few years, with remittances of Egyptian workers in the Gulf, foreign aid and Suez Canal revenues as well as increasing tourism, Egypt saw a limited economic boom (Amin 2011:15).

Politically, Sadat's dramatically different economic and political vision for Egypt faced two major challenges. On one hand there were the Nasserist elites and secular leftist critiques of the regime, and on the other the increasing power of Islamist movements and religious sensitivities in the country. These pressures led Sadat to seek rapid economic and foreign policy changes, while easing the pressure on Islamist groups and increasingly highlighting the role of Islam. With this, he could create an opposition pressure against the well-educated and organized left-leaning political groups (Kepel 2006:65). He would also be able establish legitimacy among large sections of the society that was increasingly becoming influenced by religious sensitivities and political visions. Wickham captures the shift from Nasser's secular-nationalist-socialism vision of just using Islam to Sadat's positioning of Islam at the centre of his political agenda:

Islam was central to Anwar Sadat's self-image and claim to political author-ity. Styling himself the 'Believer-President', Sadat made a public show of his personal piety; promoted Islamic programming in the media, schools and universities; expanded the government's support of official Islamic institu-tions; and used religious themes to justify the regime's policies, including the decision to go to war with Israel in 1973 (Wickham 2002:98).

Yet, none of these dramatic re-orientations would really be possible within the structures governed by officials appointed by Nasser. From 1971 onwards, Sadat started his campaign to expel, intimidate and imprison the executives under Nasser's rule (Rubenstein 1972:10). He also returned some land and businesses confiscated during Nasser's rule back to their owners to solidify his appeal to private businesses and wealthier classes. Slowly, he moved towards lifting the single-party rule under Nasser by first allowing distinct platforms within the Arab Socialist Union and then to new legal parties, yet with still-tight control and not allowing Muslim Brotherhood or Nasserists to form parties. He released a large number of members of the Muslim Brotherhood and other Islamist movements from prison, allowed the return of many other key figures who were in exile and allowed them to be active in university campuses (Ashour 2007:605).

Even though not officially accepted as a political party, the Brother-hood was able to reorganize and have an increasingly wide presence in the society outside of political party structures, including the establish-ment of a newspaper and publishing houses. Within this context, Islamic radicalization in Egypt entered a new phase, and with it, its impact on overall Egyptian politics, society and especially violence towards Copts took a worrying turn, as we will explore later in this chapter. Olivier Carre notes three periods in the story of Islamist movements in Egypt in the lead-up to the Sadat and post-Sadat eras (Carre 1995). In period one, the 1930s and 1940s, Carre observes the principal aim of the Islamist movements was the Islamization of polit-ical and social institutions with a secondary aim of jihad for national independence. In this period, Banna becomes the dominant exponent of Islamist visions. In the second period, the 1950s and 1960s, Carre observes the increasing influence of Qutb on movements and the principal aim being Islamic social justice initially, and then evolving into underground religious education and political activity with a secondary aim of ensuring *hakimmiya* over *jahiliya*. In the third period, the 1970s and 1980s, Carre notes the influence of 'Qutibists' and hardening attitudes that make their principal aim an insurrection against the 'apostate' rulers with a secondary aim of establishing an imminent Islamic state.

This transformation is clear in the wider demand for the application of Shari'a law that became much louder both across Egypt and in the Egyptian parliament in the 1970s. In 1971, a new constitution was ratified. While all previous constitutions of Egypt since 1922 acknowledged Islam as the state religion, they had not given any precedence or even mention of Shari'a. In contrast, Article 2 of the 1971 constitution stated that 'Islam is the religion of state, Arabic is the official language, the principles of Shari'a are a main source of legislation' (Scott 2010:46). The Article made Shari'a only 'a' source of legislation, not the primary basis of the state as demanded by the Islamist groups. While limited in scope, the Article 2 was enough for lawyers, judges and the courts to slowly advance a case law based upon Shari'a, and thus expand its centrality even though it might have contradicted other more secular provisions.

Changing social attitudes, eased government pressure and increasing public presence of Islamist groups as well as loud calls for jihad were to be demonstrated in 1972 on an attack at a Coptic centre in Al-Khanka, which marked the start of contemporary violence against Copts in Egypt. While the incident will be dealt with in detail later, it was symbolic that the 'rumour' that Copts were 'secretly' using the venue as a church had caused the mob attack. With this, it was becoming clear that the vision of Egypt being an Islamic state only for Muslims was now resulting in violent actions against those who did not fit in or share that vision or simply spoiled such a vision by their mere presence. The push to advance Shari'a laws emerged again in the late 1970s, when there were attempts to introduce the death penalty for apostasy from Islam (Khalil 2006:40, 41). This caused shock waves across the non-Muslims of Egypt as well as reformist Muslim thinkers, who had always been deemed 'apostate' by radicals. In the church, there were significant numbers of Copts who had at one stage officially converted to Islam in order to annul marriages or through pressure or mere economic opportunities but then wanted to be re-registered as Christians. All of them would be seen as apostates and thus face death. But more importantly, the law symbolized a reversal of the freedom of religion and the place of modern secular laws in place since the *tanzimat* reforms under the Ottoman Empire. Mass protests in Egypt and loud reactions from Pope Shenouda, who went on hunger strike, and lobbying efforts of Coptic diaspora groups especially in the United States eventually forced Sadat to block the passage of the law in 1977 (Philipp 1995:146).

It was clear that it was not only the attitude of the Egyptian state and Egyptian Muslims that changed in the 1970s. Post-Nasser Egypt also saw a dramatic shift in Coptic attitudes to and relations with the state. The newly elected Pope and the newly elected President Sadat found themselves in tension from day one. Pope Shenouda, who was elected in October 1971, was fully aware of the shift from Nasser to Sadat. Since 1952, Copts had somehow accepted a gradually declining role as a minority in postrevolutionary Egypt, but nevertheless felt protected under Nasser and did not face the risk of living in an Islamic Egypt, a disastrous possibility for them. Yet, as Sadat's programmes became clear, Pope Shenouda made a rare stand to speak up for Copts and in 1972, 'the Assembly of Christian Churches in Egypt called for an end to discrimination in personal status cases and government appointments, and for the elimination of restrictions on church construction' (Sedra 1999:225). When the 1972 attack on the Coptic charity centre in Al-Khanka happened, rather than accepting the language of 'national unity' and 'brotherhood', Pope ordered hundreds of monks and priests to hold prayer meetings on the burned site to show resolve and demand a government response (Ansari 1984:400).

In 1977, as Egypt began seeing the end of its economic boom, the Italian Chamber of Haute Couture declared Sadat to be one of the top-ten best-dressed men in the world (Hirst & Beeson 1981:211). In fact, his and his family's love of extravagance and fast-growing personal riches were all too visible and once again, the butt of jokes among the public. His lavish military costumes and self-granted glamour earned him the nickname 'King Sadat'. This stood in stark contrast to that of Nasser and his family. When Nasser had died, he had left hardly any personal fortune behind. His simplicity was paralleled by his devout wife. As Sadat continued to live a life of often-mythical luxury, for the ordinary Egyptians the promised 'opening' had only made the situation worse. For most life had not changed, but a new rich emerged and free markets brought products and lifestyles that were out of reach for many. In January of 1977, thousands of Egyptians began protesting as the government announced a decision to reduce subsidies on basic commodities like rice, sugar and cooking gas (Baker 1990:118). For many, it was clear that *infitah* which had filled the country with high-end luxury goods had only worked for the corrupt rich elite. While it was argued that Egypt could not afford paying for subsidies, the opposition groups pointed out that 'Egypt imported luxury cars at the price of 475 million [Egyptian] pounds, while the removal of subsidies from popular goods would save only 96 million' (Baker 1990:149). Amidst this worsening situation, more Egyptian migrants began returning to Egypt and emigration rates went down significantly (Amin 2011:16). Returnees brought with themselves fresh impressions, not least the increasing prominence of Islamism they had encountered in neighbouring countries, particularly Saudi Arabia.

Sadat's political and economic reforms thus ironically resulted in more frustration, the mobilization of Islamic movements, class envy and the alienation of especially large sections of educated but often unemployed or underemployed youth. Most importantly, it resulted in the demise of a robust secular opposition and the enforcement of Islamism as the only powerful opposing ideology and political possibility. The robust organizational strengths of the Islamist movements was strengthened in their capacity to offer an ideological project that not only answered temporal grievances but also provided personal, moral and eternal visions in a fast-changing and seemingly immortalizing Egypt. This was no 'passive' opium for the masses or a retreat into spiritual enclaves. On the contrary, Islamist calls were a call for social and political action as a personal religious duty. As Wickham notes 'through the medium of the *da'wa,* or "call to God", they promoted a new activist conception of Islam, claiming that it was a *fard 'ayn,* a duty incumbent on every Muslim, to participate in the Islamic reform of society and state. In sum, the Islamists challenged the dominant patterns of political alienation and abstention by promoting a new ethnic of civic obligation that mandated participation in the public sphere, regardless of its benefits and costs' (Wickham 2002:120).

Sadat had opened Pandora's Box by easing pressure on Islamists, giving more chances for them to engage with society and dominate the public sphere. While his plan to weaken the risk of leftist groups had in fact worked, it had strengthened Islamist movements and emboldened demands for an Islamic Egypt, ultimately incompatible with his rapprochement with Israel and closeness with the United States. As an act of desperation, in 1980 Sadat pushed for an amendment to Article 2, which changed Shari'a from being 'a' source of legislation into 'the' source of legislation: a small change in an article with serious ramifications for customary law. The scope of it is still debated to this day. With it, Sadat aimed to continue what I call the 'politics of defending Islam', which was also seen in the late 1970s in Pakistan and Sudan, where constitutions were also changed to give precedence to Shari'a yet without actually shifting to restructure the legal systems completely (Meral 2009:879). However, the cosmetic re-introduction of Shari'a was not enough for Islamists demanding an Islamic state. While in the early 1970s, attacks by Islamist groups were local and often targeted Copts, later in the decade militant groups were also attacking government buildings, security forces and officials across the country (Fielding & Shortland 2010:434). Sadat's rapprochement with Israel and the peace treaty that was brokered by the United States between the two countries were seen as a betrayal and a ground to declare a jihad against the 'apostate' rulers of the land. In 1981, the situation across Egypt was precarious. In desperation, in June Sadat unleashed a crackdown on all groups that were posing an opposition to him (Wickham 2002:66). The same month, an Islamist group claiming that Christians were secretly building a church triggered attacks and clashes between Copts and Muslims between 17 and 20 June in Al Zawya Al Hamra in Cairo. Kepel points to the words of Shaykh Kishk that captured the mindset of the attackers: 'Nowhere on earth is there any minority that has been accorded the rights enjoyed by the Christians of Egypt, who occupy so many important posts: ministers, chairmen of the boards of directors of banks, generals and their Pope, who sits on the throne of the Church with all its authority' (Kepel 1985: 238). During those three days, scores of Copts were killed and properties were attacked and the security forces were nowhere to be seen. As Coptic diaspora groups widely spread the news and Pope Shenouda publicly demanded justice, he was forced from his seat in Cairo and sent to exile into the Soryan Monastery in Wadi el Natrun in September 1981, where he stayed until 1985 (Fawzy 2000:35). The president had been increasingly promoting anti-Coptic views. As a Copt reminded me, 'around 1980 Sadat's tone towards Christians noticeably changed. In fact, he gave a speech that year accusing them of seeking to establish an independent state in Asyut'.

Even with such a harsh clampdown on Islamists and Copts alike, it was the beginning of the end for Sadat. His attempts to play the politics of defending Islam had not worked; he was seen as an immoral apostate in bed with the enemies of Islam. On 6 October 1981, he was assassinated by a group of Islamist military officers during the annual victory parade that celebrated Egypt's Suez Canal victory, along with twenty-eight other foreign and domestic dignitaries. Ironically, if Pope Shenouda had not been sent into exile, he would have been killed in the attack: Bishop Samuel, who had taken the Pope's place in the state protocol, died instead. His assassin, Khalid Istanbuli, a young lieutenant, 'who proclaimed with pride that he had shot the pharaoh', was appalled by the cultural price paid by Sadat to the United States and Israel (Ajami 1995:72). Istanbuli had not been a religious person, and had in fact attended a Christian missionary school, only adopting radical views not long before the assassination. Ajami argues that the incident marked a 'tension in the psyche and politics of Egypt' which persisted 'between Sadat's world, with its temptations and its window on modernity, and Istanbuli's world, with its rigours and its furious determination to keep the West at bay. A fissure has opened, right in the heart of Egypt's traditionally stoic and reliable middle class. A wing of this class has defected to theocratic politics. The rest are disaffected and demoralized. There is no resolution for this dilemma' (Ajami 1995:75). In fact, Egypt saw increased radicalization and expansion of Islamist networks after then. A key aspect of this was the emergence of 'parallel Islamic sectors', as Wickham notes: private mosques, Islamic voluntary associations and Islamic for-profit commercial and business enterprises such as Islamic banks, investment companies, manufacturing firms and publishing houses (Wickham 2002:97). These would play a much more important role as the main opposition force under the presidency of Mubarak and helped shape the context of growing attacks on Copts and their complete exclusion from the Egyptian public arena as 'Egyptians'.

Under Mubarak

In the attack that took President Sadat's life, Vice President Hosni Mubarak was slightly injured. Mubarak had been made vice president in 1975 in an attempt by Sadat to solidify his own public standing. Mubarak was a successful soldier who had rocketed through the rank and file and was head of the Egyptian air force in the 1973 campaign against Israel, which was hailed as a victory. He was not known to be politically ambitious and lacked presence and charisma, and thus was a perfect choice for Sadat. Sadat 'proclaimed that he was beginning to hand power to the "October Generation", i.e., to those who had conducted the battle with Israel in October 1973' (Waterbury 1983:47). Yet now, the twist of history carried Mubarak onto the main stage. He declared a state of emergency and served as the interim head of the state (McMillan 2013:124). As Amin puts it masterfully, Mubarak had no grand political vision:

President Nasser had a project. To put this project into effect, he attracted men who believed in his vision or at least professed a belief in it. President Sadat presented the Egyptians with a new vision, quite opposed to that of Nasser, and he in turn attracted men who believed or pretended to believe in his project. For his part, Hosni Mubarak had no project of his own. Instead, he was content to continue without any deviation on the path opened up by Sadat (Amin, 2012:16).

This meant an easy transition of allegiance of the regime officials and interest groups as Mubarak seemed to pose no threat to the system of benefits set by Sadat. This was also a matter of relative comfort both for domestic and international worried watchers. Mubarak did not seem to be on a course of remaking and reordering Egypt and its foreign policy like Nasser and Sadat did, except to signal his desire to restore Egypt's relations with other Arab nations that had been harmed significantly with the signing of the peace treaty with Israel under Sadat. In his early years, through talks and limited attempts at addressing corruption in the system, upholding the rule of law, pursuing reform, bringing stability, security and political pluralism, releasing political prisoners from the Sadat era and lifting of rigid regulations effecting syndicates and charities, Mubarak gained some public legitimacy and goodwill, including from the Muslim Brotherhood (Al-Awadi 2004:49–58). Mubarak's presidency technically began in 1984, when the ruling National Democratic Party achieved 72.9 per cent of votes and 87 per cent of the seats in the People's Assembly (Ayubi 1989:13). While the high ratio might seem to signify wide support for Mubarak, in actuality voter turnout was low. A new electoral law had helped him secure a victory, including specifically an 8 per cent threshold rule whereby parties need to get more than

8 per cent of votes in order to enter the People's Assembly, and if they fail to reach 8 per cent, all of their votes were to be added on to the winning party's tally (Ayubi 1989:13). Yet, one could not deny that Mubarak was the only actual candidate and for many voters, he represented stability and had the backing of the armed forces as well as key international allies.

Two important early promises that were to turn sour and create the political and social tensions that marred the Mubarak rule were to be economic and political reform. At the economic level, Mubarak had in fact inherited a crumbling state from Sadat. On paper, Egypt had seen an economic boom in the 1970s and official numbers seemed to affirm it. Egypt had seen an annual growth of around 8 per cent between 1974 and 1985, and per-capita income had doubled from $334 in 1974 to $700 in 1984 (Bush 1999:23). However, this 'growth', as Ray Bush argues, was not based upon industrial productive activity but was fuelled by rents from a host of external revenues from aid to tourism, remittances and foreign exchange earnings (Bush 1999:23). In fact, by the mid-1980s, more than 40 per cent of GDP was based upon foreign exchange rates and remittances, compared to 6 per cent in 1974 (Bush 1999:24). Mubarak had set up a three-day conference in 1982 to set a new course and in fact he did provide an image of commitment to economic reform. Yet, as Amin points out, in reality, until 2005 Mubarak only continued Sadat's economic policies, patching the account deficit with borrowing and addressing the rapid increase in unemployment with unsustainable levels of employment in the state sectors (Amin 2011:64). Ayubi states: 'By the mid-1980s, it was estimated that well over three million individuals were employed in the central and local government as well as in the public sector (excluding public companies)' (Ayubi 1989:7). A mixture of high-level state expenditure, resistance to undertake IMF-requested reform on subsidies and scale down on out-of-proportion budgets, and an economic growth that largely depended on 'rental' income, meant that the Egyptian state faced near-bankruptcy in 1989 as it could no longer keep up with the payments of its foreign debts (Soliman 2011:1).

But Mubarak had to find revenues to maintain the high rate of state expenditure. Ever since the 1952 revolution, while the Egyptian state under both Nasser and Sadat was a coercive and heavy-handed autocracy, its legitimization still depended on public appeasement, which often took the form of short-term-sighted expenditure. Soliman argues that the 'caretaker state' was an instrument for Nasser, utilized to entrench his political power and enabled him to maintain some sort of stability and public support, 'but its problem was the need to feed itself continuously with financial resources in order to maintain its political grip' (Soliman 2011:27). The same problem haunted Sadat and then Mubarak. The legitimacy of the Egyptian state in the eyes of Egyptians, then and even today, depended upon its capacity to deliver economic welfare far more than any other ideology. Al-Awadi's study on legitimacy in Egyptian politics demonstrates the centrality of 'eudaemenonic legitimacy', based upon the performance of a government to enable economic growth and goods and services for the consumer public, in comparison to other sources of legitimacy such as ideology, state structures and ruling personalities (Al-Awadi 2004:9). It was clear that Mubarak was facing a crisis of legitimacy, most of which he had inherited from his predecessors, but he had no long-term plan to address the crisis.

The country and the future of the regime, however, were saved by regional developments. In August 1990, as Iraqi troops entered Kuwait, the United States needed its Arab allies to back its campaign against Iraq, which resulted in the writing off of almost half of Egypt's debts, some $30 billion, and ushered in new foreign aid (Cook 2011:161). With this impetus, Mubarak maintained his ill-fated economic vision of more privatization, no fiscal tightening and unhealthy dependence on foreign direct investment, aid and undependable revenues. As domestic and international pressure for economic reform increased in the early 2000s, Mubarak had no option but to offer at least half-baked reform packages, as he depended on the goodwill of foreign actors, if not the backing of his own society. From 2005, Egypt started seeing economic growth. Foreign direct investment (FDI) in Egypt increased from $3.9 billion to $11.1 billion in 2007, caused by the initial market approval of the appointment of a new government in 2004 that seemed to finally have an economic plan (Bowker 2010:169). This lifted Egypt's GDP from 4 per cent over the last two decades to 7 per cent (Amin 2011:64). However, high figures of growth and FDI were not able to hide the fact that poverty was deepening, corruption was reaching endemic portions and life conditions were becoming more and more difficult for the average Egyptian, except the few who benefited from the system. Cook cites that there were one thousand protests staged by Egyptian workers between 1998 and

2004, and that 2004 alone accounted for more than one quarter of all protests staged in this period. In 2006, employees in the state-owned sectors staged a further 222 strikes and protests (Cook 2011:178). In 2007, an attempt at a nationwide strike was aborted, however 'demonstrations at the industrial centre escalated into rioting in which three protesters were killed. Those riots were the first since 1986 and the third since 1952' (Adly 2011:310). The increasing frequency of protests were not a surprise; as Amin notes, the widely-used expression of 'disappearance of the middle class in Egypt' would have been more accurate if it said 'lost in the crowd'. He observed that 'a whole class seem to have disappeared, or dissolved into another, to form a single large mass of people, all looking the same and having the same hopes' (Amin 2011:99).

While the economy faced serious crises and many services were underfunded, Mubarak increased the allocations to the Ministries of Interior, Culture, Information and Religious Endowments (Soliman 2011:74). The underlying functions of these ministries demonstrate that rather than addressing the grave economic problems and investing in sectors that would enable future flourishing, Mubarak was more concerned with strengthening his security apparatus and combating Islamism through a monopoly over religious provision and education. In other words, Mubarak's hodgepodge of economic policies and short-term fixes had only one aim, to maintain its *eudaemonic legitimacy* by continuing a high expenditure on subsidies, welfare and a high rate of employment in state sectors and by generously funding state expenditure that combated political challenges to the regime rather than focusing on creating long-term economic sustainability. As for Mubarak's promise of political reforms, while political liberalization in the form of multiple parties and regular elections advanced, in reality subsequent parliamentary and presidential elections were governed and controlled closely by the Mubarak regime. In her excellent study of elections and politics in Egypt, Lisa Blaydes points out that the 'authoritarian regime in Egypt has endured *not despite* competitive elections, but to some degree, *because* of these elections' (Italics in the original, Blaydes; 2001:1). Her study shows that controlled elections had the functional utility of providing a system within which resources and access to the regime's benefits could be allocated to the political constituency which assured the smooth transition of interest groups and allegiances from Sadat to Mubarak and also enabled the patron-clientele relationships which was a hallmark of Mubarak's rule. This relationship was central to the Egyptian political structures. Article 76 of the constitution, which was amended throughout Mubarak's rule to suit political concerns, meant that the People's Assembly had the right to vote for a president. Yet, the members of the Assembly, the vast majority of whom were from the ruling NDP, were vetted, if not directly appointed by Mubarak. This meant that Mubarak only appointed members to the Egyptian parliament that he could count on and those who were appointed knew that their position depended upon the president's favour (Arafat 2009:17).

However, in the April 1987 elections the only actual opposition to the Mubarak regime emerged: the Muslim Brotherhood. While legally barred from running for elections as a political party, through deals brokered with other official parties Muslim Brotherhood candidates were able to run for election and take up seats, and thus engage with mainstream politics (Tal 2005:50). In the lead up to the election, the Brotherhood pursued a wide national campaign, filling the streets with posters and banners that said 'Islam is the solution', 'Give your vote to God, give to the Muslim Brotherhood', 'God is our objective, the Prophet our leader, and the Koran our Constitution' (Ebeid 1989:43). The elections marked a turning point in Mubarak's relationship with the Muslim Brotherhood as it was clear that it was fast becoming a genuine challenge to Mubarak's rule. Thus far, Mubarak had allowed the Brotherhood's reorganization, *tanzim* and charitable work in the social peripheries where state services failed to reach and strategic positioning in professional guilds. However, in the 1990s, the prospect of an inevitable clash became visible as both the Brotherhood and Mubarak were competing for legitimacy by attempting to be the 'care-takers' of the public (Al-Awadi 2004:193).

Islamist calls for a fair and just order cloaked in the language of Shari'a were appealing to a society living in gross economic inequalities and suffering the injustices of the system. As Bowker puts it, 'Palestine and the policies of the US preoccupy Arab intelligentsia and salon society. But the core political issues of the region, almost monopolized by Islamist political forces for want of a credible political alternative, are jobs, education, food security, honest government and justice' (Bowker 2010:6). The Muslim Brotherhood not only seemed to be offering a moral alternative to a lineage of corrupt rulers, but also provided help to poor families and gave chances for social uplift through its professional and educational networks and close social solidarity in a society that had seen rapid urbanization and individual consumerism and privileged cliques who benefited from privatization. After the earthquake of 1992, when the Muslim Brotherhood's well-organized response and help to those affected drew widespread positive attention domestically and internationally, in contrast with the late and shabby work of the state, Mubarak unleashed his clampdown on the Brotherhood as well as wider political threats to the regime (Zahid 2012:119). The regime's responses ranged from attempts to assuming control over all mosques, limiting the influence of radical Islamist clerics, regulating structures of professional syndicates and banning of all political activity by groups that had no legal status as a party (Fielding & Shortland 2010:436).

As Mubarak began hardening his attitudes towards organized and deeply-rooted Islamist social movements, Egypt's social, economic and political crisis became a fertile ground for militant jihad that was emerging regionally and in the wider Islamic world in the 1990s. Egypt saw a tremendous increase in attacks on Copts, and symbols of the regime such as security forces, the ruling party NDP and official state buildings between 1990 and 2000. Worryingly, targets increasingly included tourists, who were a major revenue source. Attacks on them deeply tarnished Egypt's image. Fieldings and Shortland, who studied these attacks closely, note that 'the main series of twenty-five attacks against tourists started in August 1992; attacks occurred every 2–6 months until March 1995. Three further attacks occurred between November 1995 and March 1996, with two final attacks in September and November 1997' (Fielding & Shortland 2010:437). The 1997 attack on tourists at the popular Luxor site took eighty-eight lives, mostly foreigners, which was a shock both the world and to the regime, but also to the Islamists and even the militant groups, that things had gone beyond a line of acceptability. Following immense domestic outcry, the militant group behind the attacks, *Al-Jama'a Al-Islamiya*, declared that it would henceforth be committed to nonviolence. Yet, it was not merely self-reflexivity on their part. Between January 1990 and 2000, the regime had arrested 17,825 suspects with links to Islamist groups and in the same time period, some '592 civilians were killed and 398 wounded by the security forces' (Fielding & Shortland 2010:435). After the 1997 Luxor incident, terror attacks, especially on tourists, declined, demonstrating that both the heavy-handed response from the regime and the wide condemnation of the Egyptian public were capable of limiting such incidents.

The actual threat from militant Islamists might have been limited, but for the Mubarak regime, the process proved to be invaluable in continuing the state of emergency that had been in place since the assassination of Sadat. His economics might have been weak, but at least he provided 'security and stability' against dangerous Islamists. With this narrative, he was able to turn Egypt into a harsh police state that was much more restrictive and abusive than it has been. The state of emergency gave unprecedented power to the security services, especially to the Egyptian intelligence, State Security Intelligence Service (SSIS), and included indefinite detentions, arbitrary arrests and the denial of legal representation and official charges as well as the routine use of torture and physical and psychological intimidation. The Egyptian Organization for Human Rights (EOHR) stated that it 'monitored 263 torture cases between 2000–2006 inside police stations and detention centres, including seventy-nine cases which ended with the death of the victim believed by EOHR to be the direct result of torture and maltreatment. There were also ten incidents of torture monitored since the end of 2006 until the beginning of February 2007' (Egyptian Organization for Human Rights, 2007). During yearly fact-finding visits I conducted between 2005–2010 to Egypt to look at human rights abuses, the arbitrary use of power and the heavy-handed presence of intelligence services was truly suffocating. The effects of this on the Egyptian society meant that even victims of torture would refuse to speak out on their suffering due to fear of repercussions.

In the middle of these worsening economic, political and security conditions in Egypt, the relationship of the Copts with the state had entered a paradoxical stage. The Pope had changed dramatically in his years in the desert following his forced exile by President Sadat. His earlier political activism that had led to head-to-head clashes with late Sadat was now gone. The Pope continually sent out messages both to the Copts and wider society on national unity and the need to remain united in the difficult days and support the president. According to Sedra, the new attitude adopted by the Pope would mean that 'he would adopt a low profile, cooperate with the regime, embrace the rhetoric of national unity, negotiate with the government behind the scenes, avoid public confrontation at all costs, and consolidate his power within the church' (Sedra 1999:227). The shift in attitude and

public expressions of support as well as growing international pressure
had led Mubarak to lift the ban on the Pope and enable his return to
Cairo in 1985. During the following thirty years, both men would
enjoy a seemingly friendly relationship and a clear understanding of
what was expected from each of them to maintain that relationship.
The assassination of Sadat and increasing attacks by jihadists were an
acute reminder of the growing power and risk of Islamist networks in
the country. This was a major factor in the relationship of the Copts
with Mubarak until the end of his rule. Substantial numbers of Copts
believed and shared Mubarak's argument that without him and his
fight against Islamists, Copts would be abandoned to the attacks and
the country would be taken over by Islamists. As Michael Wahid
Hanna notes, 'the Mubarak regime willfully manipulated Christian
fears of Islamists to cultivate political quietism and support for the
government' (Hanna 2013).

The tacit agreement of a silent and cooperative relationship with the
state, however, was the start of prolonged and certain exclusion of
Copts from mainstream social and political structures. While some of
the structural and day-to-day problems faced by Copts in the Mubarak
era were the same problems faced by all Egyptians, with the exception
of a small clique of beneficiaries from the regime. Copts were victims of
the arbitrary use of force by state security services and the lack of rule
of law in the country, just as any other Egyptian. A vast majority of
Copts shared the same economic deprivation as Muslim Egyptians,
with the exception of Coptic middle classes that prioritized education
and professional qualifications as a means of a safe future for their
children, thus creating a socially-mobile Coptic generation. In addition, Mubarak's commitment to ensure no political or social movement could threaten his rule meant that every type of civil-society
engagement and activities were severely restricted, controlled and
only allowed within rigid state-set parameters, which automatically
impacted Coptic activities and organizations too. However, Mubarak's policies of trying to meet the sensitivities of Muslims as well as
using the threat of Islamism in order to maintain his rule added
additional layers of pressure on and discrimination against Copts and
placed them in a much more precarious position than under any other
previous president.

Firstly, during the Mubarak era Copts continued to be excluded
from political and state structures. Copts were by and large excluded

from the political process, except for a symbolic low-level representation. For example, in the 2007 elections, there were only two Coptic candidates out of 446 NDP candidates, and after the elections there was only one elected and five appointed members of the People's Assembly and no Coptic member of the upper house of Egyptian parliament, the 264-member Shura council (Malak 2007). Throughout Mubarak's rule, Copts were not appointed to Egypt's twenty-eight governorate posts, except for one appointed as governor in the late 2000s. No Copts held any high- or medium-level posts in government ministries, such as diplomatic and judicial services, state-owned industries, universities and the media. Coptic students regularly reported incidents of discrimination in high-level studies, especially in postgraduate exams and assessments. In the Mubarak era, there were no high-ranking Coptic officers in the armed and security forces.

Secondly, even the most basic provisions of religious freedom were denied on the basis of 'national security'. As under Sadat, no new church buildings were allowed and even the most basic church repairs required a presidential permission. In 1999, following much international attention, Mubarak had decreed that church repairs did not need presidential or any other state-level permission, and could be done under civil-construction registrations; in 2005, another presidential decree allowed repairs and constructions to be done solely following a simple notification to local authorities. Yet permission for new church buildings still had to be given by the president. In practice, not only was it almost impossible to get permission for even most basic repairs, when permissions for annexes or even repairs were given, they were stopped by the state-security services due to 'national security' reasons. In comparison, mosques needed no such regulations and private mosques were regularly opened across the country.

Thirdly, as will be clear in the reports of specific incidents below, even though Egyptian security forces were capable of stopping and containing attacks on Coptic places of worship, businesses and residences, in almost all incidents they were late in interfering. In most cases, none of the attackers were arrested even though they were widely known in small towns, and none received any criminal prosecution and punishment. Similarly, Copts were almost never compensated for serious material damage. In almost all incidents, Copts were forced into 'reconciliation' meetings where they had to sign documents waiving access to courts and letting go of their grievances for 'national unity and brotherhood'. In her study of how the state-controlled Egyptian national media reported these incidences, Iskandar found three distinct frameworks used: a) narratives of national unity, which selectively used historical narratives that spoke of Muslims and Copts being integral parts of the Egyptian social fabric; b) descriptions of 'inter-religious conflict as alien and external through the use of an "us versus them" paradigm', which 'shift[ed] responsibility for Egypt's sectarian incidents to "outsiders"'; c) discourse of 'extremists versus moderates', which aimed to unite Muslims and Christians by 'setting moderate Egyptians against the Muslim Brotherhood, and Muslims and Christians in Egypt against the Coptic diaspora' (Iskandar 2012:33). Thus, attacks on Copts continued not only with complete complacency of a state that boasted that it offered 'security and stability', but they were also relativized and utilized for political aims.

Fourthly, while the Egyptian state kept a tight rein on the media and public expressions against the state and issues deemed sensitive by the state, in the media, discriminatory and hate-speech against Copts and day-to-day discriminations went untouched. While Article 98F of the Egyptian Penal Code banned the 'insulting of heavenly religions', in actuality, it has only been used against criticism of Islam, either by non-Muslims or reformer Muslims, but never against any radical group portraying Copts and their beliefs in degrading terms. Copts were continually represented in negative terms in the media and often blamed as the root cause of even the attacks against them. In this process, the Egyptian state has de facto allowed Coptic culture and identity to be erased from the wider Egyptian culture, if not allowed Copts to be marginalized and seen as second-degree citizens.

By the mid-2000s, domestic demands for change began matching changing international trends. Soon after the initial wave of military responses to the jihadist networks behind the September 11 attacks on the United States, a wide consensus began emerging among the policy makers and experts in the United States that a lack of democracy and human rights across the Middle East led to a fertile ground for Islamist militants; thus, democracy promotion was integral to maintain both the security and interests of the United States. In 2002, the Bush administration launched the Middle East Partnership Initiative to fund efforts to strengthen the rule of law, civil society and political participation, to empower youth and women, and encourage economic growth. It had an initial budget of $29 million in 2002, which increased to $75 million in 2005 (Carothers 2005). MEPI states that it contributed over $600 million to more than one thousand grant projects across the Middle East and North Africa since its creation.[3] At the same time, the Bush administration increased pressure on its regional allies for reform, and Egypt was a major focus both for public comments and calls by US officials and also for direct funding and development of semi-underground networks for promotion of political participation.[4] Arafat points out that the Iraq campaign and the opposition of the Egyptian public to Bush's Middle East policy meant that even democracy advocates distanced themselves from the Bush agenda and the talks of democratic change even though many agreed with the need (Arafat 2009:88). This enabled the Mubarak regime to play a sophisticated game of exploitation and playing both the domestic and international actors against each other. On one hand, Mubarak intimidated 'democracy activists and independent nongovernmental organizations (NGOs) by citing national sovereignty, violations of the country's independence, and even treason'; on the other hand, he cited 'the Islamist threat to fend off the United States and the EU', which caused all pro-reform groups to go to 'great lengths to avoid any foreign contact, and even condemn external attempts to bring about reforms' (Arafat 2009:88). As for the European and American policy makers, fear of what might happen in Egypt if Mubarak's strong rule was not there forced them into accepting these mediocre reforms by Mubarak as a lesser evil than a possible Islamist takeover of Egypt. The 2003 campaign against Iraq and the subsequent surge in global militant networks enabled Mubarak to offer his services to combat terror. In the process, he once again made himself a valuable partner for the United States.

By 2005, growing tensions both within the country and from outside pushed Mubarak to undertake window-dressing reforms on a host of issues ranging from electoral law to the lifting of the required permissions for church repairs and buildings. Yet, a closer inspection of all of the 'reforms' showed their true nature. For example, while the regime seemed to open the way for multiple candidates to be nominated and run for presidential elections, Law No 174, 'On Regulating the Presidential Elections', which came into force in 2005, actually made it once again almost impossible for a legitimate challenger to emerge (Sullivan

& Jones 2008:12). Even with such preemptive legal buffers, in the lead up to 2005 elections, Mubarak intimidated and ultimately arrested his chief contender, Ayman Nour, under seemingly trumped-up charges, while security services arrested and mistreated demonstrators, parties and even voters (Brabant 2005). While it was not a surprise that Mubarak once again emerged as a president from the presidential election, in the following parliamentary elections the Muslim Brotherhood won more than eighty-eight seats (20 per cent) for the parliament through independent candidates, a massive increase from their seventeen seats in the 2000 elections (Caromba & Solomon 2008:119). Even though they were banned from politics as a party, the Brotherhood's decades of silent work among the marginal and under-the-radar was now showing itself. In March 2005, they held an unprecedented public protest against the regime. As a result thousands were arrested. Yet, far from slowing the party, later in May 2005 it showed its powerful social mobilization in multiple demonstrations across the country in a single day.

The emboldening of public expression in Egypt, however, did not only include Islamist political movements. The mid-2000s saw an increase in media outlets that kept pushing the boundaries set by the regime. Domestic human-rights and civil-society groups emerged in all sizes and capacities. Access to the Internet and global exposure was making it difficult for the generation to be simply 'tamed' by old narratives and tricks of showcase reform. Copts too were becoming louder both domestically and internationally. Following 9/11, there was a steady increase of attention on the situation of non-Muslims in the Middle East, particularly in the United States. Coptic diaspora organizations were becoming much clearer in condemning the regime as well as drawing attention to the 'Islamization' of Egypt. Yet, more dangerously, 'mainline Islamist groups, such as the Muslim Brothers, began to link their aversion to Western foreign policy, which was often depicted as a Christian crusade against Islam, with local Christian communities. The Islamists emphasized the difference of Christians from Egypt's Muslim society with references to them as "Nazarenes" and "Crusaders"' (Hanna 2013). Within such a context, attacks on Copts escalated to previously-unseen levels, as will be addressed below. President Mubarak, however, seemed more committed to maintain his grip on power than in addressing spiralling levels of violence in the country.

Following the Muslim Brotherhood's 2005 victory local elections were postponed, and through the adoption of the language of 'combating with terror', Mubarak was able to enshrine unprecedented powers granted to the state under the state of emergency into law through a series of 'terror laws' in 2007. Amnesty International reported that there were approximately 18,000 people held in Egyptian jails without any official charge or a trial; they were simply arrested and kept indefinitely by the state security (Amnesty International 2007). The heavy-handed pressure from the state and Cairo's new glamorous hotels and suburbs hid another sad factor from millions of people who visited the pyramids and Red Sea resorts; by 2009, 'over 40 per cent of Egyptians remain poor or extremely poor, with 2.6 million of the population of around 80 million unable to cover their basic food needs' (Bowker 2010:24). And yet Mubarak, who had seemed to be omnipotent and untouchable, was occupied more with securing the future of his family's rule by opening the way for his son to be the next president. President Mubarak had never appointed a vice president, and while he denied it continually, it was clear that he was grooming his son Gamal as his successor (Sullivan & Jones 2008:11). With full confidence in its power, the regime pursued another tainted election in 2010, in which it gained 420 seats against fourteen held by opposition parties and seventy by independents (Cook 2011:278). The elections were marred by widespread protests and scores of deaths and arrests.

When a Tunisian street vendor, Mohamed Bouazizi, burned himself to death in protest against his degrading treatment by his country's local authorities in December 2010, a wave of protests led to the ousting of another long-term autocrat, President Zine El Abidine Ben Ali, on 14 January 2011. While protests across the region started to spring up, rumours of a large-scale protest in Egypt was played down. Yet, on 25 January, much to the surprise of even the organizers, unprecedented numbers of Egyptians hit the streets in protest, demanding dignity and justice and fairness. After eighteen days of protests and international pressure, Mubarak had no choice but to resign when it became clear that his regime had run out of tricks to play. In a thirty-second announcement on TV, Mubarak's intelligence chief announced Mubarak's resignation and that the Supreme Council of Armed Forces (SCAF) would be taking control.

During the Interim Era from Mubarak to Field Marshall Sisi

The chaotic interim phase including Mubarak's standing down from power in February 2011, the election of a Muslim Brotherhood government in June 2012 elections and the military takeover of the government in July 2013 is truly important in the assessment of violence against Copts. As will be clear from the closer inspection of violent incidents below, the 2011–2013 era saw historic levels of violence against Copts even though all throughout the 'revolution' of January we witnessed encouraging signs of solidarity between Copts and Muslims. As Mubarak stood down from power, two important shifts happened: a) security forces, particularly the police, disappeared from the streets and the armed forces made a political stand of refusing to use force against Egyptians, resulting in a wide variety of petty crimes, including looting as well as ease of conducting any protests or vigilantes (Saleh 2011); and b) an immense competition was triggered to take credit for the revolution and shape the country's future power structures. Protests against the repressive acts of SCAF and apparent efforts to enshrine the army's privileges in the new Egypt by a wide range of secular and often left- and liberal-leaning movements, parties and youth went hand in hand with the unprecedented public boldness and presence of Salafist groups that presented a much more totalitarian vision than more modernist Islamists such as the Muslim Brotherhood (Rubin 2013; also El-Houdaiby 2012) Copts too broke the threshold of fear and launched unprecedented protests against the failure of the state to protect them, even though this was against the wishes of the Pope (Kassab 2012).

As SCAF pursued changes to electoral laws and the process of forming of new parties and writing a new constitution began, intense public debates on Article 2 of Egypt's constitution began, with Islamist blocks demanding the new constitution should be solely based on Shari'a and Egypt declared an Islamic state, and non-religious blocks demanding Egypt remain a 'civil state' (Felsberger 2014:261). As the public fixated on the debate over religion and state, attacks on Copts, Baha'is and non-orthodox Muslims such as the Sufis began. While in the lead-up to the 2012 elections the frequency of violent incidents lessened, throughout the election process Copts reported being attacked and stopped from registering and voting, especially in Upper Egypt where they were present in sizeable numbers in certain governorates. Islamist parties publicly condemned Copts to be 'traitors' and 'anti-revolutionary' for voting for Mubarak-era candidate Sahfik, as his victory would have been a return to the ousted regime (Abdelmassih 2012).

The 2012 election resulted in an outright victory for the Muslim Brotherhood through its Freedom and Justice Party (FJP) established in June 2011. The party secured 51 per cent of the votes, in comparison to the 48 per cent of votes won by former prime minister Ahmed Shafiq, who was seen as a mere continuation of the elite that governed Mubarak's Egypt (Weaver 2012). Even though the election-turnout rates for the first round of elections in May, 46.42 per cent, and in the second round of elections in June, 51.85 per cent, of Egypt's almost 51 million registered voters (Carter Center 2012:5), were rather low, in FJP's Muhammad Morsi, Egypt had its first democratically-elected and first civilian president since independence in 1952. In his inaugural speech, President Morsi 'called for national unity, vowed to preserve national and international agreements, and to protect the rights of women and children as well as Christians and Muslims alike. He said that Coptic Christians are "certainly just as Egyptian as I am, and have as much right to this homeland as I do"' (Batchelorte 2014:120). While Islam remained a central reference, the FJP 'introduced several amendments to the draft platform the Brotherhood unveiled in 2007', including the 'omission of the controversial provision giving clerics a formal role in politics and law-making' and removal of 'the article on the importance of the state's religious functions' (Al-Anani 2015:229). Al-Anani also notes that in economic policies too FJP showed a shift from the Brotherhood's thinking, by embracing economic freedom with the desire to achieve social justice while still attracting foreign investment, unlike the 2007 draft platform by the Brotherhood which promoted an Islamic economic system (Al-Anani 2015:230). These were seen as similar signs of a new Islamist politic emerging in Egypt, as it had in Tunisia and Turkey earlier.

The FJP's year-long rule was to feature fierce tensions over two crucial points: the place of the armed forces in politics, and a new constitution. Barely two months into office, 'President Morsi took a series of dramatic steps that included replacing top members of the SCAF's senior leadership' (Carter Center 2012:2). Initially both within and outside of Egypt, observers saw a positive understanding between the armed forces and Morsi (Stacher 2012). The tensions between the armed forces and the Brotherhood, however, deepened gradually due to regular public statements by Morsi that the armed forces would need to face budget cuts in line with all other government departments (Khalaf 2012). In an off-the-record conversation, an Egypt desk officer of a Middle Eastern country told me that it was in fact the continual signals from Morsi that the armed forces were going to see their budget and wider economic activities limited and political powers curbed that led them to take action towards ousting Morsi. The diplomat noted that in principle and in practice, the army's red lines were not Islam or risks of Islamization, since Egypt remained a deeply religious and conservative country, but the army's place in the system.

While such a focus on fiscal policy could have had wide public appeal, the FJP's proposals for the new constitution raised wide concerns that the party was simply seeking to establish an Islamic Egypt. The draft constitution was finalized by the Constituent Assembly dominated by the FJP and the Salafist Nour Party and was protested against widely. The draft attracted wide criticism as falling short of international standards, opening the door to discriminate against non-Muslims and blocking equality between men and women (Amnesty International 2012). In particular, Article 219 of the draft constitution declared Shari'a laws to be the 'fundamental rules of jurisprudence', in addition to the historic presence of Article 2 that defined Shari'a as the principle source of legislation. Also, Article 43 restricted religious freedom to only 'heavenly religion' (i.e., Islam, Judaism and Christianity) leaving all others outside of its protection. The draft constitution provided new powers to President Morsi, and accommodated the sensitivities of the armed forces by excluding civilian oversight over the army budget and allowing the army to try civilians before the military tribunals (Sika 2014:81). However, the fears of the general public that Egypt was now heading for an Islamist authoritarian state increasingly triggered protests and street clashes between supporters and opponents of the FJP. Then the Defence Minister General Abdel Fattah al-Sisi warned that it was the military's duty to 'prevent Egypt from slipping into a dark tunnel of civil unrest' (Caristrom 2013). Finally, following protests attended by millions of Egyptians throughout the summer, on 3 July the Egyptian Army, led by General Sisi, removed President Morsi from power, suspended the constitution, installed an interim government and promised new elections (BBC News 2013). The televised announcement featured General Sisi standing in front of a small group of key military officials, the head of Al-Azhar University and the Coptic Pope. The popularity of the overthrowing of Egypt's first democratically-elected president by the military was hailed as a revolution, with both the Egyptian state and intellectuals harshly condemning the naming of the incident as a military coup. Arafa expresses that sentiment strongly;

The dismissal of the Muslim Brotherhood's President Morsi cannot be considered a *coup d'etat* because the Egyptian military sided with the will of more than thirty million Egyptians by compelling Morsi to step down, leaving everything to a civilian government. Although Morsi was forced to leave office because of the army, it cannot be called a coup because it is what the people wanted, and power was placed in a civilian government (Arafa 2014:862).

The ousting of Morsi caused wide protests by his supporters, which were brutally put down, and triggered a clampdown on the Brotherhood and increasingly all forms of opposition across the country. Egypt entered a year of protests, violence, terror attacks and gross human rights abuses committed by the armed forces, including a redeclaration of a State of Emergency. The official National Council for Human Rights noted that between 2013–2014 violence in the country had resulted in about 2,600 deaths, including 700 security personnel, 1,250 supporters of the Muslim Brotherhood and 500 other civilians (HRW 2015). Human Rights Watch noted that 'the authorities detained, charged, or sentenced at least 41,000 people between July 2013 and May 2014' (HRW 2015). All rights organisations issued worrying reports on torture, extra-judicial killings, arbitrary detentions and failures of justice. Amidst all the chaos and a publicly-declared 'war on terror', General Sisi was promoted to the status of a Field Marshall: a military title that is given to a general with actual combat experience, which he did not have. In March 2014, he announced his resignation from the military to be able to run for the presidency. The May 2014 elections saw Sisi contesting against a weak candidate, and according to official statements, he won the elections with 96.1 per cent of the votes on a 47.5 per cent turnout rate, which critics challenged as a highly inflated result (Kingsley 2014). While the turnout might be lower than stated by officials, it was true that a substantial proportion of Egyptians, including liberals and secularists who had played a key role in ousting Morsi, supported

Sisi's presidency due to fears of insecurity, the need for stability in the country and to stop an Islamist takeover.

Both the ousting of Morsi and Sisi's election were met with wide enthusiasm among Copts. Morsi's victory had caused grave concerns for Copts due to the history of a clear Muslim Brotherhood stand on Coptic issues. Morsi's initial promise to appoint a Coptic vice president was never followed up, and when Morsi set the dates of parliamentary elections with dates that coincided with the Coptic Easter, Copts saw insincerity in many initial promises by Morsi (Sedra 2013). As Sedra notes, it would be a mistake to think that Copts acted in a united political block, and that even though the majority in fact voted against Morsi, some had voted for him reluctantly out of a desire to not return to the old regime (Sedra 2013). Yet Morsi's reluctance to protect Copts and respond to violent incidents against Copts, including the historic incident of an attack on the main Coptic cathedral by mobs in April 2013, led Pope Tawadros to publicly state that while President Morsi had called him and promised protection, in reality he did not, and Copts wanted 'action, not words' (Al Jazeera 2013). While state failures to protect Copts were not new, the increasing power and control of the Muslim Brotherhood and other Islamist groups in Egypt caused a clear sense of threat. When it became clear that the proposed new constitution would strengthen the place of Shari'a laws and give more powers to the president, Copts saw a dire future ahead. During the debate over the constitutional referendum in 2012, Muslim Brotherhood figures regularly accused the Church of mobilising the clergy for a 'no' vote by the public and often argued that it was mainly Copts who were opposing the new constitution (Fahmi 2014). That is why, even though large number of Copts did not want to see a return to the Mubarak-era rule under the army, the threat of an Islamist-governed Egypt made the Coptic Church and large number of Copts publicly back the military takeover. The historic number of attacks unleashed against Copts following Morsi's ousting in the summer of 2013, which we will address in Chapter 4, was seen as yet another proof of the risk caused by Islamists. Throughout 2014–2015, Coptic diaspora organisations and activists regularly issued statements and sent private e-mails to their networks (which included me) supporting the brutal 'war on terror' by the Egyptian military, and often criticized the West for not understanding Egypt and for condemning the excessive use of force and human-rights abuses by the Egyptian military.[5] During an interview in Egypt, a high-ranking clergyman in the Coptic Orthodox Church said that he was aware of the brutality of the armed forces and how they were only interested in protecting their interests; however, he said that the Coptic Church had no alternatives in the face of the real risk of worse conditions under Islamists. Yet Sisi's election and iron fist in dealing with Islamist networks did not result in stopping the attacks on Copts and, so far, a radical change to the limitations brought against Copts in Sadat and Mubarak years (Fayek 2014). Copts remain vulnerable targets as the 'war on terror' in the country is producing a new wave of radicalisation and militant jihad (Perego 2014).

Religious Violence in Egypt

As already noted above, attacks against Copts evolved and escalated throughout the twentieth century as Egypt went through major changes and was impacted by regional and global developments. Leading Egyptian scholar Saad Eddin Ibrahim provides a list of attacks on Copts between 1953 to 1993, showing 111 attacks in total and marking 1972 as the first year since independence when attacks against Copts took place (Ibrahim 1996:22). From 1972 to 1992, there are a limited number of sporadic attacks. A sharp increase in numbers is seen in the early 1990s, with thirty-three incidents in 1992 alone. While the violence seems to calm down in the late 1990s, it picks up again from 2005 and onwards and increasingly reaches unprecedented levels. The leading Egyptian human-rights organization Egyptian Initiative for Personal Rights states that 'from January 2008 to January 2010, there have been at least fifty-three incidents of sectarian violence or tension – about two incidents a month – that have taken place in 17 of Egypt's 29 governorates' (EIPR 2010b:5). Therefore, before the historic level of attacks against Copts in the summer of 2013 following the ousting of the Muslim Brotherhood government, there were already worrying signs of increasing frequency of such incidences.

The Al-Khanka incident of 11 December 1972 marks the start of contemporary ethno-religious violence in Egypt. A group attacked and burned a Christian charity in Al-Khanka, Cairo, during the Eid El-Fitr holiday (Brownlee 2013:7). The group claimed that the charity was being used to hold Christian prayers and worship even though it was not a church. In response to the incident, the following Sunday, Christians protested in large numbers by holding a prayer service on the site. Their protest was met by a large group of Muslims marching towards them under the leadership of a Sheikh. In the chaos that followed, numerous Coptic houses and businesses were burned and looted and the charity site attacked once again, and scores were arrested. An investigative committee set up by President Sadat urged the government to ease restrictions on Christian places of worship, so as to allow Christians to build new churches and thus not attract suspicion from and clash with Muslim neighbours (Mohieddin et al. 2013:9). If the recommendations had been followed, much of what was to follow could have been prevented. The next major incident caused by inaction on the issue of church permits was on 12 June 1981, when protests by a group claiming that Christians were secretly planning to build a church on a plot allocated for a mosque triggered violence which escalated between 17–20 June in Al Zawya Al Hamra in Cairo. The security forces did not attempt to stop the attacks on Coptic properties. As a result seventeen people were killed (Amer 2010).

The underlying tensions began showing themselves again in the 1990s in the Mubarak era. The city of Kosheh in Upper Egypt saw fatal incidents between 1998 and 1999. Following the ill-fated ways President Sadat used to downplay and brush the increasing signs of violence under the carpet, President Mubarak too started showing signs of handling the grave matter similarly. In the 1998 incident, the state opted to downplay it and did not seek to enforce law and order. On 31 December, the violence was triggered again and nineteen Copts and one Muslim were killed and more than forty were wounded (*Economist* 2000). Officially, the narrative was that the clashes were triggered because of a dispute between a Christian vendor and a Muslim customer that eventually extended to various villages around Kosheh. As the international outcry intensified, the Egyptian government eventually arrested more than ninety Muslims and some were accused of murder, only for all but four to be released and acquitted a year later. The only charges faced by the remaining four were manslaughter and possession of a gun without a licence; one of the accused was sentenced to a ten-year sentence and the other three sentenced to one to two years in prison, but in a subsequent retrial two more were freed (Hibbard 2011:99).

There was a rapid increase in frequency and scope of attacks on Copts between 2005 and 2011. During my fellowship at USCIRF, we were able to confirm some thirty incidents across Egypt in this period from English sources and Arabic media through the use of a translator.[6] The first major incident was in October 2005, when rumours spread that a play produced by Christians was insulting Islam and the Prophet. As reactions to it grew, a Coptic nun was stabbed in front of a church in Alexandria (BBC News 2005). The play told the story of a poor Copt who became a Muslim then reverted to Christianity when things did not work out. The protests escalated on 22 October 2005, when more than five thousand Muslims marched to the church after Friday prayers. Security forces dispersed the crowds, arrested fifty-three people, but three Muslim demonstrators were killed in the process (Tanner 2005). On 20 January 2006, rumours that a house was being used as a church by Copts in Udaysat village in Luxor province resulted in a group attacking and burning down the house. One Copt died and fourteen people were injured (Morrow 2006). Thirty people were detained and but all were released without charge. The government sought to defuse the situation by enforcing a 'reconciliation' meeting, which was to be used increasingly throughout the escalation period. During this meeting, representatives of communities were been brought together under the chairmanship of a state official and forced to sign documents that waived any further access to justice or demands. No criminal cases were brought against criminals, and no reparations were paid.

On 14 April 2006, three churches were attacked almost simultaneously in Alexandria (BBC News 2006a). Twelve people were injured and one died, 78-year-old Nioshy Guergis. The government blamed the attacks on a mentally-unstable individual. Coptic sources and witnesses pointed out that a group of people attacked the churches and this was no undertaking of a mentally handicapped person (BBC News 2006b). On 16 December 2007, the congregation of the Church of the Holy Virgin in Esna in Luxor was attacked with stones. On the same day, scores of Coptic residences and business were attacked. Shops were torched and looted. Following the refusal of the Copts to engage in a reconciliation agreement, the governor's office offered and provided financial reparation (Shortt 2012:18, 19). In April 2008, a Coptic congregation leaving the Palm Sunday celebrations in the church in the village of Qasr Hur was attacked by a large group of

men, leaving five injured. Copts were forced to sign an official 'reconciliation' agreement, and again none of the attackers were charged and
none of the injured Copts compensated (CSW 2009:18). The link
between the impunity shown to attackers on Coptic properties and
the increasing number of attacks became visible in an attack on the
historic Abu Fana monastery in al-Minya province on 31 May 2008 by
a group of Beduoin villagers living nearby. I had visited the monastery
and interviewed monks and local witnesses in 2008.[7] The monastery
had been a target of such attacks before from the same small village
nearby. The monastery and the monastery's farming area was ran-
sacked and looted. Monks were beaten severely, some suffering from
gunshots. During the attack on the monastery, a Muslim man was
killed from a gunshot from a fellow attacker. Two monks were kidnapped and kept by the villagers the entire night and were subjected to
torture and physical mistreatment in an attempt to convert them to
Islam. Even though the security forces had deployments nearby, they
not only did not come to the monastery for a few hours after the
attack, but also did not do anything to free the kidnapped monks,
who were released by the villagers the next day. Given the fact that the
monastery and the small village are on the edge of a desert area with a
small population, all of the attackers were known and yet, while a
small number of actual attackers were arrested, a number of civilian
Coptic workers at the monastery and Copts from the nearby town
were arrested at random. Arrested Copts were forced to confess that
the monks opened fire on villagers. The issue was reduced to a land
dispute between the monastery and the villagers, who claimed certain
rights over the monastery grounds. A reconciliation meeting was
forced once again.

On 20 June 2008, several houses and businesses that belonged to
Copts were set on fire, looted and damaged in al-Nazla in the Fayoum
governorate (CSW 2009:18). The attack followed rumours that a
Coptic woman who had converted to Islam was kidnapped by Christians. Those who were arrested were eventually released and after
an initial refusal, Copts agreed to partake in a reconciliation agreement. This was one of the rare incidents where a small but symbolically important level of financial reparations was eventually paid
to the Coptic community. Yet violence continued throughout 2008.
Following a call by a local Sheikh to protest against the permission
given to a local church to build an extension, a large crowd attacked a

church in Ain Shams, Cairo, leaving several Copts injured and the church damaged. Police questioned some sixty rioters, and briefly arrested eight suspects, three of which were Copts, but did not bring any charges against any of them (CSW 2009:17).

Violence continued across 2009 and 2010. While some seven attacks took place against Copts between July and August 2009 in Upper Egypt, targeting Christian properties and chapels, there were also attacks on the small community of Baha'is in March and April, causing serious material damage and forcing Baha'is to leave their villages (CSW 2009:17). Salafi clerics and media had continually put out inciting messages that portrayed Baha'is as a 'threat to national stability'. (Mohieddin et al. 2013:12). On 20 October 2009, Copt Farouk Henry Atalla, 61 years old, was shot dead in Dairut village, fifty kilometres south of Assiut, following rumours that his son raped a Muslim girl. Following the arrests of the accused murderers, on 24 October hundreds of Muslims protested against the arrests in front of the municipality building and the protest developed into a large crowd of two thousand Muslims attacking and looting houses, churches and shops belonging to Copts (EIPR. 2009:12). On 6 January 2010, a major incident occurred during the Christmas celebrations at a church in Nag-Hammadi in Qena. The church was attacked by a group of men, who killed six Copts and one police officer (Brownlee 2013:12). Attackers were arrested and were found guilty, one of whom was hanged in 2011 by the SCAF. On 7 January Copts, angered by the attack and the lack of protection and support offered to them, gathered in thousands outside the hospital where the dead bodies of murdered Copts were being kept. In a procession from the hospital to the church, Coptic youth attacked various buildings, cars and individuals, and clashed with the police (El-Naggar 2010). From then onwards until 9 January, a wave of attacks on houses and properties belonging to Copts broke out. In a fact-finding visit to the area, the EIPR noted grave failures of security forces in preventing the escalation of violence but also numerous stories of rumours spreading among Muslims, such as that Copts had killed a Muslim or burned a mosque, that led many Muslims to partake in attacks (For a detailed account see EIPR 2010a). In November of the same year, 'at least one Coptic Christian was killed and 120 wounded when violent clashes ensued between Egyptian police and Christians protesting a municipal decision to halt construction of a new church on the outskirts of Cairo' (OSAC 2011:4).

The turbulent year of 2010 ended with an attack on the Church of Two Saints in Alexandria on New Year's Eve. This showed a completely different pattern and evoked an unprecedented reaction against the state by the Copts. A car bomb killed twenty-one and left more than ninety people injured (BBC News 2011b). The sophisticated use of the car bomb as well as the timing of the attack amidst growing pressure on the Mubarak regime led many within and outside of Egypt to believe that the attack was undertaken by Mubarak's agents. In interviews and conversations with Copts, there was a widespread belief that with this incident President Mubarak wanted to give weight to the argument that kept him in power so long: that without him, Islamists would unleash harm and chaos. During the memorial service for the victims of the bomb attack, Copts stunned both the church and the public by their protests and booing of the state officials. There were protests across the country and clashes between the police and Copts (BBC News 2011c). A church leader I interviewed in Egypt noted that the reactions of the Copts showed that a threshold had been passed in Egypt.

In the period between the ousting of President Mubarak and the military coup that made Field Marshal Sisi the president, the breakdown of law and order allowed attacks on Copts and other vulnerable groups such as Sufis to unfold with no personal risk whatsoever to the perpetrators. This was something both the Copts and secular Egyptians circles had always been afraid of. For a while, it did in fact look like Mubarak was in fact right, that he was the dam holding the pressure from Islamist groups from bursting out into the open. However, on 9 October 2011, Copts found themselves not victims of loosely-related extremist groups but the armed forces, whom they had looked to as the protectors. The Egyptian Army used brutal and disproportionate force against a group made up of mostly Coptic youth but supported by various Muslims and liberal and secular activists, all protesting against the state handling of the Imbaba and other recent attacks on Copts. I was present both in Maspero and Tahrir Square that night and witnessed the brutality of the army first-hand. Army trucks drove speedily into the crowd to disperse them and fired countless rounds and tear-gas canisters into the crowd. Twenty-seven Copts died during the clampdown, mostly crushed by the military vehicles (BBC News 2011a). This was the first time in the history of Egypt that the Copts had been being killed directly by the military and security officials. Meanwhile, official state television channels aired statements and clips from military officers urging Muslims to come out and protect the armed forces, which were said to be under attack from Copts (Zuhur & Tadros 2015:120).

Minor incidences continued to occur following the Muslim Brotherhood victory, but it was a particular incident that would be the beginning of never-seen-before levels of violence against Copts in the history of Egypt since 1952. On 6 April 2013, violence erupted in the town of Khusus, following a group of Coptic children drawing what looked like a swastika on the walls of an Islamic institute. In the tensions that followed, four Copts and one Muslim were killed, several shops owned by Christians were attacked and a Coptic day centre was burned (Dalsh 2013). A funeral service was held at the country's main Coptic Cathedral in Cairo's Abbiseya district. While the Coptic mourners were leaving the cathedral, they came under attack by Muslims throwing rocks at them, which led to fights. Large numbers of Copts took refuge in the cathedral. Stones and Molotov cocktails were thrown at the church for hours, resulting in some ninety people being wounded and at least two people killed (Taylor 2013). This was the first occurrence of an attack on the Coptic Cathedral in the history of Egypt. Following the incident, Pope Tawadros condemned President Morsi for his failure to protect Copts, and stated that life under Morsi for Copts has 'a sense of marginalisation and rejection, which we can call social isolation' (Cesari 2014:177). The Pope issued a list of demands for protection and equal treatment of all religious minorities, including Shiites, as they too were facing similar conditions. On June 23, hundreds of people led by a Salafi preacher attacked Shiites living in a village near Cairo, killing four Shiites, whom they accused of being infidels and spreading debauchery (El Gundy 2013). H. A. Hellyer notes that the police were present but did not intervene during the lynching, and unchallenged statements about Shiites in the media and by clerics contributed to this incident (Hellyer 2013).

Within such a violent context following months of Muslim Brotherhood attempts to alter the constitution and seize more presidential powers, fears of Copts over their future under Muslim Brotherhood rule and thus their support of the military takeover in the summer of 2013 were understandable. For almost a century they had found themselves being seen as a problem to be dealt with by Islamists, and Morsi's brief time in the office only seems to have confirmed their fears.

But it was mostly what happened following the 2013 coup that has pushed large numbers of Copts to publicly and strongly support Field Marshal Sisi's takeover of the country. Rayna Stamboliyska documented that on 14 August 2013 alone some thirty-seven churches, five schools, seven offices belonging to Christian institutions and tens of homes and businesses belonging to Copts were 'either burnt down or at least badly damaged. In none of these cases was there confirmation of the presence of police or security forces in the vicinity of the buildings' (Stamboliyska 2013). Eshhad, a new project based at the Tahrir Institute for Middle East Policy aiming to document cases of religiously-motivated violence in Egypt, began cataloguing all incidents in the country starting from 14 August 2013. It recorded some thirty-eight further attacks on Coptic places of worship, personal properties and businesses and individuals from 15 August to the end of 2013.[8] Throughout the summer of 2013, Islamist preachers and Muslim Brotherhood figures continually put out inciting language against Copts in their media outlets, with dangerous accusations including Pope Tawadros employing sorcery to bring down the Islamist president, Copts working with Israel as spies, churches and monasteries full of weapons ready to attack Muslims, and Copts planning to create a Coptic country in Upper Egypt working with the United States (Zuhur & Tadros 2015:121). The Eshhad database includes some thirty-seven incidents in 2014, and in the first half of 2015, the number of incidents recorded has passed 120, including fatal attacks on individuals, properties and places of worship. While the incidents from 2014 and 2015 were not part of the research process of this book, their astonishing levels point to how the ousting of President Morsi and the brutal clampdown on Islamist networks by President Sisi have resulted in historically-exceptional levels of violence against Copts. While the intensity and number of incidents are new, there is a deeply old pattern in play; Copts remain blamed and targeted by Islamists for their fate and the fate of Egypt. As Bishop Angelos of the Coptic Orthodox Church noted, 'When Morsi was overthrown the Brotherhood wanted a scapegoat and they held the Christians up as a scapegoat' (Quoted in Malnick 2013).

A Vulnerable Minority Amidst Fierce Political Tensions

A closer look at the incidents listed above starts bearing interesting insights into the dynamics of violence in Egypt. The majority of attacks happen in Upper Egypt, with high levels also in Cairo and Alexandria; thus, while the attacks naturally show themselves in areas with higher Coptic populations, they are still nationwide in character. There are three important observations that can be made from the chronological account of attacks: *what triggered the attacks, what the profiles of the attackers are,* and *the timing of the attacks.*

The largest number of incidents until 2013 were triggered by rumours, mostly about places of worship. These were either rumours that Copts were secretly building new sections to their churches, holding prayer meetings in non-designated church buildings or expanding the land of religious centres by building walls. One incident was caused by rumours of blasphemous comments about Islam made by Copts. Two incidents were caused by rumours that Copts held Christian converts to Islam against their will and tried to forcefully convert them back to Christianity. Four incidents were triggered by rumours of shameful acts by Copts, all involving sexual allegations, from indecent relations to rape to allowing prostitution. At least two incidents was triggered by a mundane incident, one a traffic accident and the other a disagreement between a Copt and Muslim over a purchase of a good. One incident was caused by the appointment of a Coptic governor, which was protested against by Islamists. More worrying are the incidents that were unprovoked. These include organized attacks by small groups with arms, some indiscriminate and unprovoked mob attacks following mobilization of crowds by clerics after the Friday prayers. There was one incident suspected to be an act of state agents, an unprecedented bomb attack. There were three incidents where protests by Copts against the state's handling of prior incidents triggered attacks on the protesting groups, including one incident of a brutal use of force by the Egyptian Army.

In addition to the diverse range of triggers, there is also a diverse profile of attackers. In some cases in Upper Egypt, we see local Bedouins looting and attacking with more temporal interests. We also see Islamist groups attacking either to enforce morality or ideology or because of religious sentiments such as accusations of blasphemy and conversion or church activities. In nine cases we see senseless mobs comprising youth, the unemployed and zealots incited by a trigger, such as rumours of immorality, fiery sermons or a traffic accident. In at least two cases, we see well-organized small groups of attackers with unknown backgrounds. In one case, we suspect state agents planting a bomb, and in two cases of attacks on Copts protesting in 2011, we see thugs often thought to be paid by the police to intimidate protesters. In attacks between 2013 and onwards, Islamist zealots play a more dominant and organized role.

The most widespread series of attacks on Copts often overlap with major political and social developments in the country that are independent from Copts. This can be seen in both the lead-up to the events of Mubarak's ousting and in its follow-up. They also show themselves in eras in which the Egyptian state finds itself either clamping down on Islamist networks or responding to overall terror risks in the country. In other words, attacks on Copts either emerged in times of serious overall security challenges in the country or amidst serious macro-level changes in the country. What a close inspection of all accounts has revealed is how little protection has been given to the Copts by the state. Not only the Islamists but also the state itself has seen Copts as an expediency in their political projects of responding to challenges to their rule from grassroots discontent. By not protecting them and punishing their attackers, actively removing Copts from public office and not including their historic presence in the land in education and mainstream culture, the state has put Copts into a vulnerable position. This has encouraged a wide range of attackers, from looters to resentful neighbours to Islamists to irrational mobs, to attack Copts with great impunity while the country saw moments of lapse in the rule of law and order or a wave of terror attacks in line with regional trends in the 1970s and 1990s. That is why, even though Nasser was not keen on addressing Coptic rights, his strong-man rule and brutal enforcement of security meant hardly any major attacks on Copts occurred during his period of rule.

Neither the silent submission of Copts to Egypt's military rulers, nor the Pope challenging or supporting them, nor Coptic youth following the church's lead or protesting against church's wishes seems to have a conclusive impact in stopping these attacks. The impact of activism among Coptic diaspora groups, particularly in the United States and Europe, on ethno-religious violence has also not resulted in substantial positive change to the conditions faced by Copts. On the contrary, some Coptic groups in the United States have engaged in inflammatory language against Muslims and Islam, and closely associated their activism with conservative groups in the United States which have deep worries about the global threat caused by Islamism (Hanna 2013). Such short-sighted types of Coptic activism that aligns with particular partisan politics and agendas in the United States only provide Islamists with more fuel to accuse Copts of working with the presumed enemies of Islam, thus puts Copts in Egypt into a vulnerable position. All of these point out that without a genuine commitment to protect Copts by the state by enforcing the rule of law and justice, providing adequate protection and pursuing positive steps to lift all restrictions and limitations before Copts, ethno-religious violence in the country will continue with varying levels of intensity depending upon local, national and regional developments.

Conclusion

This chapter has demonstrated that while Copts are in no way responsible for the economic, political and foreign-policy failures that haunted Egypt since World War I, and while their presence in the land predates Islam, they have assumed a symbolic role by simply being there and being religiously different. Throughout the macro-changes in the country from a failed monarchy to an attempted nation-state experimenting with socialism, then to a free-market economy yet ending as a poor authoritarian regime with weak ideological appeal, there have been immense tensions between two opposing visions for Egypt: on one hand, an autocratic regime whose main interest is maintaining its power through any means and on the other hand, theo-political visions that promote theocracy as a solution for the failures of the 'secular' regimes, though one can legitimately argue that the word secular does not really apply to the Egyptian context, given how the state incorporates, manages and controls religion.

Copts have been caught up in these tensions, not only in the Islamist calls to purify the land, but in the 'secular' regimes' denial of cultural, economic, political and religious freedom to Copts. They went from being an integral partner in the story of liberation of Egypt from the colonial powers in the early twentieth century to being comrades of Arab nationalism under Nasser that sought to underplay religion, but then increasingly became non-equal citizens and nuisances under Sadat and Mubarak both for the regime and for the grassroots religious movements. Violence against Copts was not a given consistently across the twentieth century, nor were Copts the actual focus of Islamist violent extremists in the country whose main targets were always state officials and state interests. While the Egyptian state combated effectively all threats to its own existence, including jihadists that directly harmed Egypt's interests by attacking tourists, no official campaign to stop violence against Copts was ever launched and all attacks on Copts were relativized as 'communal clashes' within the 'united family' of Egypt. In other words, allowing violence was an important political expediency for the regime to defuse tensions and meanwhile maintain its self-serving narrative of defending Egypt from an Islamist take over. For the attackers, Copts became de facto officially-sanctioned targets on whom to take out frustrations and discontent. Attacking them would pose no personal risk or the wrath of the state.

Regional trends and global trends, whether from the momentum of the late 1970s that saw a resurgence of Islamic revolution ideals, or the aftermath of the 9/11 terror attacks, the invasion of Iraq in 2003 or the 'war on terror' declared by the United States, directly contributed to the escalation of violence against Copts in the period 2005–2011. The country saw a rocketing of anti-American attitudes and terror attacks as well as a deepening perception of a 'Christian' West on a 'crusade' against 'Muslims'. Salafist groups which had no prior geopolitical ambitions or public presence and often saw politics as dirty, now became visible in violence against the Copts. In fact, the historic level of violence that followed the ousting of the Muslim Brotherhood government in 2013 was an accumulation of a decade-long build up of ethno-religious violence in the country and global and regional trends. With the almost total collapse of law and order from 2011–2013, clashes between state security forces and protesting public, as well as attacks on non-Muslims and non-orthodox Muslim groups, sky-rocketed. Since then, President Sisi have continued Mubarak's policies identically in using violence against Copts as a political utility while promising to be their protector. Copts remain as a vulnerable minority vilified by the Muslim Brotherhood and others as a scapegoat for their own conditions and agendas. Yet, Copts also have agency and have taken clear public and political stands, at times directly contributing to deepening risks they face, which could have been contained to a certain extent with more careful approaches.

4 | *Comparative Analysis of Violence in Nigeria and Egypt*

In previous chapters, cases of ethno-religious violence in Nigeria and Egypt were addressed in detail and preliminary conclusions about each case were presented as the conclusions at the end of each chapter. It is clear that even though Nigeria is a complicated federal state where multiple ethno-religious groups associated with strong geographical locations compete for power and access to state revenues, whereas Egypt is a nation-state with a single language and well-enforced state structures run by a clientele-elite network utilizing a rentier economy with mass poverty in the wider population with grassroots political challenge from religious movements, they both see high levels of violence between Muslims and Christians. While Muslim and Christian communities in Nigeria are of roughly equal population and both have considerable power, in Egypt the Christian population is a minority with a mere 8 per cent to 10 per cent of the population. The Christian population is also economically and socially marginalized and largely excluded from politics and state roles. However, even given these deep local differences, the ethno-religious violence seen in both countries are regularly used as examples of the declared clash between the Christian world and House of Islam, as shown in both case chapters.

Therefore, the task that now follows is reflecting on the similarities between the two cases, with *the logic of agreement* that is most suitable to establish factors that are similar in the two cases. Such a comparison will be able to test the arguments about the link between religions and violence as outlined in the introduction, given that those arguments depend on assumptions about declared intrinsic qualities of religious beliefs that somehow inescapably result in violence. If such assumptions are valid, what we should be witnessing in our comparison is that religion is the core similarity in the factors triggering violent clashes independent of the difference in contexts. However, a thorough comparison of both cases demonstrates a much more complicated series of key factors that form the necessary conditions for such conflicts to become possible. Below are the key commonalities that are observable from the data presented in each case chapter.

Colonial Heritage and State Formation

The first similarity in the two histories is their colonial experiences. Both Egypt and Nigeria emerged from colonial rule in which their populations and structures were run directly by colonial authorities. In both cases, the United Kingdom was the colonial power, but Egypt had previously been run by an Ottoman colonial administration which adds an additional layer. Both British and Ottoman authorities worked with social, political, ethnic and religious structures to be able to control their populations and in this process, played key roles in establishing the parameters of the relations between different ethno-religious communities and their place and aspirations in the subsequent governance of their countries. In both countries, national emergence and struggles for independence began in reaction to the colonial powers and their policies, which resulted in tensions between particular communities and elites over presumed or actual privileges the other did or did not enjoy under the colonial powers. Emerging as and becoming nations from the colonial era has been a continual quest in the politics of both countries. While what is Nigeria and who is a Nigerian and whether there is such a shared collective vision for the country is still debated, prebendal politics continually undermine the vision for a shared nation and fair state. In Egypt since the end of the colonial era, politicians have been attempting to develop a vision for the nation, whether in the form of the secular nationalism and socialism of the Nasser era, or the open-market but religious politics of Sadat, or economic interests and maintenance of status quo of Mubarak, or the short-lived Islamist future of Morsi. The result was a brutal state and never-ending cycles of authoritarian heads of state promising economic development and stability at the expense of rule of law and democratic reform. The tensions between Islamists and non-Islamist but conservative populations and the place of minorities means the same questions about identity and the future of Egypt have continued from the start of the twentieth century to the present day.

Political Instability and Poor Governance

One of the most striking similarities between the two countries is the instability of their state structures and their poor management. Within the relatively short period of fifty years, both countries have seen numerous revolutions, military coups and mass protests leading to impeachments. While Nigeria declared a new republic after each period of military government to mark the return to civilian rule, Egypt has seen four military officials assuming leadership of the country with the only civilian president to be elected, Morsi, ousted in a widely-backed military coup. All phases of military rule in both countries have seen what Giorgio Agamben (2005) names a 'state of exception', a formal suspension of the application of law and the bestowing of grave unprecedented powers on to the rulers of the countries under declared states of emergency. While in both countries such iron-clad military interventions based their initial public support on promises of stability, an end to corruption and the protection of the nation from ideologues with dangerous agendas, in actual terms, their rules too have seen the creation of powerful economic and political elites, corruption, exploitation of state revenues, gross human rights violations and worsening economic conditions for the wider sections of their societies. The speed of fundamental changes to state structures, and their unsatisfactory long-term outcomes for society in general, and the insecurity and unreliability they create are important factors in the emergence of ethno-religious violence in both countries.

Deprivation and Fierce Competition

What the prebendalism of Nigeria and the clientelism of the Egyptian economies signal is the exclusivist nature of economic and political opportunities in both countries. In both countries, whom you know, whom you are associated with, which ethnic or religious group you are affiliated with, which family line you came from, where you live and what socio-economic classes you are in have direct implications for your political and economic access. These include access to civil service posts, scholarships, economic incentives, academic appointments, political party participation and representation on local councils and in national parliaments. The background to such an exclusive social, economic and political structuring of the society is the limitations of unhealthy economies with a disproportionate dependency upon rentier revenues coming from sectors such as oil, the Suez Canal or tourism, as opposed to healthy and diversified robust economic activities. Geographically, desert conditions in both countries, poor water-management and low agricultural productivity amidst deforestation and difficult terrain have meant many people have moved to urban centres with more economic opportunities. Yet, given the limitations of both economies such migration patterns have created widespread poverty and large settlement on the fringes of cities. The increasing unprecedented richness of the elite and their benefactors are contrasted to the despair seen in the levels of poverty in both countries. Such realities make politics and access to opportunities a high stakes process, thus competition for them and attempts to maintain interests are equally fierce.

High Levels of Violence by State and Non-State Actors

A comparison also highlights an important factor: ethno-religious violence is only part of a wider picture of violence in both cases. Both Nigeria and Egypt have seen wars since their independence in the mid-twentieth century. Terror attacks, brutal state security and military clampdowns on opposition groups or any security threat have been a common feature. In Nigeria, separatism triggered a civil war and armed militias in the Delta state have sought to achieve a share of oil revenues, and common criminal activities in cities and rural areas have reached truly violent levels. Whereas, in Egypt, the Sinai area often formed a safe haven for militant groups, terror networks emerging to continually challenge the state, army and state security apparatus regularly deploying torture, disappearances and executions. In fact, while violence against Copts has been largely damaging in material terms, the single incident with the highest fatalities was the soldiers killing Copts in the Maspero protests. Similarly, some 800 supporters of the Muslim Brotherhood were brutally killed by the Egyptian security forces in a single day as they protested against the coup that ousted president Morsi. Both countries see 'thugs' deployed in critical political events, such as protests or elections, to intimidate and attack people. In both countries, such thugs are seen as being directly paid by politicians or the security establishment to intimidate the masses, and such worries have a legitimate basis. All of these experiences lower the threshold for new violence to emerge and that violence is sometimes seen as the only option to defend, assert, establish or maintain interests as well as express grievances and opposition.

Dynamic History of Place of Religion in Politics and Society

It is clear that in both countries religious beliefs, identities and networks have deep historic roots. Such roots maintain the narratives of communities, whether in helping them protect their identities in a positive way or maintaining their grievances and historic experiences in the face of contemporary challenges. They also provide social support in the absence of state structures that are able to offer welfare services. The societies of both countries are deeply conservative and religious values and readings of the world are widely held, though the majority of both populations have come to incorporate religious values into modernity and its technological and scientific offers. Yet, what the closer study of Nigeria and Egypt has revealed is how dynamic the role of religious identifications, religious dignitaries, religious visions and religious appeals are in politics. In Egypt, the lead up to the 1952 Revolution and the entire Nasser era saw wide support given to a secular nationalism with a blend of socialism. It was only since the defeat in the 1967 war and the beginning of the Sadat era that we see a wider appeal to and accommodation of religious politics as well as religious framed demands for fairness in the society. The late 1970s saw a strong presence of religion in politics and wider society tensions in Egypt, forcing Sadat to change the Egyptian constitution to accommodate Shari'a laws.

Nigeria went through a similar period of development. The era of the First Republic and initial politics of Nigeria up to the 1970s was primarily about ethnicity. The religious grouping of such ethnic communities with a split between the Islamic North and Christian South together with demands for the restoration of mythical Islamic eras became more dominant in the 1970s with demands for Shari'a law to be applied and nationalized. Therefore, while religions do have deeply entrenched places in both countries, the playing out of their political significance and emergence as points of contention are not a given, and both countries have seen prolonged phases of peaceful co-habitation among religious communities.

Impact of Political Developments on Religions

A comparison of both cases reveals that changes in context not only alter the place of religions in politics and conflicts, but they also alter the religions themselves. In both countries, religious institutions have found themselves at times as the only permitted and often independent form of civil society network and platform, with all other non-religious networks and platforms seeing fierce government clampdowns. This has been both due to the resilience of religious networks and the sensitive approaches that governments have shown in handling them as well as their desire to utilize them for political aims. In the process, in both countries, religious leaders have increasingly played important roles in the public realm. This has been particularly so because of growing disillusionment with the political elite and its widespread corruption and unfairness. The prophetic voice gained by religious actors in this process has accommodated a wide range of types: officially-sanctioned or politically-supported clergy supporting particular political leaders or ideas, opposition groups using religious platforms to promote their politics based on religious ideals to establish a fair society and religious entrepreneurs simply garnering personal power, influence and money. While some of these have incorporated positive roles that religions can play, such as offering social and material support to the marginalized, it has also taken a direct toll on religions. Religious ideologies, identities and solidarities have become primarily about 'us' and the restoration of a new moral order – a utopia, in opposition to the 'them' who do not share that religion or its interpretation. This is particularly clear in the emergence and modification of Islamist thought in both countries: first focusing on spiritual reform, then political impact, then revolution and then direct physical confrontation with the state and communities seen as standing in the way of achieving a pure society, either other Muslims who do not share such Islamist views or Christians who are in a minority or competitors. Thus the religious mandates of 'loving your neighbour as one's self' and helping those in need became about group solidarity and not extended easily outwardly. The positive religious significance of offering support for the needy in two countries sharing such dire conditions has overlapped with religious identification and exclusion shaped by the same prebendalism and clientelism. Alignment with the powerful has been rewarded and particular networks formed out of perceptions of threat and animosities that other religious communities might have to undermine them. Thus religious actors also accommodated the deployment of violence and tribalism. Therefore, religious groups are far from being the mere root causes of tensions or politics of identity boundaries and mobilization in Nigeria and Egypt. Instead they are also vulnerable to emerge as victims of such interferences. Religions pay the high price of losing their self-declared moral beliefs in a spiritual sense of 'state of exception' when beliefs are suspended for the welfare of their believers and supporting bad things done in the name of security and protection become necessary evils. This can be seen in the support of the Coptic Church of brutal clampdown of Muslim Brotherhood by President Sisi or in active participation of Christians in violence in Nigeria while preaching New Testament beliefs on loving one's neighbour.

Patterns of Ethno-Religious Violence

In both countries, ethno-religious violence follows similar patterns. There are moments of aspirations to national unity which ethno-religious communities are able to share in the face of common dangers. This may be in the case of independence from the colonial authorities, or revolutions and military coups in both counties; there are numerous such moments of shared political stands and a sense of brotherhood. Yet, in both countries elections and sudden shifts in power structures have been preceded or followed by violent clashes, including those between ethno-religious communities and towards religious minorities. For example, in Nigeria, almost all elections have seen violence, and in Egypt we have seen how violence against Copts and other religious minorities reached historical levels contemporaneously with the ousting of Mubarak and then Morsi. In both countries, we see prolonged eras of no ethno-religious violence during strong military or heavy-handed state rules. However, in both countries periods of weaker or civilian governments following such authoritarian rule see fierce episodes of violence. For example, in Egypt, while the Nasser era saw no major incident of violence against Copts, the Sadat era saw the beginning of fierce attacks on them. Likewise in Nigeria, large scale clashes and fierce ethno-religious conflicts emerged particularly after shifts to civilian rules. While one could raise the warning of logical fallacy *post hoc ergo proctor hoc* in arguing for causal relations between events that follow one another in chronological order, in both countries, it is clear that ethno-religious conflicts are directly correlated to political changes and political uncertainty in contexts where elections and the taking or losing control of state structures are high-stake competitions.

Multiple Actors and Motivations Involved in Violence

In both countries, the profiles of people inciting or partaking in violence differ in similar ways, even though the overall categorizations of events place them within the same phenomenon. While there are some ideologues with clear visions and political entrepreneurs with clear agendas to incite violence, and though the vast majority of people deploying violence are young and middle-aged men, their individual aims are complicated. Some clearly see ideological necessities in the deployment of violence to protect or remove their communities from danger, some are clearly opportunists seeking to achieve personal material or sexual gains or settle personal vendettas; some are clearly paid actors or those who benefit politically by partaking in such acts through prebendalism and clientelism, while some are simply individuals caught up in the euphoria and attraction of such large scale events. Thus, in ethno-religious violence in both countries we do not simply see religious zealots experiencing a loss of control and simply harming those who do not share their beliefs, but the common experiences of violence we see in all contexts across the world from revolutions to wars, uprisings to gang violence.

Rule of Law and Impunity

In all the interviews I conducted in Nigeria and Egypt, the answers given to two key questions used to enquire about respondents' thoughts on causes and prevention of ethno-religious violence 'What is the primary reason for these violent incidents to continue?' and 'What needs to be done to stop violence and conflict?' – were nearly identical. The primary answer given to the first question was always 'impunity', that attackers and those who incite violence face no punishment. The primary answer given to the second question was always 'rule of law', that there has to be justice for the victims and punishment for the attackers to stop violence and conflict. The lack of impunity and rule of law are major problems in Nigeria and Egypt. As shown in the chapters on the countries, perpetrators and inciters of violence almost always walk away free. Rather than enforcing the rule of law, faith investigations, establishment of acts, and culpability, in both countries authorities either demonstrate no lack of will to handle such a politic-ally sensitive process, or at worse, tolerate and utilize such incidents for their own political ends. When action *is* taken, the authorities often pursue languages of brotherhood, pushing reconciliation meetings or calls for harmony. This makes victims feel unheard, pushed aside and left alone to their own suffering, and makes the risk of deploying or inciting violence miniscule for those who partake in them. Thus, attacking Copts to seize or harm their material belongings and clergy is an act that can be done in the full knowledge that the robust security establishment that would show no hesitancy in responding harshly to political dissent will not stop such attacks nor punish the attackers. While being a numerical minority limits Copts' sense of revenge, the resentment and sense of vulnerability it builds and its outcome for international advocacy and sharp political alignment is clear. In con-trast, a sense of lack of justice and security pushes communities in Nigeria to take matters into their own hands. Thus cycles of violence continue with a long list of episodes of being victims leading to violence deployed on others. The more violence continues unchallenged, the more facts of incidents are not established and culpability punished, the more violence becomes a common occurrence and a normalized expression. The impact of this on religions themselves and the accom-modation and justification of violence in religious terms to protect the community is visible in both cases. Thus, justice and rule of law not provided by state structures becomes a challenge for religious commu-nities to address theologically and practically.

Broken Social Trust

In both countries, we see widespread conspiracy theories and deep mistrust of officials, politicians, security forces and people of other religious and political persuasions. Some of these reach almost surreal levels. In Nigeria, a Muslim said in an interview that he heard some Christians were cannibals and purposefully seduced Muslim women to disgrace them. Christians in Nigeria told me of elaborate plans by Muslims to lure Christian women into Islam and get them pregnant.

Several people told me that there were Muslims who would inject HIV-positive blood into Christians with a syringe in crowded markets and that some Muslim leaders pay for HIV-infected 'loose women' to sleep with Christian men. Both Muslims and Christians were always certain of the other's evil intentions to destroy, including cunning plans and stockpiling of arms in places of worship. In Egypt, conspiracy theories are wide and media and Islamic clergy continually put out dangerous stories about Jews and Christians and their secret aims in the Middle East. Beliefs about the wealth of Copts and their secret dealings with foreign powers continue unchallenged. Copts, too, believe a wide range of unreliable stories about Muslims and Islam, Islamists. These include numerous accounts of organized kidnapping of Christian girls by Muslims. While this is sometimes true, some of these cases in reality seem to involve young Copts willingly leaving their communities to marry or be with a Muslim, or to escape family oppression and conditions of poverty. Yet sexual aggression and abuse towards Copts is a fact indeed. In Egypt, such a deep lack of social trust and beliefs in theories of grandeur are supplemented with fears of an all-knowing and all-powerful state as well as extreme expressions of emotive nationalism. In both countries, while ethno-religious communities live in close proximity and share economic and social activities, deep mistrust and fear of the other create relational ghettos and close-quarter living of communities. This creates conditions for rumours and half-truths to spread fast through religious networks, creating wider tensions and disproportionate responses. In the example of fighting in Jos which I experienced, a mundane dispute between a Muslim and Christian at the marketplace had spread to both communities as each accused the other of killing innocent people, thus triggering young people to rush to protect their kind. Mistrust of the other, and the expectation that they are somewhat united in evil intentions, are sustained by clerics and the religious terminology used to dehumanize the other in both countries. This way, tensions and misperceptions become reified in an imagined eternal basis for assumed differences between Muslims and Christians due to their religious beliefs.

Religious Counter-Violence Initiatives

In both countries, there are numerous initiatives for grassroots peace building and reconciliation and high-level clerical and faith-based initiatives to de-escalate tensions and stop the conflicts. In Nigeria, this is especially visible in Plateau State where Christians and Muslims are in equal numbers and where violent clashes are common. A group of Muslims, who have been involved in communal projects, when interviewed told of projects that bring young Muslims and Christians together and reach out to victims and perpetrators to process the events and talk to one another to seek absolution in the Jos area. Similarly, a high-ranking Anglican bishop told of numerous such initiatives and personal engagement with high-ranking Muslim clergy to calm down tensions and promote understanding as well as attempting to challenge political manipulation of their youth. The internationally celebrated case of a Nigerian imam and a pastor promoting peace is commonly raised as an example (Joseph 2013). I observed the two of them sharing their experiences with a group of Egyptian civil society activists in Cairo.

In both countries, all faith actors talked about their hope for peace and the need to help their communities to ease tensions, show maturity, forgiveness and kindness and not pursue further violence. This happened in Egypt after the attacks on Copts and the brutal murder of Copts by ISIS in Libya. In response, the Coptic Church and victims' families issued emotional messages of forgiveness and not holding all Muslims accountable (Burke 2015). Given the very real physical risks involved in such projects and areas, and given the long history of grievances and resentment, and the legitimate lack of trust in state authorities to protect and uphold justice, such individuals and their faith-inspired attempts to counter violence are truly remarkable. This does highlight that while it is tempting to pursue a line of enquiry to locate violence in an imagined value within religions, religious beliefs can also inspire people in the most vulnerable positions to pursue peace and moral responses to other faiths and ethnicities, when all factors should lead them to deploy violence and escalate conflicts.

Impact of Global Developments

In both Nigeria and Egypt, it is clear that global political, social and religious developments directly impact local developments. Both countries have been shaped by the colonialism of the nineteenth and early twentieth centuries. They were also impacted by the same anti-colonial and nationalistic visions that emerged in the early twentieth century across the world. The political aspirations in both countries as they began their independence echoed their milieu in aspirations of nation-hood and the 'right to self-determination'. In the 1960s and 1970s, there were similar political movements with socialist visions for eco-nomic redistribution as well as the wide appeal of Islamic movements that promised a fair society. The impact of the Iranian Islamic revolu-tion in 1979 is seen in both countries in galvanizing Islamic movements and their aspirations for a revolution. In the same time period, both countries saw wide demands for application of Shari'a law and its integration into formal structures. This coincided with identical calls across North Africa, the Middle East and South Asia, with the consti-tutions of Pakistan, Bangladesh and Sudan changed to accommodate Shari'a law, as it was the case in Egypt and in the calls for Shari'a law in Nigeria. Such calls created conflicts and violence in both countries between Muslims and non-Muslims and secular elites seeking to sus-tain their rule. The 1980s saw religiously motivated terror attacks in both countries. While such attacks eventually decreased in frequency and size, in both countries, the late 1990s and 2000s saw a return of Islamic terror organizations. These coincided with the rise of global Islamic terror organizations, such as Al Qaida, which, among its many recruits and supporters, had many Nigerians and Egyptians join its ranks. The 9/11 attacks, and most importantly, the 'war on terror' that was launched after them, had a direct impact and outcomes in both countries. It triggered support for and reaction against Al Qaida and the United States, and subsequent US military campaigns became referred to domestically in 'Christian West' versus 'the Muslim world' language, with many Muslims increasingly seeing US aggression as a battle against all Muslims. This not only caused more friction between Muslims and Christians in both countries, but violence in both coun-tries between Muslims and Christians was also given much more attention internationally in the media, and by non-governmental organizations and faith-based networks. As a result, now in both countries we see Muslims and Christians interpreting and representing their domestic conflicts through post-9/11 discourses of a global clash between the West and Islam.

Conclusion

The book has demonstrated thus far that the particular contexts of Nigeria and Egypt highlight a much more complex history of how and when ethno-religious violence and conflict emerged, escalated and at times ceased, than would be expected from some simplistic theories. Both cases pose a serious challenge to the view that somehow what we are witnessing are the local, intrinsic and inescapable outcomes of violence caused by religious belief and the values and identities of ethno-religious communities defined as civilizations. A closer look at the cases has shown that such a conflict is not a given and that it is triggered and sustained by multiple causes. The outcome of our comparison of both cases for features of agreement to be able to trace claimed universal factors across such conflicts that establishes the *necessary conditions* for such conflicts to occur also points to the difficulties of maintaining reductionist views on how such violent conflict emerges and continues.

It is clear that in both cases, religious beliefs, religious actors, institutions, sensitivities, social visions and mobilization channels play important roles. Yet, what the comparison reveals is that the reality of the importance of religion and its interactions with social, economic and political spheres is dynamic and evolves and changes over time. Thus, rather than being an unmoved mover in the Aristotelian sense, religions themselves are impacted by macro and micro pressures, national and global developments and more often than not, rather than being the primary engine of politics and conflict, they themselves become impacted and guided by them. The context within which religions become a vital aspect of individual or communal responses and visions to better or correct the world or seek protections from the chaos and failures of states that are always in flux and failing to meet the needs of their populations is where the primary causes of ethno-religious violence lies. Neither in Nigeria nor Egypt do we see theological beliefs or imagined notions of civilizational identities being the starting point of violent conflicts or even political tensions, but such beliefs and identities have developed in response to conflicts and tensions which are deeply local and contextual. In both countries we also see numerous religious initiatives to de-escalate conflicts and pursue peace, thus, while it is tempting to merely focus on religion and violence, religion's role in enabling the breaking down of cycles of violence is often overlooked.

What is peculiar to observe in both countries is how global developments – whether from the 1970s wave of Islamic revolution, ethno-nationalism and separatism, or the post-1990s religious militancy and post-2000s Manichean battles between 'us' vs. 'them' – have directly impacted local conflicts or at times triggered new ethno-religious clashes and violence and fuelled deep local animosities. This demonstrates that not only the view that what we are witnessing in Africa and Middle East is an outcome of religions is not supported by two of the most cited cases, but that the view that these are somehow local expressions of a given global problem is also not correct. On the contrary, international developments and globalized narratives of animosities between Islam and Christianity directly impact local conflicts, which are created and sustained by local factors.

5 | *Religion and Violence in a Global Age*

What the cases of Nigeria and Egypt and their comparison reveal is that there is in fact a correlation between religion and conflicts, and also a correlation between such local conflicts and global developments, but that neither the causal relationships argued by the three essentialist views presented in the introduction of the book nor imageries of global Manichean battles unfolding in local theatres of conflict are sustainable. The challenge that remains is to provide a much more grounded and healthy explanation of how religion, violent conflict and global developments interact with each other as we see in the cases dealt with in this book. This chapter seeks to build upon the insights gained from the case studies by offering an alternative way of conceptualizing *religion, violence* and *the relationship between the two in today's world.*

Religion

The challenge of providing a definition of religion that can accommodate both Theravada Buddhism (which does not hold a belief in a god) with Christianity (with its Trinitarian theism) and that with animistic beliefs in Africa, without including systems of thought, culture and ideology that might have religion-like qualities but no belief in deities or life hereafter, such as Marxism or Confucianism, is real.[1] Peter Berger divides definitions of religions into two approaches: substantial: defining religion 'in terms of the meaning contents of the phenomenon', and functional: 'in terms of its place in the social and/or psychological system' (Berger 1974:126). While Berger acknowledges the validity of functionalist definitions of religion, he sees an ideological use of such analyses which often 'serves to provide quasiscientific legitimations of a secularised word view' by reducing religions to 'social or psychological functions that can be understood without reference to transcendence' (Berger 1974:129). Thus Berger calls for a return to 'a perspective on the phenomenon "from within", that is, to viewing it in terms of the meanings intended by the religious conscious-ness' (Berger 1974:129). An attempt to move beyond an understanding of religion merely from its beliefs, through its social and political outworking into an approach that seeks to understand religion 'from within' but which also decodes the complex ways it plays itself out beyond the challenges of providing a universal definition of religion is in fact truly helpful for this book. What the Nigeria and Egypt case studies have revealed is the fundamental place of religion in the lives of individuals and communities, as well as their wider social and political realities. They prove the necessity of moving beyond any typology that reduces religion to merely issues of personal belief or simply vulner-abilities exploited by religious or political elites and mental deficiencies allegedly caused by lack of education.

For Berger, religion starts with human beings' attempt to make sense of the universe. Berger sees an anthropological necessity in human existence to grant the world and his/her experiences with meaning. Thus he defines religion as 'the human enterprise by which a sacred cosmos established' (Berger 1990:25). By sacred, Berger means 'a quality of mysterious and awesome power, other than man and yet related to him' (Berger 1990:25). This enterprise is ultimately about establishing an order – a nomos – to human existence in the face of death, chaos and meaninglessness. Berger notes that 'the sacred cosmos, which transcends and includes man in its ordering of reality, thus provides man's ultimate shield against the terror of anomy. To be in a "right" relationship with the sacred cosmos is to be protected against the nightmare threats of chaos. To fall out of such a "right" relationship is to be abandoned on the edge of the abyss of meaning-lessness' (Berger 1990:26). Thus the sacred both fills a vacuum while providing boundaries and hence order. As Wydra noted, 'while the sacred is a symptom of disenchantment and crisis, it also is the yard-stick for the just measure and the limit that restore boundaries. Voids of meaning have to be kept in check by transcendental signifiers, symbols, or rituals' (Wydra 2015:9).

The construction of such a sacred cosmos is as societal as it is personal. In *Social Construction of Reality,* Berger and Luckmann (1966) established the framework of the process through which social order, and with it definition and experience of reality, is constructed and maintained. Through the process of socialization, the individual is confronted with the subjectively created nomos as an objective reality, resulting in its internationalization by the individual, which demands continual maintenance by society and the individual through rituals, plausibility structures, institutions and significant individuals in the life of human beings. That is why the pursuit and maintenance of a sacred cosmos is intrinsically linked to politics, making any language of 'keeping religion out of politics' an ideological preference but an impossible reality. As Wydra states, 'if politics is not engaged with the sacred, it is not politics. People need to recognize good and evil in order to find markers of orientation, meaning, and reassurance in a world full of ethical proclivities and predispositions to identity' (Wydra 2015:16). The anthropological necessity of such needs show themselves in the question of theodicy, which shakes the assumptions of the order and poses experiences that need to be explained from categories of 'evil' to 'fate' to secular narratives developed to enable the individual to regain confidence in the social reality and process extraordinary experiences. Edkins captures this idea in his concept of 'trauma time': 'the disruptive, back-to-front time that occurs when the smooth time of the imagined or symbolic story is interrupted by the real of "events"' (Edkins 2003:230). These experiences include violent episodes such as terror attacks and wars, shaking the foundations of our perceptions of the world and beliefs about values or strength of our communities. 'Trauma time' needs to be 'tamed' in order to sustain the present order (Edkins 2003:176). Thus, religion and politics of the sacred become fundamental ways to respond to disruptions in experience, time and order. This is simply because 'people need to turn chaos and nothingness into a cosmos. In order to cope with the extraordinary, they rely on symbolic signs, ritual practices, and collective performances. They require a constitutive outside that provides stability, comfort, and a sense of unity' (Wydra 2015:22).

This attempt to give the world a meaning and respond to the challenge of theodicy has demonstrated itself as a fundamental aspect of human history from the primitive societies of thousands of years ago to today. It signals the depth of beliefs in human beings, in their attempts to make sense of the world and respond to it. Justin Barrett, in his *Born Believers: The Science of Children's Beliefs* (2012a), argues that children are born with a preparedness to believe in God, not through the indoctrination of their parents nor a particular theological belief, but rather a general belief in the supernatural that is observable in the natural development of children. Drawing from research in developmental psychology and cognitive anthropology, he argues that 'the vast majority of humans are "born believers", naturally inclined to find religious claims and explanations attractive and easily acquired, and to attain fluency in using them. This attraction to religion is an evolutionary by-product of our ordinary cognitive equipment, and while it tells us nothing about the truth or otherwise of religious claims it does help us see religion in an interesting new light' (Barrett 2012a:39). An assessment of Barrett's argument is beyond the limit of the scope of this book, but it does raise some interesting possibilities for the anthropological realities of *Homo sapiens*. Thus, it is legitimately right to question whether God ever actually died in the nineteenth and twentieth centuries, and consequently, whether he has returned or unleashed revenge on the world in the 1970s or 1990s.

Instead, what seems to have altered is the trajectory of the modernism project, and in particular, the social and political contexts in which religious visions, religious actors and religious networks have regained significance and preeminence in current affairs. The political significance of religion, as well as the theo-political visions utilized by political actors, emerges from the realities of their context. Both the cases of Nigeria and Egypt have shown changes in regards to the place of religions in politics in the 1970s and 1990s. In both countries, the 1970s witnessed renewed demands for Shari'a laws in line with regional and global trends. The dramatic defeat of Nasser and his Arab allies in the Six-Day War fought against Israel in 1967 resulted in the 'collapse of secular pan-Arabism and its replacement by Islamic extremist ideas' (Oren 2002:337). Then, the 1979 revolution in Iran gradually turned into an Islamic project with a supreme leader that represented a counterimage to the brutal secular elite that governed Iran in authenticity, morality and a radical vision to re-establish a fair society. In 1990s, Islamic networks have demonstrated not a vision for a particular geographical location as Islamists did until 1970s, but the utopia of a global Islamic rule with a global caliphate and a global war against the forces that stop and hinder its emergence. In both eras we see the search for reordering meaning and a fair nomos, first domestically and then globally. This is also why failed and weak states produce such radical groups that attempt to provide alternative worlds for masses disenfranchised and excluded from social, political and economic opportunities and why sudden changes in political structures results in violent episodes. As Richard E. Wentz put it, 'Much of the violence done in the name of religion is an ideological response to change. Human beings, in their effort to discern some kind of order and meaning for existence, observe change and have to come up with some way of handling it' (Wentz 1993:87). We have seen this in the story of radical groups including Boko Haram in the Nigeria section and Islamist thought and politics in the Egypt section of this book. In other words, religions and religious actors are deeply shaped by the very context they seek to respond to, as the answers they provide and steps they promote in the service of their aims are developed within their contexts, just as we see how the Islamic 'revolutions' of the 1970s gave way to globalized militancy in the 1990s.

No matter what their roles are in politics at any given moment, religions remain as constant attempts to make sense of and respond to a world that seems chaotic and destructive, and to offer their members an anchorage of meaning amidst macro developments outside their control – in Peter Berger's term, 'a shield against terror' (Berger 1990:22), a belonging to receive support and solidarity, and a language to formulate grievances and solutions. Given that in Africa and the Middle East religious identification overlaps with national, tribal and communal identifications, it provides 'in' and 'out' group boundaries, and thus creates both solidarity and differentiation. Religion also facilitates mobilization, since religious networks and places of worship are often protected from political interference, have a high level of legitimacy among wide swathes of the populations, and 'can often bring together diverse groups of people that could not be organized under another format' (Fox & Sandler 2004:49). In fact, in authoritarian states, as we saw during the strong military rules in Egypt and Nigeria, religion serves as the only possible platform for civil society and opposition mobilization. Thus, religion is not simply a personal theological orientation towards an eschaton, or rituals that serve an individual's needs; it is deeply social and political and it is about here and now. As Jürgen Moltmann noted:

Eschatology was long called the 'doctrine of the last things' or the 'doctrine of the end'. By these last things were meant events which will one day break upon man, history and the world at the end of time ... These end events were to break into this world from somewhere beyond history, and to put an end to the history in which all things here live and move. But the relegating of these events to the 'last day' robbed them of their directive, uplifting and critical significance for all the days which are spent here, this side of the end, in history. (Moltmann 1993:15)

Moltmann, one of the twentieth century's most influential protestant theologians, a German prisoner of war in the UK after World War II, argues that 'from first to last, and not merely in the epilogue, Christianity is eschatology, is hope, forward looking and forward moving, and therefore also revolutionizing and transforming the present' (Moltmann 1993:16). What Moltmann observes about Christianity can be said for all forms of religions and all-encompassing eschatological visions promoting a perfect moment in the future such as communism, socialism and even nationalism: the promise of a future defined as fulfilment ultimately shapes and alters how one lives here and now. Thus, religions could very well be seen as maintaining the order of the status quo with effectiveness. But, they also give birth to revolutionary projects that attempt to completely reorder the here and now. In fact, both aspects of this are visible in Nigeria and Egypt; religious actors and visions can be seen as maintaining a political and social status quo, but also radical visions for opposition to the status quo. Both opposing visions claim a basis and legitimacy based upon the same sacred authorities, such as holy books, significant clergy and traditional beliefs.

Violence

Violence has been an integral aspect of human history from the emergence of homo sapiens in the world to this day. From state brutality in the forms of torture to gang crimes, homicide, domestic abuse, terrorism, wars, genocides and territorial expansion now and throughout history, one constant variable remains unchanged: human beings. It is the human being that deploys violence and its track record raises a serious question of whether or not human beings have a predisposition to deploy violence. Two lines of enquiry have sought to pursue this question within the evolutionary realities of human beings.

The first line of enquiry has focused on the biological evolution of homo sapiens. Such arguments often focus on observations inferred from animals that share a close relation to homo sapiens in the evolutionary process. For example, in *Demonic Males: Apes and the Origins of Human Violence* (1996), Wrangham and Peterson draw on their decades-long work among the apes, and observe some disturbing facts particularly about chimpanzees, which share the closest genetic outlook with human beings. After witnessing an incident in which a chimpanzee was killed by a group of other chimpanzees in an unprovoked attack, they articulated that the flaw in the commonly held view that humanity's violence against its own species is unique in the natural world, because animals' killing 'is directed toward other species, toward prey. Individual animals, often males in sexual competition – fight with others of their own species, but that sort of contest typically ends the moment one competitor gives up' (Wrangham & Peterson 1996:6). They note a multitude of similarities in human and chimpanzee behaviour from menopause to mourning for dead children to close friends to the capacity to use weapons, but most importantly social worlds and relationships of power. They state that 'only two animal species are known to do so with a system of intense, male-initiated territorial aggression, including lethal raiding into neighbouring communities in search of vulnerable enemies to attack and kill. Out of four thousand mammals and ten million or more other animal species, this suite of behaviours is known only among chimpanzees and humans' (Wrangham & Peterson 1996:24). One of the possibilities raised by their work is 'a long term evolutionary inertia' in the human beings, which makes them still maintain certain capacities such as violence (Wrangham & Peterson 1996:24). Further studies on chimpanzees and bonobos have used much wider data and argued that lethal violence is a result of *adaptive strategies* which conceptualize killing as an evolved tactic that enables increased access to territory, food, mates and other benefits. They discovered that while 'lethal aggression occurs within a diverse set of circumstances', it is committed commonly by males towards other males and directed at 'particularly members of other groups' and 'committed when overwhelming numerical superiority reduces the cost of killing' (Wilson et al. 2014:414). In *Anatomy of Violence* (2013), Adriane Raine poses interesting arguments about the criminal behaviours of human beings, building on evolutionary insights. He notes that 'in evolutionary terms, the human capacity for antisocial and violent behaviour wasn't a random occurrence. Even as early hominids developed the ability to reason, communicate and cooperate, brute violence remains a successful 'cheating' strategy. Most criminal acts can be seen, directly or indirectly, as a way to take resources away from others ... Many violent crimes may sound mindless, but they may be informed by a primitive evolutionary logic' (Raine 2013:14).

None of the scholarship on the evolutionary basis of human violence argues for a deterministic understanding of human beings. Liddle, Schelford and Weeked-Shackelford warn 'that we must avoid committing the naturalistic fallacy and concluding that people today ought to be violent because it served an adaptive purpose for our ancestors' (Liddle et al. 2012:33). After all, not only human beings but also many other species demonstrate cooperation with and support to others, not merely violence. However, as they argue, studying violence from an evolutionary perspective reveals that 'violent behaviours in humans and other animals are not arbitrary' (Liddle et al. 2012:33). Accordingly, they argue that the findings of evolutionary psychology acknowledge 'the important interactions that take place between one's genes and one's environment'; thus, 'psychological mechanisms that have evolved to produce particular behaviours will only do so when the necessary environmental inputs are present and registered. In fact, since violent behaviours are potentially very costly, evolutionary accounts suggest that we should only expect these behaviours under very specific conditions (i.e., in response to a specific and limited set of environmental inputs)' (Liddle et al. 2012:25).

The second line of enquiry focuses on the social evolution of human beings as a way of creating the tension within which the evolutionary roots of human violence is suppressed, which creates tensions for the individual and poses an ever-present threat for the societies. An interesting account of this can be seen in the writings of Sigmund Freud. Freud points out that a truth 'one so eagerly denied' is that 'men are not gentle, friendly creatures wishing for love, who simply defend themselves if they are attacked, but that a powerful measure of desire for aggression has to be reckoned as part of their instinctual endowment' (Freud 1929:24). Thus, one's neighbour is 'not only a possible helper or sexual object, but also a temptation to them to gratify aggressiveness on him, to exploit his capacity for work without recompense, to use him sexually without his consent, to seize his possessions, to humiliate him, to cause him pain, to torture and kill him' (Freud 1929:24). According to Freud, this 'aggressive cruelty usually lies in wait for some provocation, or it steps into the service of some other purpose' and in 'circumstances that favour it, when those forces in the mind which ordinarily inhibit it cease to operate it also manifests itself spontaneously and reveals men as savage beasts to whom the thought of sparing their own kind is alien' (Freud 1929:24). Freud argues that 'this tendency to aggression which we can detect in ourselves and rightly presume to be present in others is the factor that disturbs our relations with our neighbours'; thus 'civilised society is perpetually menaced with disintegration through this primary hostility of men towards one another' (Freud 1929:25). This aggression is contained within the boundaries, laws and enforcement of the civilization, which protects man from the free exercise of this aggression, yet at the same creating a suppression and denying the individual the instant gratification desired, causing both neurosis and a constant tension.

A similar argument can be seen in Walter Burkett's work *Homo Necans,* in which he focuses on ancient sacrificial systems and myths. Burkert makes the observation that the 'age of the hunter, Palaeolithic, compromises by far the largest part of human history. No matter that estimates range between 95 per cent and 99 per cent: it is clear that man's biological evolution was accomplished during this time. By comparison, the period since the invention of agriculture – 10,000 at most – is a drop in the bucket. From this perspective, then, we can understand man's terrifying violence as deriving from the behaviour of the predatory animal, whose characteristics he came to acquire in the course of becoming man' (Burkert 1983:17). Thus Burkert defines the human being as the 'hunting ape', but notes that the success of the 'hunting ape' in survival was dependent on both its capacity to cooperate and partake in a communal hunt life. For this reason, 'man ever since the development of hunting has belonged to two overlapping social structures, the family and *Mannerbund*; his world falls into pairs of categories; indoors and out, security and adventure, women's work and men's work, love and death' (Burkert 1983:18). The man continually moves between these two pulls, and throughout history has adapted into societal roles and cultural boundaries, learned to postpone his gratification, 'curbing his individual intelligence and adaptability for the sake of societal predictability', which has bound him 'in an irreversible process analogous to biological "imprinting"' (Burkert 1983:19). Through sacrificial practices, 'civilised life ensures only by giving a ritual form to the brute force that still lurks in men' (Burkert 1983:45). Yet, the tension remains and the same behaviour mechanisms show themselves in the contemporary world. For Burkert, there is the 'far more serious way to divert aggression toward the outside world: by integrating large groups of men in a common fighting spirit, i.e. war' (Burkert 1983:47). Burkert argues that 'war is ritual, a self-portrayal and self-affirmation of male society. Male society finds stability in confronting death, in defying it through a display of readiness to die, and in the ecstasy of survival' (Burkert 1983:47). Thus, the learned and internalized strategies of the 'hunting ape', though tamed and adopted, still show itself as an undercurrent tension in human interactions and outcomes in search of 'blood'.

Both of these lines of enquiry, whether locating human violence in the biological legacy of the evolutionary process or in the unsuccessful containment of it through the evolution of human societies, point to a very real condition of human existences: that under the right circumstances and with the right stimuli, homo sapiens deploy violence not only in a mere adaptive strategy to ensure their survival but in the pursuit and satisfaction of primordial urges, known and unknown to the person. As Raine puts it, 'there is an evolutionary root to actions that run the gamut from bullies threatening other kids for candy to men robbing banks for money' (Raine 2013:15). An insightful exploration of this has been seen in Rene Girard's mimetic theory. Starting with his reflections on major literary texts in *Deceit, Desire, and the Novel* (1965), Girard argued that human beings learn through copying a model, whether learning a language or a skill, but also learning to desire an object. Girard observed that this was done through a 'triangular' dynamic, where the relationship is not merely between the subject and object of desire, but through the presence of a mediator, who serves a model for the subject through the object of their desire. As Girard observed, literary texts reflected that the 'object changes with each adventure but the triangle remains' (Girard 1965:2). As Flemming notes, in Girard's theory 'the object is desired neither because of its intrinsic value (like, say the Freudian maternal object") nor as a result of being consciously "invested in" or "chosen" by the will of an autonomous subject – it is desired because the subject (consciously or non-consciously) imitates the desire of another (an Other), real or imaginary, who functions as a model for that desire' (Flemming 2004:11). An example of this triangular dynamic is seen in how Nigerian Christians wanted and demanded the Nigerian state to pay for pilgrimage to Rome or Jerusalem just as Muslims were being paid by the state to go to Mecca for pilgrimage, even though such a pilgrimage is not a religious obligation for Christians like it is for Muslims.

This mimetic process turns the model into a rival, since 'the subject desires the object because the rival desires it. In desiring an object the rival alerts the subject to the desirability of the object' (Girard 1979:145). The rivalry inevitably results in tension and conflict. Girard observes that 'two desires converging on the same object are bound to clash. Thus mimesis coupled with desire leads automatically to conflict' (Girard 1979:146). This conflict has the potential to destroy the rivals, but also societies, in a spiralling violence, in which rivals mimic one another in actions and violence, and seek the ultimate destruction of the other. Girard uses the term *reciprocity* for this dynamic: 'just as a good reciprocal gesture might defuse a conflict (for example, if one rival offers the hand of friendship), so an expression of hostility or bad reciprocity by one of the parties will be imitated and probably amplified by the other, thus causing the antagonism to escalate' (Kirwan 2004:42). In Nigeria, we have seen this dynamic regularly, in which each incidence of violence evokes more violence from the other group, turning a relatively small dispute between a handful of people to a citywide out-of-control violence where thousands of houses are burnt down and hundreds of people killed. Such an escalation has no end, thus, in order to defuse the tension, a *surrogate victim* is found: 'any community that has fallen prey to violence or has been stricken by some overwhelming catastrophe hurls itself blindly into the search for a scapegoat. Its members instinctively seek an immediate and violent cure for the onslaught of unbearable violence and strive desperately to convince themselves that all their ills are the fault of a lone individual who can be easily disposed of' (Girard 1979:80). The society 'tends towards persecution since the natural causes of what troubles it and transforms it into a *turba* cannot interest it. The crowd by definition seeks action but cannot affect natural causes. It therefore looks for an accessible cause that will appease its appetite for violence' (Girard 1986:16). The victim is the scapegoat, someone innocent, yet different, often from a minority or an outsider to the society, that can easily be disposed of without fear of repercussions, but whose sacrifice ultimately is thought to affect external causes such as plagues, droughts and calamities (Girard 1986:43). Girard points that religious minorities particularly attract persecution during a time of crisis (Girard 1986:6).

Minorities often become objects that appease collective anguish and frustration (Girard 1986:39). With the establishment of a scapegoat that serves as a surrogate victim, violence vanishes, since all previous acts of violence between mimetic rivals only compounded the violence (Girard 1979:85). We see a clear example of the surrogate-victim mechanism and scapegoating of religious minorities in moments of crisis which have nothing to do with them in the persecution of Copts in Egypt.

As Wolfgang Palaver notes, however, mimesis not only results in negative consequences; in addition, 'violence and murder can ensure from mimetic desire – just as easily can devotion to one's fellow man or openness to God. The difference lies in the varying ways mimesis can manifest itself in the human relations, ranging from acquisitive desire and rivalry to imitation resulting in the spreading of peace' (Palaver 2013:37). That is why, as Palaver draws our attention to, Girard remains somewhere between the poles of optimistic views of human beings, as seen in the maxim *homo homini amicus,* and the pessimistic view of the human beings as captured in the maxim *homo homini lupus* (Palaver 2013:37). This provides the human being with a chance to break free from the escalation of mimetic rivalry, even through the very dynamic of mimesis, by modelling ourselves in the ideal of the gospel of Christ that chooses to not respond with vengeance but, in meekness, chooses to forgive. Thus, Girard ends *The Scapegoat* by arguing that 'in future, all violence will reveal what Christ's Passion revealed, the foolish genesis of blood stained idols and the false gods of religion, politics, and ideologies. They, too, know not what they do and we must forgive them. The time has come for us to forgive one another. If we wait any longer there will not be time enough' (Girard 1986:212). Yet, while such a personal moral stand might be possible it often stands against the power of mimetic desire and the escalation of violence. As Girard observes, 'only violence can put an end to violence, and that is why violence is self-propagating. Everyone wants to strike the last blow, and reprisal can thus follow reprisal without any true conclusion ever being reached' (Girard 1979:26).

Girard acknowledges that what has stopped mimetic violence spiraling has been social institutions: 'our judicial system, which serves to deflect the menace of vengeance. The system does not suppress vengeance; rather, it effectively limits it to a single act of reprisal, enacted by a sovereign authority specializing in this particular function. The decisions of the judiciary are invariably presented as the final word on vengeance' (Girard 1979:15). However, even within social structures where the rule of law and a strong state enforce boundaries to mimetic escalations and stop the spiralling of violence, mimetic rivalries and scapegoating mechanisms regularly show themselves in contemporary politics universally, and in violent forms when such controls and boundaries collapse. Transitory political phases shake our perceptions of security and exacerbate tensions: 'as groups begin to fear for their safety, dangerous and difficult-to-resolve strategic dilemmas arise that contain within them the potential for tremendous violence' (Lake & Rothchild 1996:41). That is why the liminal[2] phase in Egypt, with historic changes of political structures, saw a tremendous increase of incidents of attacks on Copts. There was no longer a strong state apparatus containing the violence, and thus the Copts were not only scapegoated for the fate of Egypt, but also could be easily attacked with no fear of reprisal for the attackers. Similarly, that is why the never-ending political instability in Nigeria with coups and brief stints of civilian government almost always gave birth to fierce ethno-religious violence when the transitions between strong military rules to ethnic-agenda-driven political parties unfolded. Mimetic mechanisms were fuelled and left unchecked. The stakes were made higher by fears of not being able to have what the other might have. In fact, beyond the two case studies, one can argue that both Muslim and Christian attempts to make sense of a chaotic world through Manichean imageries and intrinsic clashes are anxious projects to provide quick, clear boundaries in an age that melts away old certainties. As Wydra, Horvarth and Thomassen note, 'the uncertainties created by globalization processes have triggered new divisions and antagonisms. In some cases they spur desperate attempts to recover old certainties; in others, they create new differences' (Wydra, Horvarth & Thomassen 2015:1).

Perhaps, Solzhenitsyn was right about the ambivalence of human beings, trapped between the poles of the legacy of the violent evolution of their biological conditions and the inspiring visions of humanity that aspires to achieve higher ideals. In his reflections on his own actions and all the brutality he witnessed in the gulags, Solzhenitsyn noted:

Gradually it was disclosed to me that the line separating good and evil passes not through states, nor between classes, nor between political parties either – but right through every human heart – and through all human hearts. This line shifts. Inside us, it oscillates with the years. And even within hearts overwhelmed by evil, one small bridgehead of good is retained. And even in the best of all hearts, there remains ... an uprooted small corner of evil. (As quoted in Scruton 2008)

It is clear that multiple urges, instincts and desires, as well as religious, political and ideological ambitions can result in human beings deploying violence under the right circumstances. That possibility is never far away, whether in the 'civilized' world or in a 'developing' country, in the streets of world capitals or in the deserts of failed states with vacuums of power and no rule of law. When violence becomes a low-risk possibility, an effective and sometimes the only strategy to meet desires, ambitions and secure resources, or gain a sense of security and control or assert political agency, its outcomes are disastrous. As Wentz notes, 'violence breeds violence. Not only does it do harm to the other person, it encourages the violence already present in him. Oppressed people are nurtured on violence, and the violence waits inside, often unrecognized, for the tables to be turned. Unless the oppressed person has a way of restraining or converting that violence, it will find expression whenever the opportunity is provided' (Wentz 1993:61). Thus, violence only creates further violence, normalizing its presence, escalating its levels, and in the process creating new grievances, fears of being victims of it and thus the need to deploy it preemptively or in retaliation. This echoes the 'security dilemma' concept applied to ethnic conflict whereby 'what one does to enhance one's own security causes reactions that, in the end, can make one less secure' (Posen 1993:28). It finds new and innocent victims who have no actual involvement with the initial causes that triggered the violence. As human history demonstrates, violence is not alien to human beings, nor arbitrary; it is an ever-present potential in human interactions that shows itself regularly in varying forms and levels.

Relationship between Religion and Violence

The sections above on religion and violence signal the fact that there is indeed a deep relationship between religion and violence – but not in the way that it has been speculated by the arguments cited in the introduction – that presents religions to be the main cause of the violence. A common scholarly approach that moves on from the failures of such popular explanations can be seen in the instrumentalist understanding of religions. As Stein explains, 'instrumentalism rejects the view that differences in religion are real causes of political conflicts' but recognizes 'that religion can play a part in violent conflict' as a 'tool used by self-interested elites to mobilize support and fighting power for conflict'. (Stein 2011:23) In fact, the case-study chapters in this book have demonstrated the elite use of religion for political mobilization and legitimization in both Nigeria and Egypt. That is why this book too has used insights gained from instrumentalism in the case-study chapters through language and discussions of 'political entrepreneurs', 'violent specialists' and 'religious entrepreneurs' that have sought to achieve personal gains from a resurgence of public interest in religion. While such approaches are correct in rejecting the causal role given to religion in popular explanations challenged by this book, often they run the risk of minimizing, or at times overlooking, the deep relationship between religion and violence beyond simplistic claims of a causal role. In fact, since they categorize violent conflicts with religious characteristics as 'best subsumed under political conflict and violence in general', often this leads to a problematic implication that 'religion does not require special analytic treatment'. (Brukaber 2015:2) As Hasenclever and Rittberger point out, there are countless markers in each nation that can be utilized by political actors, may they be ethnic, cultural or religious and elites can draw from abundant 'pre-existing raw materials such as common myths, common language and common religions'. (Hasenclever & Rittberger 2000:646) Thus, for a strict instrumentalist, religion 'amounts to a spurious correlation, and there is no point exploring the political consequences of the revival of religion any further' (Hasenclever & Rittberger 2000:646). In fact, instrumentalism often stops decoding the relationship between religion and violence at the point of stating its use by conflicting parties. This tendency is inadequate for the interests of this book. The elite use of religious sensitivities, imageries and languages to achieve desired political outcomes does not explain fully why such religious sensitivities, imageries and languages are so powerful in moving human beings to risk their own lives. Similarly, it does not explain why it is that calls for or experiences of violence seem to find an effective space in religions at the first place and why and how local conflicts with religious characteristics are able to interact with and impact global developments. Thus, while helpful in explaining the use of religion, instrumentalist approaches fall short in exploring answers to questions pursued in this book beyond contributions to specific aspects of case analysis.

As Burkert notes, 'blood and violence lurk fascinatingly at the very heart of religion' (Burkert 1983:2). In fact, religion in human history emerged from the sacrificial rituals that were utilized by primitive communities as a response to both human conflict and also to the violence of inhospitable natural conditions. Girard observes that 'the objective of ritual is the proper reenactment of the surrogate-victim mechanism; its function is to perpetuate or renew the effects of this mechanism; that is, to keep violence *outside* the community' (Girard 1979:92). Through sacrifice, and spilling of blood, the ritual aims to satisfy demands for absolution and provides a *surrogate victim* to be able to end violence, thus 'the sacrificial process furnishes an outlet for those violent impulses that cannot be mastered by self-restraint: a partial outlet, to be sure, but always renewable, and one whose efficacy has been attested by an impressive number of reliable witnesses' (Girard 1979:18). Therefore, unlike the common argument that religion necessarily results in violence, historical studies on sacrificial systems point to an interesting dynamic whereby violence has actually given birth to religion, and religion is ultimately engaged in responding to violence, which is a deeper understanding of the relationship between the two than merely a focus on elite manipulation of religious sensitivities at particular conjunctures. Girard affirms this by saying that 'the sole purpose of religion is to prevent the recurrence of reciprocal violence' (Girard 1979:55). In today's world, such a task is taken away from religions by the legal use of violence by sovereign states, but even contemporary forms of rule of law and enforcement mimic religious rituals throughout the court procedures and promise a final settlement of justice. Yet, the role the state assumes in today's world means neither the eradication of human potential for violence and human drives and social mechanisms that escalate risks of violence, nor that religions do not play a central role in the human experience of and addressing of violence.

In fact, the intrinsic relationship between religion and violence shows itself in multiple levels from the emergence of violent conflicts to their aftermaths. In the emergence period of a violent conflict, religion becomes visible in multiple ways. Religious language is often used in appeals for a fairer system and redistribution of justice. The demands for Shari'a, as explained in the cases of Egypt and Nigeria, were not merely ideological preferences, but theo-political visions to address deep grievances. It is the accumulation of certain conditions that make violence a possibility that results in the accommodation of violence as a necessity or an outcome. However, even though violence is no stranger to homo sapiens, given the contemporary forms of social and political frameworks that keep violence in check and containment and distance violence from the average human being, it still remains as an extraordinary act. Exposure to blood and killing is a psychologically demanding experience for most human beings. As Clarke notes, 'most people who commit violent acts do so reluctantly and only after they have overcome internal constraints that would ordinarily make them feel guilty about harming others. When they do act violently, they do so in the belief that what they are doing is justifiable, all things considered' (Clarke 2014:13). Therefore, such an extraordinary call to inflict violence demands out-of-the-ordinary psychological and social processes to enable the individual to both process the trauma that the common order has been altered – making violence a viable if not the only option – but also provide a moral suspension and authorization to move beyond socially and religiously enforced inhibitions that forbid violence.

This can be broken down into two crucial social mechanisms that are intrinsic to any deployment of violence, whether through its legal use by a state or by mobs, militants and crowds: *legitimation* and *dehumanization*. Peter Berger defines legitimation as 'socially objectivated "knowledge" that serves to explain and justify the social order' (Berger 1990:29). Acts, institutions and deployment of violence need an explanation, an answer to the question of 'why' and whether one has the 'right'. Legitimation is not simply limited to religion: countless utilitarian, moralistic or ideological attempts are used to legitimatize murder in the name of a nation, a people group, a revolution or a political outcome. As Steve Clarke points out, 'the religious generally justify their activities in much the same way as the secular and these justifications generally follow the same canons of logic as secular justifications. Religious arguments justifying violence are structurally similar to secular ones, but the religious are able to feed many more premises into those structures than the non-religious' (Clarke 2014:7). That is why Berger argues that there is an important relationship between legitimation and religion, since 'it can be described simply by saying that religion has been the historically most widespread and

effective instrumentality of legitimation' (Berger 1990:32). This is
because religion plays a key part with its unique role 'to "locate"
human phenomena within a cosmic frame of reference ... Religious
legitimation purports to relate the human defined reality to ultimate,
universal and sacred reality. The inherently precarious and transitory
constructions of human activity are thus given the semblance of ultimate security and permanence. Put differently, the humanly constructed
nomoi are given a cosmic status' (Berger 1990:36). As Benedict Anderson noted, 'all the great classical communities conceived of themselves
as cosmically central, through the medium of a sacred language linked
to a superterrestrial order of power' (Anderson 1991:13). And since
religious ideas are legitimized by virtue of emerging from a transcendental source, 'they are hardly subject to negotiation and compromise
given their accepted supernatural origin' (Basedau, Struvers & Villiers
2011:7). That is why 'whenever a society must motivate its members to
kill or to risk their lives, thus consenting to being places in extreme
marginal situations, religious legitimations become important ...
Killing under the auspices of legitimate authorities has, for this reason,
been accompanied from ancient times to today by religious parapher-
nalia and ritualism. Men go to war and men are put to death amid
prayers, blessings, and incantations' (Berger 1990:44).

Clarke observes this by noting that 'although most modern wars are
prosecuted by armies of secular states, it is striking how religious
formally secular armies often seem to be' (Clarke 2014:102). This fact
takes us back to anthropological perspectives that have been able to
trace the emergence of religion to sacrificial rites, which emerged
following violence, reminding us that the legitimation powers of religion are based upon the powers religion has to contain and respond to
human violence. Therefore, even 'secular' languages are deeply religious, albeit without the figure of a deity, as they face the need to move
beyond the scope of propositional truths of rational calculations to
much deeper cognitive and emotive appeals that can ultimately force
an individual to act against the very rational calculations of a mechanic
world and sacrifice their own and the life of another. In the case of
Nigeria, we saw the destructive power of religious legitimation at play
in the lead up to and after local elections, when what was being
contested was merely the issue of which political actor will assume
what political office, not a cosmic war between Islam and Christianity
as declared by multiple actors.

Legitimation for the act of violence still faces the difficulty of the *Imago Dei* in the Other that forces all moralizations of the act of violence in conflict, and all abstractions of legitimation into a crisis. Religion, which gives the human being a cosmic significance, is also able to remove it from the human being by reducing the ability to split biological life from political life, as Agamben (1998) demonstrated, and in the process deny the dignity and value of a human life by reducing it to a mere biological existence. Firstly, it does this by serving as a boundary line between 'us' vs. 'them', in the process not only creating fixed and eternal categories of 'us' but also 'them'. Anthias and Yuval-Davis note that such an 'imagined community which divides the world between "us" and "them", is maintained and ideologically reproduced' by symbolic 'border guards' (Anthias & Yuval-Davis 1993:33). In the definition of such border guards, they include a wide range of factors from behaviour to customs, language and religion, that are used to identify different groups and determine who is 'in' or 'out' of whatever the constructed 'we' is. Volkan, building on the work of Erik Erikson, names this process *pseudospeciation*, which enables groups to develop a distinct sense of identity, convincing each group that it was 'the sole possessor of the true human identity' with an attitude of superiority over other groups (Volkan 2006:15). Religion, with its ability to articulate why the other is not simply different due to the products of culture and language, but due to an eternal reason whereby the Other, with his false gods, is eternally separate from us, becomes far more effective in establishing differences and solidarities. That is why Durkheim has a valid point in saying religion is 'eminently a collective thing': rituals of religion bring individuals together physically as well as socially and emotionally into a shared identity, 'into one single moral community' (Durkheim 1912:44).

Secondly, it does so through representation and effacing of the other in the languages of enemies of God – evil, heresy, abomination, impure – all of which serve to dehumanize the other. In northern Nigeria, we saw how minority Christians were regularly called names, such as *arne* – godless – and how in Egypt Islamist media outlets regularly used derogatory words for Copts. Once a person or a community is abstracted by such categories and language, we are no longer dealing with human beings. The Other has been effaced of his human face: 'the owner of the face is nothing more and nothing less than the treatment reserved for the *category* of which the owner of the face is but a *specimen'* (Bauman 2002:54, italics in original). Thus, religion is not only able to provide grounding for why violence needs to occur, and why it is morally acceptable, but also why morality can be suspended and all theological provisions on the dignity and value of human life denied in pursuit of combating an 'evil'. One 'regrets' that bad things had to be done as a 'lesser evil' in a 'just war' in which violence deployed by us is 'different' in nature than that of our enemies. Thus, even nonreligious campaigns of violence use religious descriptions about their enemies and their motivations and aims. Ultimately, one can argue that the moment of the use of violence, with blood spilt and power felt, ushers one into a euphoria and ecstasy in a religious experience, albeit a dark, destructive one. In fact, partaking in violence can create what Durkheim named *collective effervescence,* in which those who deploy violence feel grandeur, a sense of the extraordinary, and an entrance into a new phase (Verkaaik 2003:17). Such experiences are intrinsically religious. As Appleby notes, the 'ability of religion to inspire ecstasy – literally, to lift the believer psychologically out of a mundane environment – stands behind the distinctive logic of religious violence' (Appleby 2000:91). It is this ability of religion to enable violence that causes intensification of conflicts. Jo-Eystein Lindber (2008) presents a study of identity-based religious cleavages in 241 intrastate conflicts between 1946–2004, which demonstrates that religious conflicts are found to be longer-lasting and more intense on average that nonreligious conflicts.

Religion maintains its essential relationship with violence not only in the prevention, emergence and escalation of violence, but in its aftermath too. Violence always leaves a legacy behind in the individual psyche and body as well as in the psyche and body of the community. The damage it caused demands a response. The damage done to others and withdrawal symptoms from the euphoric experiences of deploying violence demand a response. The gains and losses, the sufferings inflicted and the sufferings experienced, the boundaries collapsed and re-drawn, need a response. All of which takes us back to the central role of religion in human experience as explained above. Thus, even the secularized politics of 'truth and reconciliation commissions' and transitional justice projects use and mimic deeply religious concepts such as forgiveness and reconciliation and deploy ritualistic ceremonies of confession, expiation and absolution for oppressors and the oppressed alike. Politics of regret and public apologies within national politics and within international politics are all quasi-religious practices (Olick 2007). As Daniel Philpott put it, 'the language of faith comes through strongly in performances of apologies and forgiveness. It is often the religious who conduct civil society efforts to deal with the past and repair the body politic' (Philpott 2007). In other words, religion becomes a central aspect of projects of redeeming the legacy of violence, just as it was a central aspect of projects of preventing if not containing violence as explained above, as Marc Gopin (2000) demonstrates in his *Between Eden and Armageddon*. In both Egypt and Nigeria we saw how religious actors and their calls for forgiveness, unity and brotherhood have been utilized by their states and communities in the aftermaths of violence. In fact, in both places we see deeply altruistic attempts by religious actors to protect people from other faiths and risk their own lives in the violence unleashed by their own brethren.

Yet, since religions are also carriers of collective memories (Hervieu-Leger 2000) and promise an eschatological redemption and justice for wrongs done and an ultimate victory over the enemy even if all the realities of the here and now signal the impossibility of such an absolution, religion is also often able to prolong the impact of violent memories and serve as a language to evoke ancient rivalries and eternal offenses with the promise of the arrival of the prophecies about their eschatological fulfilment. As Juergensmeyer notes, the framing of conflict in cosmic terms prolongs conflicts and crosses beyond the time limitations of nonreligious conflicts, since 'there is no need to compromise one's goals in a struggle that has been waged in divine time and with the promise of heaven's rewards' (Juergensmeyer 2001:221). Thus, in Serbia we saw how the narratives of the 'resurrection' of a Christian nation after the suffering of their Friday at the hands of Muslim Ottomans hundreds of years ago became grounds to unleash ethnic cleansing against Bosnian Muslims (Judah 2002:56; Mertus 1999:184). The fact that such a Christian narrative and its aims and outcomes contradicts the very tenets of the Gospel of Christ – the innocent scapegoat, who accepted out-of-control rage so as to offer a path to break human violence with a call for human beings to mimic his model, was an irony not visible to its creators and consumers. Deep theological truths about the value of human life and the mandate to 'forgive' can often be suspended with the message of 'never forget' and waiting for vengeance in patience, carried through religious symbolism, teaching and ceremonies across generations. It is clear, therefore, that religion might be able to respond to violence effectively, but it is also vulnerable to be shaped by it and continue its legacy at the expense of the self-destruction of its declared tenets.

This takes us to the recognition that the relationship between religion and violence is ultimately ambivalent, simply because religion remains as a mediated attempt in the relationship of the human beings with that of the sacred, which is always the holy other, apart from clear human cognition, shrouded in a 'cloud of unknowing' (Walsh 1981). That is why Appleby states that 'religion is both powerfully disclosive of the sacred and radically limited in its ability to understand what it discloses' (Appleby 2000:29). Thus there is always a distance between the believer and the object of their beliefs: 'from a religious point of view, then, living with ambiguity is the consequence of the distance between the infinite God and the contingent human being' (Appleby 2000:29). And in the course of a human life that ambiguity remains, forcing individuals to take decisions according to facts and options and choose from explanations available to them, which 'fosters a state of ambivalence' with contradicting emotions and urges (Appleby 2000:29). Thus, religion contains within itself both the capacity to unleash violence, but also to prevent it and stop it from re-emerging. It is within such complex and ambiguous settings that religious ideals are realized (Appleby 2000:35). That is why while religions portray themselves as 'changeless entities, existing above the fray of the temporal, immune to vicissitudes of history', 'history shows that religious communities, in their self-understanding and in their orientations to the world, change constantly' (Appleby 2000:41). The hermeneutics of Hans Gadamer, as cited in the introduction, highlighted the fact that the context dictates the way in which a community interprets a text as they approach a text with a wide range of questions, anxieties, needs and assumptions deeply shaped by their own experiences. It is this *all too human* condition of religious experience, beliefs and ideals that makes any essentialist argument of an intrinsically violent or intrinsically peaceful core of any religion based upon particular passages in sacred texts problematic to maintain.

Rethinking the Relationship of Religious Violence with the Global Age

The cases of Nigeria and Egypt have highlighted how regional and international developments, as well as political ideals in different eras, have shaped religious views and ignited religious mobilizations. We have seen this in modern assumptions of the nation-state and visions of Islamists across the twentieth century, 'revolutionary' vocabularies with Marxist readings of class and economy adopted by religious visions in the 1970s, and the internationalization of militancy and the emergence of global religious networks in the 1990s. This trend continues in the contemporary world, which Albrow (1996) argues to be in a global age. According to Albrow, the shift from the modern age with its political horizons to the global age occurred when the nation-state started not being 'able to control new forms of social organizations', as 'the social takes on a meaning outside of the frame of reference set by the nation state' (Albrow 1996:58). Albrow provides a helpful breakdown of key concepts that relates to the global age: *global*: the natural environment on which human beings depend; *globality*: objectification of the outcomes of human interaction with the world; *globalism*: assumed obligations towards the world as a whole and values that take the globe as a frame of reference; and *globalization*: the historical transformation constituted by the active dissemination of practices, values, technology and other human products throughout the globe (Albrow 1996:82–89). He notes five major ways in which the world has moved from modernity into globality: 'the global environmental consequences of aggregate human activities; the loss of security where weaponry has global destructiveness; the globality of communication systems; the rise of a global economy; and the reflexivity of globalism, where people and groups of all kinds refer to the globe as the frame for their beliefs' (Albrow 1996:4).

This reality gives birth to new global risks that impact everyone, but also new horizons beyond nationalism, such as 'globalism, the commitment to values which reference globality, mobilizing opinion and identifying with likeminded people on a worldwide scale' (Albrow 1996:140). Globality enables new networks, and with it new opportunities for activism beyond the limits of nation-states and international institutions: 'globality itself became the resource and medium through which the movements could operate. Communication at a distance serves as the needs of opposition as much as it does of dominant institutions. It became realistic to mobilize support elsewhere in the world to bring pressure to bear on one case in one country, even on a whole system, as was the case with the anti-apartheid movement' (Albrow 1996:143). Albrow argues that this has resulted in a multiplication and diversification of the world rather than homogenization or hybridization of cultures (Albrow 1996:149). Globalization does not operate in a single dimension, 'nor is it a process which has altered every pre-existing tendency in culture and society' (Albrow 1996:144). Therefore globality includes a variety of different phenomena 'sometimes contradictory ways and which may be even on occasion be directly anti-global', and does not negate locality (Albrow 1996:145). Thus Albrow uses the concept of *disconnected contiguity* to describe 'relationships between people living in the same area under globalized conditions', which are 'neither disorganized nor meaningless. On the contrary they are engaged in intense social construction generating activities whose geographical scope reaches as far as the globe' (Albrow 1996:157). Albrow acknowledges that whether this is a world or global society yet is to be questioned, and that the world society is not yet something counterposed to the nation-state, but a parallel to it (Albrow 1996:167).

While one can legitimately challenge conceptualizations of a new age, or the abstraction of a world society, the process of globalization is real. As Cesare Poppi noted, 'The literature stemming from the debate on globalization has grown in the last decade beyond any individual's capability of extracting a workable definition of the concept. In a sense, the meaning of the concept is self-evident, in another, it is vague and obscure as its reaches are wide and constantly shifting' (Quoted in Al-Rodhan & Stoudman 2006:8). It is indeed difficult to provide a final and conclusive definition. Al-Rodhan and Stoudman make an interesting attempt by providing a chart that includes how globalization has been defined in more than eighty cited sources, from leading academics to journalists and international bodies. As a result of their survey, they offer a simple definition of globalization as 'a process that encompasses the causes, course, and consequences of transnational and transcultural integration of human and non-human activities' (Al-Rodhan & Stoudman 2006:5). They add that 'globalization is not an endpoint to be discussed and then forgotten. Rather, it is a process, a current that has been impacting communities, cultures and economies for hundreds of years. It is a result of the transnational and transcultural integrations that have occurred globally throughout human history. It encompasses the causes, the course, and the consequences of these integrations' (Al-Rodhan & Stoudman 2006:5).

The process of globalization has brought new dynamics to ethno-religious violence. We see this in multiple ways in the cases of Nigeria and Egypt. Technological advancements in communication and travel have enabled an increasing flow of ideas across the world. We have seen how religious ideas and theo-political visions developed in Saudi Arabia and Iran increasingly spread in Nigeria and Egypt through clerics educated there, expatriate workers returning home, and aggressive state-sponsored proselytism and promotion of ideas. Thus, both Salafism, with its vision of rediscovering a pure Islamic life, and visions of Islamic revolutions to re-order a country upon Islam galvanized local grievances and political movements (Fox & Sandler 2004:83–114). Increasing awareness of developments in the world and within the same countries through mass media have intensified religious boundaries and senses of solidarity among people with shared faiths. This has caused religious conflicts to cross borders, through two universal patterns: *contagion* – where a conflict can spill into another country which hosts populations that are the same as the majority or minority group in conflict in a neighbouring country; and *diffusion* – where a rebellion in one place can inspire people from similar groups to rebel (Fox & Sandler 2004:71). Both mechanisms of contagion and diffusion can be seen locally, too. Attacks on Christians in north or middle Nigeria resulted in attacks on Muslims in other parts of Nigeria by Christians who were dismayed by the news. Likewise, attacks on Copts across Egypt skyrocketed following news of the ousting of the Islamist President Morsi and the seeming complicity of the Coptic church with the Egyptian military regime in the coup. The same mechanisms also show themselves in the pulling of external actors into the conflict. Since the 1990s we have seen a globally mobile network of Muslim militants fighting in emerging local battles, sometimes igniting them as local theatres of conflict in their global fight against the Christian West (Fox & Sandler 2004:75). The suffering of co-religionists at the hands of people of other religions has been a key mobilizing factor for jihadists.

Interestingly, such a religious affinity with the victims has also been a cause of political and military interventions by states. Fox and Sandler surveyed 275 conflicts between the years 1990 and 1995 recorded in the Minorities at Risk dataset to test their hypothesis that religious affinities are an important aspect of interventions of foreign states in conflicts in other countries (Fox & Sandler 2004:63–82). They acknowledge that the study can in no way establish motivations behind interventions, whether military or political, but that it is able to 'assess whether conflicts between groups differ, religious or minorities of particular religions attract more intervention and whether interveners are more likely to be religiously similar to those groups on whose behalf they intervene' (Fox & Sandler 2004:65). Their findings demonstrate that religious conflicts attract more political intervention by foreign governments than do regular ethnic conflicts, and that 'foreign governments who intervene both politically and militarily are likely to be religiously similar to those minorities on whose behalf they intervene' (Fox & Sandler 2004:69, 70). Fox and Sandler acknowledge that 'while non-religious conflicts also cross borders, the potential for religious conflicts to do so is much greater. This is because while all the factors that cause nonreligious conflicts to cross borders apply to religious conflicts, religious conflicts involve additional and unique factors that cause them to cross borders' (Fox & Sandler 2004:81).

A key aspect of this is the ability of religions to move beyond the limits of particular ethnicities and nation-states and bring much larger numbers of people into a shared identity, and religions also give a spiritual mandate to care for people who are part of the Body of Christ or the Islamic Umma. This has become a truly important factor in the rise of international organizations that pursue humanitarian aid or advocacy both on internal platforms and across the world on issues and conflicts of concern. We have seen traces of this in how Catholic organizations played a part in spreading the news of the Biafra war in Nigeria by bringing aid but also substantially shaping the narrative of what was happening in religious terms, as discussed in the Nigeria section of the book. We also mentioned how Coptic diaspora communities in the United States and Europe played a role in raising the profile of the persecution of Copts, at times supporting the strong military regime in Egypt, such as in Sisi's takeover from Morsi, and at times directly challenging it, such as during the time of Sadat and the later years of Mubarak, as discussed in the Egypt chapter.

A very important case of this is how American evangelicals and wider faith communities began to pressure the US government to address issues of religious persecution around the world. Allen Hertzke traces how diverse religious groups launched campaigns to push the United States to promote the defence of people suffering from religious persecution around the world, which triggered a much larger trend beyond their initial focus on persecution of Christians abroad: 'the engines unleashed by this campaign have injected a shot of adrenalin into the broader human rights quest. The movement plucked the tragedy in Sudan from the backwaters of international concern and into a high level of focus for American government. It is doing the same for the humanitarian tragedy in North Korea' and a wide range of issues from international sex traffic to 'slave labour practices and exploitation' in multiple countries from India to Thailand to Eastern Europe (Hertzke 2004:5). Jonathan Agensky demonstrates how the evangelical Christian movement globalized the conflict in Sudan, garnering widespread international attention and solidarity with Sudanese Christians (Agensky 2010). Since persecution of Christians around the world was clustered in communist and Muslim-majority states, increasingly American constituencies began perceiving these developments through the fault lines of culture and civilizations. This meant that increasingly the religious freedom movement in the United States came to be seen 'as an overt attempt to protect the frontiers and outposts of Western Christian civilisation in a world where civilisational conflict may take on the dynamic of "the West versus the rest". In the literature of Christian advocacy groups, in fact, we see the twin spectres of militant Islam and the Communist remnant as the key threats to faithful abroad' (Hertzke 2004:15). Thus we see cases of religious persecution and conflict in Africa and the Middle East regularly being used by right-wing politics not only in the United States but also in Europe as such 'West vs. Rest' imaginations play themselves out in contemporary politics of migration, the cohesion of migrants and the risk of Islamic terror attacks on Europe and North America. The politics of religious persecution and solidarities are matched by the politics of Africa and the Middle East as various political actors, particularly the fast-spreading number of Christians in Africa, use the sensitivities of American and European audiences to use their Christian identities by way of shoring up support for their domestic political aims (Agensky 2013:14).

Use of these incidences for political activism and culture wars in North America and Europe results in a type of *double hermeneutic* (Giddens 1984:284), a risk that social scientific research carries in the relationship between the object and subject of research, whereby cases of ethno-religious conflict and violence are not only studied, reported and advocated by international actors, but also that such a process also impacts the local conflicts themselves. We see this in the *reification* (Berger & Luckman 1966:106) of cosmic war narratives in Nigeria and Egypt, where local Christians or Muslims adopt into their languages inherent clashes and the idea that they are on the front lines of an imagined war between the Christian Western civilization and the World of Islam. As mentioned in both of the cases in this book, local Muslims and Christians have often used such language in describing the events they saw in their localities. The outcome of reification of cosmic languages is clear. As discussed above, such perceptions that seem to be validated through the presence and support of international actors only entrench local problems further, alter the real-life time limits and communicate conflicts beyond their immediate culprits and victims. It deepens mistrust and gaps between local ethno-religious communities, whose shared lives within a state become fractured through imagined solidarities with co-religionists elsewhere. This echoes Albrow's *disconnected contiguity* idea explained above. In this way, a global ecosystem is established, in which local incidents of ethno-religious violence are communicated onto international platforms and promoted and advocated by co-religionists in the Muslim world or in Europe and North America, triggering humanitarian, political and military intervention by outsiders, and thus reifying narratives that promote the idea that a Manichean battle is unfolding. This in turn directly impacts theatres of local conflict through solidarity, aid and confirmation of the perceived rightfulness of a particular community's cause, thus deepening distances and prolonging conflicts.

In other words, while there might not be a 'clash of civilizations' to begin with in an empirical reality, there is now a de facto clash of civilizations unfolding as a *self-fulfilling prophecy*, i.e., the 'phenomenon of social beliefs affecting social facts or creating a social reality' (Craighead & Nemeroff 2004:862). Therefore what we are witnessing in the global ecosystem that sustains ethno-religious violence in today's world is a sign of the evolving nature of global politics, where bipolarity remains 'the dominant mode of aggregation in politics' (Farneti 2015:28). Within this picture, both the local and global exist simultaneously, and multiple mimetic tensions between dyads play a complex relationship in local contexts as well as in the global arena (Farneti 2015:46). In this picture, the Islamic world and the West become twins, as they imitate one another in their rivalries, losing all differences, and escalating tensions to the extreme. The mimetic understanding of drivers that maintain the attractiveness of concepts such as 'clash of civilization', 'West' vs. 'Islamic world', takes us back to anthropological truths, such as the friend-enemy separation that lies at the heart of politics (Schmitt 1996:26), scapegoating, rivalries over resources, and the intrinsic aspects of the human ways of making sense and responding to an ever increasingly chaotic world: religion and violence. Their prominence in human affairs, as well as their problematic framings as discussed above, are intrinsically linked to the shift observed from the certainties of modernity, and the never-ending uncertainty that comes in the 'liquid modernity' (Bauman 2006) with its constant fears of risks, calamities and domestic political responses that create an illusion of response to global challenges beyond their control.

Conclusion

This chapter sought to provide an alternative explanation of the complex relationship of religion with violence in a global age, drawing from insights gained by case studies of Nigeria and Egypt and their comparison. It did so by offering a different conceptualization of religion beyond popular explanations and instrumentalism. It demonstrated that religion as defined as an attempt to establish a sacred cosmos is an integral aspect of the human experience of the world. It serves both to provide individual meanings to decipher the challenges of living in a chaotic world, but also as a key factor in the construction and maintenance of communal and national identities, as well as the establishment of global networks. Therefore, religions are major social and political forces that impact and engage with all aspects of human enterprise from economy to war to humanitarianism. Similarly, the chapter argued that violence is an integral aspect of human experience of the world. Its roots lay in the biological realities of human evolution that have only been possible through adaptive strategies in ensuring survival. We pointed out that the human potential for violence demonstrates itself at all levels, and that it is only the emergence of strong modern states that has enabled large numbers of people to be protected from the exposure and use of violence through the state's monopoly over the use of violence. It argued that when a state fails, anarchy emerges, sudden political shifts occur, the rule of law collapses and violence becomes a possible strategy for human beings once again. It also demonstrated that constructs of civilizations and the 'other' that is portrayed to be more violent and somehow less developed than 'us' are deeply anthropological urges that human beings have in formation of group identities; thus, rather than helpful analytic approaches, such theories have only served political aims in establishing new imagined global iron curtains.

This chapter argued that religion does indeed play a central role in violence. It noted that religion plays a key role in the unfolding and aftermath of violence in both legitimation as well as the socio-psychological support needed in its execution and coping with its legacies due to religion's fundamental role in providing a meaning to human experiences of the world. However, it also pointed out that violence alters and shapes religion, so that the more frequently it is present, the less risky its deployment becomes; and that more religious visions for the betterment of a chaotic context can accommodate its use as a 'necessary evil' and sometimes a divinely sanctioned move beyond good and evil. It was noted that religion also plays a fundamental role in both the prevention of violence, and post-violence projects of recon-ciliation and peace-building; therefore, it maintains an ambivalence towards human violence, making any argument that religions are essentially violent or essentially peace-making problematic. The chap-ter drew attention to the alarming effect of the globalization process in not only amplifying awareness of local instances of ethno-religious conflict, which have deeply local reasons behind their emergence, but also triggering the contagion and diffusion of such conflicts to other theatres. It also creates chances of solidarity, as well as humanitarian, military and political intervention by international actors. The use of suffering of co-religionists in globalized narratives of Christian West vs. the world of Islam creates *a global ecosystem*. Local incidents are brought to the attention of international platforms by groups focus-ing on specific issues and religious minorities. They not only shape the narratives of events, but in the process, reify cosmic narratives deployed for temporal aims in particular localities. This results in deepening of tensions and fixing of imagined boundaries that cannot be bridged between communities. Therefore, what we see is not an outcome of an intrinsic clash between imagined civilizations, but a very real case of self-fulfilled prophecies that create new fault lines across the world, in structures that are identical to the perceptions of the world as constituting two or three blocks during the Cold War.

6 | *Conclusion*

I will never forgot his teary eyes, as he told me how he was tortured for days with his friends in a notorious desert jail in Egypt. Their crime was simply converting from Islam to Christianity, a scandalous betrayal in the narratives of 'us' versus 'them', defiling the identity boundaries and short circuiting all definitions. His torturers laughed at his screams; one of them even told him to scream as loud as he can as there was no one out there to hear him. He said it was not the physical pain but the recognition that his torturer was right that finally broke him. His friend who also suffered immensely told me that he still wakes up in the middle of his sleep at the same hour the secret police came to arrest him. A researcher that gets exposed to the human face of violence can never overlook the fact that what is being discussed is not simply a theoretical speculation or a rhetorical device to score a political agenda. It is about understanding an extremely worrying trend and looking for ways to prevent such violence in a milieu that seems to be more driven by creating new boundaries between people of different religions, nationality and culture than addressing root causes of complex issues we are facing.

This book has tried to challenge popular explanations of increasing violent conflicts with religious characteristics in the world to enable the start of conversations on religion and violent conflict based on the right premises and the right questions. It did so by tracing the history and context of ethno-religious violence in two of the most influential countries in Africa and the Middle East. It explored the questions of why and how violent conflicts related to religion emerge, whether they represent an intrinsic clash between civilizations (or whether such civilizations and primordial identities exist at all) or point to inevitable outcomes of religion with its claimed denial of rationality or with its exclusivist truth-claims. It also sought to answer the petrifying question of whether or not we are witnessing a global war between Islam and Christianity.

Its findings have highlighted twelve similarities between the two cases beyond the most visible religious characteristics that seem to dominate popular discussions: *colonial heritage and state formation, political instability and poor governance, deprivation and fierce competition, high levels of violence by state and non-state actors, dynamic history of place of religion in politics and society, impact of context on religions, dynamic patterns of ethno-religious violence, multiple actors and multiple motivations involved in violence, rule of law and impunity, broken social trust, religious counter-violence initiatives and impact of global developments.* Both cases have demonstrated that it is the context shaped by these similarities that makes the emergence of violence a possibility, if not sometimes the only or most effective option to assert agency, establish order, push for a sense of justice and propitiation and protect and advance interests in political, communal and personal aims. The book is a reminder of a historic truth that cannot be easily ignored: violence is a natural potential of human beings. Yet, its deployment is still costly, demanding and life altering for us. When the boundaries between peaceful human interaction and violence are crossed, the powerful social and psychological boundaries that keep human potential for violence under control are broken. Frequent exposure to violence numbs individuals living in such contexts, in other words, violence is routinized. For the average citizen of the stable countries of Europe, violence – just like the social and political importance of religions – might feel like an alien factor that is only explainable by extraordinary lapses in human development. This is why we often see frequent allusions to the 'medieval ages' or 'dark ages' in popular discussions and articles discussing religious violence. Or perhaps it can be said that those of us who live in Europe and North America have been sanitized to the realities of human violence. As this book has argued, violence as an adaptive strategy has been a reality for *Homo sapiens* and shared by the mammals with the closest genetic relationship to human beings. It is only the effectiveness of modern policing and the rule of law that hides various levels of violence from the eyesight, whether it be domestic abuse or gang crime, creating the illusion that somehow people of the 'developed' world are less violent than those of 'developing' world. Yet, some of the world's most developed countries also have historically highest rates of incarceration, and their armed forces continually deploy brutal force across the world to assert national interests and foreign policy preferences. In fact, European and North American states have only been able to maintain the peace and order taken for granted by their citizens with their effective use of violence and its threat across the globe. Therefore, any argument that suggests the 'other' is somehow intrinsically predisposed to violence unlike 'us' is a mere illusion.

What has been interesting to observe in both cases is how precarious contexts impact religion, both shaping theo-political visions, making religious networks valuable channels for political mobilization and demanding religious responses to violence, chaos, uncertainty, corruption and unfairness. While much intellectual capital has been spent on the question of whether religion leads to violence, the findings of this book highlight that a more meaningful enquiry would have to start on how violent conflict settings impact religion. In fact, as this book has pointed out, when the anthropological roots of the religious rituals of sacrifice are considered, a much more fascinating line of enquiry opens up to reveal how it might be that violence gave birth to religion, and it is the former's continuity in human experience that ensures the central role of the latter.

If there is an essence of religion, as this book has argued, it is religion's ability to provide meaning and order in a world which is chaotic, threatening and full of questions. Its points of reference that transcend the naked reality of here and now enable individuals to cope with the demanding deployment and aftermaths of violence. It also enables calls for violence to be heard and heeded against all the odds, even if it ultimately means the sacrifice of one's life. Its power is not merely destructive: the same mechanisms religions can use to enable violence also enables peace, conflict resolution and chances to break cycles of revenge. Its moral teachings and rules enable boundaries, rights and wrongs and provide order through services such as arbitration. It is, therefore, no surprise, that religion becomes the most effective response given to challenges in ungoverned spaces, failed states and corrupt systems. It is also no surprise that religious visions and solidarities emerge as strong solutions offered in the insecurities of a global age. Thus, yes, there is an intrinsic relationship between religion and violence that runs deep, but not a causal one. The absence of religion in the same contexts would not stop violence, but only push for some other all-encompassing framework to fill the role of religion, whether it is nationalism, ethnic separatism, tribalism or communism.

Rene Girard is perhaps right in his personal conclusions when he notes that 'history has meaning, and that its meaning is terrifying' (Girard 2010:xvii). Human history is indeed a history of violence.

From the emergence of *Homo sapiens* on the earth to this day, a few things remained consistent as part of the human experience, and violent conflict is one of them. Neither the scientific developments of the twentieth century, nor the transformations brought by globalization in the twenty-first, have taken away the human potential to deploy violence against their own kind. On the contrary, it can be said that far from a linear progression towards a utopian eradication of violence, developments in both the previous and current century have instead triggered new forms of violence and enabled it to be deployed on mass scales and with wider implications and contagion risks beyond local boundaries. Thus, one can assert, following Clausewitz' separation of the nature of war versus the characteristics of war (Clausewitz 1976), that while the nature of human violence remains the same, its characteristics, intensity and frequency have altered at particular moments and locations. Violent conflicts with religious characteristics in the world do in fact reflect such a pattern. The capacity of religions to adapt in the global age with networks that go beyond the limits of a local and national unit and spread violence beyond its initial context to faraway places are clearly visible characteristics of the phenomenon we are witnessing. At the same time, the causes and basic mechanics of ethno-religious violence share the same nature as any other expression of collective human violence. To this end, arguments that single out religious violence as an extraordinary human experience or that completely omits unique characteristics of violent conflicts with religious tones are both mistaken.

While the book has been able to provide answers to the research questions it pursued, one hopes, more research will be done to uncover why and how ethno-religious violence emerges and escalates in a global age. The book only scratched the surface of the important theoretical reflections on how religion responds to human violence and is impacted by it. Additional cases of ethno-religious violence in Africa and Middle East brought into analysis with wider qualitative and quantitative studies would enable a more mature theory of ethno-religious violence. A research project that compares ethno-religious violence in Muslim-Christian contexts with that in Hindu and Buddhist contexts in South Asia would provide further comparative insights. Further research needs to be undertaken on how religious ideas are developed in response to violent contexts and how such theologies that accommodate violence interact with the orthodox traditions of their own religions. Similarly, the impact of diaspora groups and international interest groups on ethno-religious conflict requires greater attention.

What is significant, however, are the implications of the arguments put forward by this book. They are both worrying and hope-giving. It can be argued that the apocalyptic visions offered by arguments cited in the introduction are right to worry about the developments across the globe. Those arguments are right to note that we see an escalation of violence with religious characteristic across the world, but they are wrong in the basis they provide as an explanation. The complexities of those violent conflicts cannot simply be explained away in the imaginations of an 'other' that is somehow more predisposed to violence or less developed, less rational and less accommodating than we are. What is worrying, as this book demonstrated, is how globalized imageries of Manichean battles between the West and Islam are becoming self-fulfilled prophecies, fuelling a mimetic escalation between global dyads with serious implications domestically, both in theatres of conflict and in places far away from them. Fatal incidents in distant localities are picked up selectively, framed and consumed by domestic political agendas in other parts of the world as yet more proof for their *a priori* position. In the process, the further discussions get from the actual conflict, the more categorical the claims they infer from domestic conflicts become, and the more easily they are used against people associated with a particular religion. The cycle is completed by religious actors in conflict zones internalizing images of global wars as they see the legitimization of and support to their own stands in the narratives promoted by international actors There is no end in sight for such a worrying "global ecosystem" that enables and spreads religious violence and deepens animosities. In fact, the nature of global risks and unknowns create deep fears for the future, only sharpening mimetic mechanisms of envy, scapegoating and escalation to extremes.

Yet, the implications of this book are also hope-giving because where there is the escalation of animosities and violence, there is also the 'possibility of positive imitation' (Girard 2010:109). The same processes that escalate violence and conflict, if decoded right, can be used to de-escalate and stop them. Violence can be contained, and underlying tensions ultimately calmed down through strategies such as establishing rule of law, fair political and economic systems, reconciliation and forgiveness. Therefore, while there are real issues that need to be addressed, we are not doomed to an inevitable religious Armageddon. If religion is seen as a powerful force that can enable, escalate and prolong a violent conflict, the same force can also serve to stop it. This points back to the argument made in this book that religions are ambivalent about violence and contain both the capacity to enable violence and the ability to stop it from occurring. That is ultimately because human beings are ambivalent: they carry the potential to inflict great violence but also to cooperate, make peace, heal and to move beyond urges to exclude, dominate, demonize and scapegoat the other. Which side of human potential wins the day depends on both the external factors caused by the context and also by an internal decision each community and individual makes on how to respond to the external factors. What is clear is that the direction of global politics, scarcity of resources, mass population movements and other deep and real grievances are providing fertile grounds for unprecedented forms of violence to emerge in an age where the same benefits provided by globalization are also providing us with globalized risks and vulnerabilities. How we respond to such challenges and limit their gross implications might proceed through deglobalizing ethno-religious tensions, refusing to promote any images of the 'other' to be intrinsically different than us and deconstructing grand narratives that promote unbridgeable distances between religious, ethnic and national communities. I sincerely hope that this book will contribute to such an effort to unmask and deconstruct worrying agendas and narratives and replace them with actual analysis of religious violence along with tangible strategies to prevent it.

Notes

Chapter 1

1 Global Terrorism Index 2015 notes 'there has been a dramatic rise in terrorism over the last 15 years. There are nine times more people killed in terrorist attacks today than there were in 2000. In 2014, 32,658 lives were lost to terrorism, the highest number recorded, and an 80% increase from 2013'. www.visionofhumanity.org/#/page/our-gti-findings (Accessed on 22 February 2016)

2 All of the data cited from Pew Research Center are from the report 'Religious Hostilities Reach Six-Year High', 14 January 2014: www.pewforum.org/2014/01/14/religious-hostilities-reach-six-year-high/ (Accessed on 22 February 2016)

3 See Pew Research Center, 'Global Restrictions on Religion Rise Modestly in 2015, Reversing Downward Trend', 11 April 2017: www.compassion.com/multimedia/religious-restrictions-trends-pew-research.pdf (Accessed on 2 January 2018)

4 In this book, the term 'ethno-religious violence' is used to capture violence between ethnic communities differentiated from each other through the religious identification of the majority of their members. The definition of an ethnic community assumes self-identification of a community and their members as an ethnic community with a shared history and cultural, linguistic and/or religious traits.

5 See Berkley Center for Religion, Peace & World Affairs, 'Sudan: Race and Religion in Civil War', August 2013: http://repository.berkleycenter.georgetown.edu/130801BCSudanRaceReligionCivilWar.pdf (Accessed on 1 January 2016)

6 See Council on Foreign Relations, 'Global Conflict Tracker: Violence in Central African Republic', updated on 12 April 2016: www.cfr.org/global/global-conflict-tracker/p32137#!/conflict/violence-in-the-central-african-republic (Accessed on 13 April 2016)

7 See Los Angeles Times, 'Egypt: Religious Conflict Becomes the Revolution's Biggest Enemy'; 9 May 2011: http://latimesblogs.latimes.com/babylonbeyond/2011/05/egypt-sectarian-conflict-becomes-the-revolutions-biggest-enemy.html (Accessed on 13 April 2016)

8 See John Campbell & Asch Harwood, 'Why a Terrifying Religious Conflict Is Raging in Nigeria', *The Atlantic,* 10 July 2013: www.theatlantic .com/international/archive/2013/07/why-a-terrifying-religious-conflict-is-raging-in-nigeria/277690/ (Accessed on 13 April 2016)

9 See Nicole Bibbins Sedaca, 'The Religious Component of the Syrian Conflict: More than Perception', *Georgetown Journal of International Affairs,* 21 June 2013: http://journal.georgetown.edu/the-religious-compo nent-of-the-syrian-conflict-more-than-perception-by-nicole-bibbins-sedaca/ (Accessed on 13 April 2016)

10 See Vaely Arya, 'Afghanistan: One Conflict, Three Faces', *Open Democracy,* 2 July 2010: www.opendemocracy.net/valey-arya/afghanistan-one-conflict-three-faces (Accessed on 13 April 2016)

11 See Rod Nordland & Suadad Al-Salhy, 'In Iraq's Sectarian Violence, a Show of Each Side's Worst', *The New York Times,* 23 June 2014: www .nytimes.com/2014/06/24/world/middleeast/in-iraqs-sectarian-violence-a-show-of-each-sides-worst.html?_r=0 (Accessed on 13 April 2016)

12 See Times of Israel/AFP, 'Growing Number of EU States Say They Prefer Non-Muslim refugees', 8 September 2015: www.timesofisrael.com/eu-states-increasingly-say-they-prefer-non-muslim-refugees/ (Accessed on 16 January 2016)

13 See Amy Davidson, 'Ted Cruz's Religious Test for Syrian Refugees', *The New Yorker,* 16 November 2015: www.newyorker.com/news/ amy-davidson/ted-cruzs-religious-test-for-syrian-refugees (Accessed on 16 January 2016)

14 For a summary of thoughts of Auguste Comte, see Jonathan Turner, et al. (2012), 'chapter 3: The Sociology of Auguste Comte'

15 For example, see the lead article in *Newsweek* by Ayaan Hirsi Ali, 'The Global War on Christians in the Muslim World', 2 June 2012: http:// europe.newsweek.com/ayaan-hirsi-alithe-global-war-christians-muslim-world-65817?rm=eu; as well as myriad others, such as Wolff Bachner, 'Christians Being Killed by Islamists in Egypt and Nigeria', 21 August 2016: www.inquisitr.com/307894/christians-being-killed-by-islamists-in-egypt-and-nigeria-2/; Raymond Ibrahim, 'Attacks on Christians Escalate in Egypt, Nigeria', 19 September 2013: www.gatestoneinstitute.org/ 3977/egypt-nigeria-attacks-christians, *The Economist*, 'Looking Within', 28 February 2015 – an article written on Islam and jihad in Cairo and Lagos, engaging with the issue in both countries: www.economist .com/news/international/21645205-there-heated-debate-about-role-islam-jihadism-will-it-make (All accessed on 2 February 2016)

16 Nigeria fits the definition of a 'cleft country' by Huntington, who argues that countries with distinct civilizations sharing the same space thus remain 'territorially bestride the fault lines between civilizations' and

suffer from internal conflicts and struggle to maintain their unity (Huntington 1996:137). Nigeria, like other countries of the Sahel region, has the demographic challenge of having a Muslim and Christian population trapped between a predominantly Muslim North Africa and predominantly Christian Southern Africa. Egypt, however, fits into Huntington's 'torn country' definition. Here there is a single dominant civilization, but the leaders of the country want to shift it to another civilization, thus creating tensions with their constituencies who do not want to follow their leaders on such a project (Huntington 1996:138). Egypt since its creation has followed an elite project of first pursuing a secular Arab nationalism, siding with the Soviets during the Cold War, then undergoing rapid economic liberalization and foreign policy shifts in line with the United States and its allies, both creating tensions with its deeply conservative Muslim population. Egypt is often seen as a key country where the conflict between Islamism and modernity plays itself out, and its impact is seen all across the Middle East and North Africa.

Chapter 2

1 For a discussion on the religions of Nigeria, particularly traditional religions at the time of colonial administration, see Meel (1943).

2 For example, US government analysts and experts considered the following possibility for Nigeria: 'Other potential developments might accelerate decline in Africa and reduce even our limited optimism. The most important would be the outright collapse of Nigeria. While currently Nigeria's leaders are locked in a bad marriage that all dislike but dare not leave, there are possibilities that could disrupt the precarious equilibrium in Abuja. The most important would be a junior officer coup that could destabilize the country to the extent that open warfare breaks out in many places in a sustained manner. If Nigeria were to become a failed state, it could drag down a large part of the West African region'. *Mapping Sub-Saharan Africa's Future: A US National Intelligence Council Conference,* 2005, brief report can be accessed at www.dni.gov/files/documents/africa_future_2005.pdf (Accessed on 1 December 2015)

3 Ahmadu Bello's fundraising was to have long term implications for Muslim and Christian relations. Many Christians continued to believe that Muslims receive secret funds from the Middle East. A Muslim man and woman interviewed in Jos said that Christians think that there is so much money coming from Arab countries to Muslims, but the woman said 'we have no money, they say we get Saudi money, but we even buy our own drugs'.

4 See Appendix 2.3 for a map of Nigeria which highlights states that apply Shari'a laws.

5 Francis, Lapin & Rossaiasco note that 'more than 20,000 delta freedom fighters initially agreed to disarm, persuaded by generous terms and the direct involvement of the president. the government reported that it collected 18 gunboats, 299,032 rounds of ammunition, 3,831 weapons, 4,377 magazines, 2,072 explosives, and a number of rocket launchers' (Francis, Lapin & Rossaiasco 2011:17).

6 There are also examples of violent clashes between smaller ethnic groups in the Middle Belt outside of the dominant tension of Hausa-Fulani versus the indigenes. Ukiwo notes that 'in Nasarawa State, there were violent clashes between the Azare and Tiv over issues of political domination in June 2000. The war led to massive loss of lives as combatants from both sides mounted road blocks, killing innocent travellers whose only crime was that they belonged to the "enemy" ethnic group' (Ukiwo 2003: 126).

7 See Badejogbin (2013) on the links and continuum from Othman Dan Fodio's jihad, its legacy and Boko Haram.

Chapter 3

1 See, for example, the article by former US Ambassador to the UN during the George Bush administration: John Bolton, 'Egypt's President Is a Courageous Warrior Who has the Guts to Confront Radical Islam' *New York Daily News,* 14 January 2015, www.nydailynews.com/opinion/john-bolton-egypt-courageous-warrior-article-1.2076747 (Accessed on 1 December 2015).

2 See, for example, Eliza Griswold, 'Is This the End of Christianity in the Middle East?' *The New York Times Magazine,* 22 July 2015, www.nytimes.com/2015/07/26/magazine/is-this-the-end-of-christianity-in-the-middle-east.html?_r=0 (Accessed on 1 December 2015) and Jane Corbin, 'These May Be the Last Christians of the Middle East – Unless We Help', *The Guardian – Comment Is Free,* 15 April 2015, www.theguardian.com/commentisfree/2015/apr/15/middle-east-christians-islamic-persecution-iraq-war (Accessed on 1 December 2015).

3 Source: US Middle East Partnership Initiative, 'About Us'; www.mepi.state.gov/about-us.html (Accessed on 14 January 2015)

4 See Cook, 2011: 210–271 for a detailed discussion on change in US policy and its direct relations with the Egyptian regime.

5 See a selection of quotes from Coptic Christian community leaders criticizing the Western calls against brutal clampdown on Muslim Brotherhood here; Carl Olson, 'Beleagured Egyptian Christians Express Deep Frustration with US Policies, Actions', *The Catholic World Report,*

19 August 2013, www.catholicworldreport.com/Blog/2511/beleaguered_egyptian_christians_express_deep_frustration_with_us_policies_actions.aspx (Accessed on 5 January 2015).

6 The incidents listed in the following section for the 2005–2011 period derive partially from a much larger unpublished data set I gathered during my USCIRF fellowship together with an Arabic translator. However, only incidents with reports in English have been re-checked, edited and used here. They also derive from professional work between 2006 and 2010 as a full time researcher for Christian Solidarity Worldwide (CSW) conducting regular research trips in Egypt, use of which can be seen in incidents citing CSW publications as the source. Some of the data from USCIRF and CSW research was also used in an unpublished briefing I co-authored for the Becket Fund, 'Religious Freedom and the Egyptian Transition: An Analysis' in 2013.

7 My findings were published in detail in the briefing I authored for Christian Solidarity Worldwide, 'Egypt-Attack on Abu Fana Monastery, el Minya', 26 September 2008.

8 All of Eshhad's database is available in English at http://eshhad.timep.org/database/ (Accessed on 1 November 2015).

Chapter 5

1 For a brief survey and alternative views on definitions of religion, see Harrison (2006).

2 For a discussion on concept of liminality that first emerged in anthropology but has tremendous importance for discussions on violence and conflict in today's world, see Thomassen (2015).

Bibliography

Abdelmassih, Mary (2012) 'Islamists in Egypt Blame Christians for Voting', *Assyrian International News Agency*, 28 May 2012: www.aina.org/news/20120528191505.htm (Accessed on 6 January 2015).

Abou-El-Fadl, Reem (2015) 'Early Pan-Arabism in Egypt's July Revolution: The Free Officer's Political Formation and Policy-making, 1946–54', *Nations and Nationalism*, 21:2, pp. 289–308, The Association for the Study of Ethnicity and Nationalism.

Achebe, Chinua (1984) *The Trouble with Nigeria*, Oxford: Heinemann.

Adamolekun, Taiye (2012) 'Main Trends in the Church Growth in Nigeria', *European Scientific Journal*, 8:23, European Scientific Institute.

Adebanwi, Wale & Ebenezer Obadare (2010) 'Introducing Nigeria at Fifty: The Nation in Narration', *Journal of Contemporary African Studies*, 28:4, pp. 379–405, Routledge.

   (eds.) (2013) *Democracy and Prebendalism in Nigeria: Critical Interpretations*, New York: Palgrave Macmillan.

Adebayo, R. Ibrahim (2010) 'Ethno-Religious Crises and the Challenges of Sustainable Development in Nigeria', *Journal of Sustainable Development in Africa*, 12:4, pp. 213–225, Clarion University of Pennsylvania.

Adly, Amr Ismail Ahmed (2011) 'When Cheap Is Costly: Rent Decline, Regime Survival and State Reform in Mubarak's Egypt (1990–2009)', *Middle Eastern Studies*, 47:2, pp. 295–313, Routledge.

Adogame, Afe (2010) 'How God Became a Nigerian: Religious Impulse and the Unfolding of a Nation', *Journal of Contemporary African Studies*, 28:4, pp. 479–498, Routledge.

Agamben, Giorgio (1998) *Homo Sacer: Sovereign Power and Bare Life*, Stanford, California: Stanford University Press.

   (2005) *State of Exception*, Chicago: University of Chicago Press.

Agensky, Jonathan (2010) 'Evangelical Globalism and the Internationalization of Sudan's Civil War', Draft Paper, available at: www.academia.edu/352162/Evangelical_globalism_and_the_internationalization_of_Sudan_s_civil_war (Accessed on 28 March 2016).

   (2013) 'Dr Livingstone, I Presume? Evangelicals, Africa and Faith-Based Humanitarianism', *Global Society*, 27:4, pp. 1–21, Taylor & Francis.

Ajami, Fouad (1995) 'The Sorrows of Egypt', *Foreign Affairs*, 74:5 (Sept.–Oct., 1995), pp. 72–88, Council on Foreign Relations.

Akwara, Azalahu Francis & Benedict O. Ojomah (2013) 'Religion, Politics and Democracy in Nigeria', *Canadian Social Science*, 9:1, pp. 65–78. Canadian Academy of Oriental and Occidental Culture.

Al-Anani, Khalil (2015) 'The "Anguish" of the Muslim Brotherhood in Egypt', in L. Sadiki (Ed.), *Routledge Handbook of the Arab Spring*. Oxford: Routledge.

Al-Arian, Abdullah (2014) A State without a State: The Egypt Muslim Brotherhood's Social Welfare Institutions, Project on Middle East Political Science, Elliott School of International Affairs.

Al-Awadi, Hesham (2004) *In Pursuit of Legitimacy: The Muslim Brothers and Mubarak, 1982–2000*, London: Tauris.

Aloa, Abiodun (2009) Islamic Radicalization and Violence in Nigeria: Country Report, *Economic and Social Research Council*.

Aloa, Abioudun (2013) 'Islamic Radicalisation and Violent Extremism in Nigeria', *Conflict, Security & Development*, 13:2, pp. 127–147, Routledge.

Albrow, Martin (1996) *The Global Age*, Cambridge: Polity Press.

Al Jazeera News (2011) 'Dozens Dead in Religious Clashes in Nigeria', 2 September 2011: www.aljazeera.com/news/africa/2011/09/20119216170786566.html (Accessed on 14 January 2016).

(2013), 'Egypt's Coptic Pope Blasts Morsi's "Negligence"', 9 April 2013: www.aljazeera.com/news/middleeast/2013/04/20134994910991737.html (Accessed on 1 January 2015).

(2014) 'Nigeria: Dozens of Boko Haram Fighters Killed', 9 January 2014: www.aljazeera.com/news/africa/2014/01/nigeria-dozens-boko-haram-fighters-killed-201419172155263747.html (Accessed on 14 January 2015).

Al-Rodhan, Nayef & Stoudmann, Gerard (2006) Definitions of Globalization: A Comprehensive Overview and a Proposed Definition, Geneva Centre for Security Policy.

Aluko, Olajide (1977) 'Nigeria and Britain after Gowon', *African Affairs*, 76: 304, pp. 303–320, Oxford University Press.

Amer, Pakinam (2010) 'Chronology: Egypt's Sectarian Violence', *Egypt Independent*, 12 January 2010: www.egyptindependent.com/news/chronology-egypts-sectarian-violence (Accessed on 14 January 2015).

Amin, Galal (2011) *Egypt in the Era of Hosni Mubarak: 1981–2011*, Cairo: American University in Cairo Press.

Amos, Valerie (2013) 'Foreword' in D. Mazurana, K. Jacobsen & L. Gale (Eds.), *Research Methods in Conflict Settings: A View from Below*, pp. xv–xvii, New York: Cambridge University Press.

Amnesty International (2007) 'Egypt: Systematic Abuses in the Name of Security', April 2007: www.amnesty.org/en/documents/mde12/001/2007/en/ (Accessed on 14 January 2015).

(2012) 'Egypt's New Constitution Limits Fundamental Freedoms and Ignores the Rights of Women', 30 November 2012: www.amnesty.org/en/latest/news/2012/11/egypt-s-new-constitution-limits-fundamental-freedoms-and-ignores-rights-women/ (Accessed on 14 January 2015).

(2013a) 'Egypt: Christians Scapegoated after Dispersal of Pro-Morsi Sit-Ins', 9 October 2013: www.amnesty.org/en/press-releases/2013/10/egypt-christians-scapegoated-after-dispersal-pro-morsi-sit-ins/ (Accessed on 14 January 2015).

(2013b) 'Shell's False Claims on Niger Delta Oil Spills Exposed', *Amnesty International*, 7 November 2013: www.amnesty.org/en/latest/news/2013/11/shell-s-false-claims-niger-delta-oil-spills-exposed/ (Accessed on 14 January 2015).

Anderson, Benedict (1991) *Imagined Communities: Reflections on the Origin and Spread of Nationalism*, New York: Verso.

Aniedobe (2014) 'The Girls of Chibok by Aniedobe', *Sahara Reporters*, 28 April 2014: http://saharareporters.com/2014/04/28/girls-chibok-aniedobe.

Ansari, Hamied (1984) 'Sectarian Conflict in Egypt and the Political Expediency of Religion', *Middle East Journal*, 38:3, pp. 397–418. Middle East Institute.

Anthias, Floya & Nira Yuval-Davis (1993) *Racialized Boundaries*, London: Routledge.

Appleby, R. Scott (2000) *The Ambivalence of the Sacred: Religion, Violence, and Reconciliation*, Oxford: Rowman & Littlefield.

Arafa, Mohamed A. (2014) 'Whither Egypt? Against Religious Fascism and Legal Authoritarianism: Pure Revolution, Popular Coup, or a Military Coup D'etat?', *Indiana International and Comparative Law Review* 24:4, pp. 859–897, Indiana University.

Arafat, Alaa Al-Din (2009) *The Mubarak Leadership and Future of Democracy in Egypt*, New York: Palgrave.

Arendt, Hannah (2002) 'Eichmann in Jerusalem: A Report on the Banality of Evil' in A. Hinton (Ed.), *Genocide: An Anthropological Reader*, pp. 91–110, Oxford: Blackwell.

Armajani, Jon (2012) *Modern Islamist Movements: History, Religion, and Politics*. Chichester: Wiley-Blackwell.

Arquilla, John (2012) 'Sorry, Steven Pinker, the World Isn't Getting Less Violent', Foreign Policy: http://foreignpolicy.com/2012/12/03/the-big-kill/ (Accessed on 1 April 2015).

Ashour, Omar (2007) 'Lions Tamed? An Inquiry into the Cause of De-Radicalization of Armed Islamist Movements: The Cade of the Egyptian Islamic Group', *Middle East Journal* 61:4, pp. 596–625, Middle East Institute.

Ayubi, Nazih N. (1989) 'Government and the State in Egypt Today', in R. Owen & C. Tripp (Eds.), *Egypt Under Mubarak*, pp. 1–21, London: Routledge.

Badejogbin, Oluwatoyin (2013) 'Boko Haram: An Enquiry into the Socio-Political Context of Nigeria's Counter-Terrorism Response', *Law, Democracy & Development* 17, pp. 226–252, University of Western Cape.

Baker, Raymond William (1990) *Sadat and After: Struggles for Egypt's Political Soul*, London: I. B. Tauris.

Balogun, M. J. (1997) 'Enduring Clientelism, Governance Reform and Leadership Capacity: A Review of the Democratization Process in Nigeria', *Journal of Contemporary African Studies* 15:2, pp. 237–260, Routledge.

Barash, Jeffrey (1999) 'The Politics of Memory: Reflections on Practical Wisdom and Political Identity', in R. Kearney et al. (Eds.), *Questioning Ethics: Contemporary Debates in Philosophy*, pp. 33–44, London: Routledge.

Barrett, Justin L. (2012a) *Born Believers: The Science of Children's Religious Belief*. New York: Free Press.

(2012b) 'Born Believers', *New Scientist*, 17 March 2012, pp. 38–41.

Bartlett, Duncan (2008) 'Japan Looks Back on 17th Century Persecutions', *BBC News*, 24 November 2008: http://news.bbc.co.uk/1/hi/world/asia-pacific/7745455.stm (Accessed on 1 January 2015).

Basedau, Matthies, Georg Struver, Johannes Vullers & Tim Wegenast (2011) Do Religious Factors Impact Armed Conflict? Empirical Evidence from Sub-Saharan Africa, GIGA Research Programme: Violence and Security, Hamburg: German Institute of Global and Area Studies.

Batchelorte, Daud Abdul Fattah (2014) 'Post Arab Spring: Beneficial Lessons in Governance from Recent Events in Egypt and Tunisia', *The Politics and Religion Journal* 1, pp. 115–133.

Bauman, Zygmunt (1989) *Modernity and the Holocaust*, Cambridge: Polity Press.

(2002) 'Holocaust', in D. Goldberg & J. Solomos (Eds.), *A Companion to Racial and Ethnic Studies*, pp. 46–64, Oxford: Blackwell.

(2006) *Liquid Fear*, Cambridge: Polity Press.

BBC News (2005) 'Three Killed in Egypt Church Riot', 22 October 2005: http://news.bbc.co.uk/1/hi/world/middle_east/4366232.stm (Accessed on 1 December 2015).

(2006a) 'Egypt Church Attacks Spark Anger', 15 April 2006: http://news
.bbc.co.uk/1/hi/world/middle_east/4911346.stm (Accessed on 1 December 2015).

(2006b) 'Sectarian Tensions Flare in Egypt', 16 April 2006: http://news
.bbc.co.uk/2/hi/middle_east/4914172.stm (Accessed on 1 December
2015).

(2008) 'Riots "Kill Hundreds in Nigeria"', 29 November 2008: http://
news.bbc.co.uk/1/hi/world/africa/7756695.stm (Accessed on 1 December 2015).

(2011a) 'Cairo Clashes Leave 24 Dead after Coptic Church Protest',
10 October 2011: www.bbc.co.uk/news/world-middle-east-15235212
(Accessed on 1 December 2015).

(2011b) 'Egypt Bomb Kills 21 at Alexandria Coptic Church', 1 January
2011: www.bbc.co.uk/news/world-middle-east-12101748 (Accessed on
1 December 2015).

(2011c) 'Alexandria Church Bomb: Egyptian Copts and Police Clash',
3 January 2011: www.bbc.co.uk/news/world-middle-east-12106177
(Accessed on 1 December 2015).

(2011d) 'Nigeria's Muhammad Buhari in Profile', 18 April 2011:
www.bbc.co.uk/news/world-africa-12890807 (Accessed on 1 December
2015).

(2013) 'Egypt Crisis: Army Ousts President Mohammed Morsi', 4 July
2013 www.bbc.co.uk/news/world-middle-east-23173794 (Accessed on
1 December 2015).

Beattie, Tina (2007) *The New Atheists: The Twilight of Reason and the War
on Religion*, London: Darton, Longman and Todd.

Beck, Ulrich (2010) *A God of One's Own*, Cambridge: Polity Press.

Beck, Ulrich & Natan Sznaider (2006) 'Unpacking Cosmopolitanism for the
Social Sciences: A Research Agenda', *The British Journal of Sociology*
57:1, pp. 1–23, Wiley-Blackwell.

Beinin, Joel (1989) 'Labour, Capital, and the State in Nasserist Egypt,
1952–1961', *International Journal of Middle East Studies* 21:1,
pp. 71–90, Cambridge University Press.

Berger, Peter (1974) 'Some Second Thoughts on Substantive versus Functional Definitions of Religion', *Journal for the Scientific Study of Religion* 13:2, pp. 125–133, Wiley.

(1990) *The Sacred Canopy: Elements of a Sociological Theory of Religion*,
New York: Anchor.

(ed.) (1999) *Desecularization of the World: Resurgent Religion and World
Politics*, Grand Rapids, MI: Eerdmans.

Berger, Peter, Birgitte Berger & Hansfried Kellner (1977) *The Homeless
Mind: Modernization and Consciousness*, New York: Penguin.

Berger, Peter & Thomas Luckmann (1966) *The Social Construction of Reality: A Treatise in the Sociology of Knowledge*, London: Penguin.

Berman, Bruce (1998), 'Ethnicity, Patronage, and the African State: The Politics of Uncivil Nationalism', *African Affairs*, 97, pp. 305–341, Royal African Society.

Blaydes, Lisa (2011) *Elections and Distributive Politics in Mubarak's Egypt*, Cambridge: Cambridge University Press.

Bowie, Leland (1977) 'The Copts, the Wafd, and Religious Issues in Egyptian Politics', *The Muslim World* 67:2, pp. 106–126, Hartford Seminary.

Bowker, Robert (2010) *Egypt and the Politics of Change in the Arab Middle East*, Cheltenham: Edward Elgar.

Brabant, Malcolm (2005) 'Jailed Nour Tests Egypt's Democracy', *BBC News*, 8 March 2005: http://news.bbc.co.uk/1/hi/world/middle_east/4328353.stm (Accessed on 1 August 2015).

Brownlee, Jason (2013) Violence against Copts in Egypt, Carnegie Endowment for International Peace, Washington, DC.

Brubaker, Rogers (2015) 'Religious Dimensions of Political Conflict and Violence', *Sociological Theory* 33:1, pp. 1–19, American Sociological Association.

Bryman, Alan (2012) *Social Research Methods: 4th Edition*, Oxford: Oxford University Press.

Burke, Daniel (2015) 'Coptic Christian Bishop: I Forgive ISIS', *CNN*, 20 February 2015: http://edition.cnn.com/2015/02/20/living/coptic-bishop-isis/ (Accessed on 6 January 2016).

Burkert, Walter (1983) *Homo Necans: The Anthropology of Ancient Greek Sacrificial Ritual and Myth*, Berkley and Los Angeles: The Regents of the University of California.

Bush, Ray (1999) *Economic Crisis and the Politics of Reform in Egypt*, Boulder, CO: Westview Press.

Cady, Linell & Sheldon W. Simon (eds.) (2006) *Religion and Conflict in South and Southeast Asia: Disrupting Violence*, New York: Routledge.

Campbell, Ian (1994) 'Nigeria's Failed Transition: The 1993 Presidential Election', *Journal of Contemporary African Studies* 12:2, pp. 179–199, Routledge.

Caristrom, Gregg (2013) 'Anti-Morsi Protests Sweep Egypt', *Al Jazeera*, 1 Jul 2013: www.aljazeera.com/news/middleeast/2013/06/2013630212512626804.html (Accessed on 6 January 2016).

Caromba, Laurence & Hussein Solomon (2008) 'Understanding Egypt's Muslim Brotherhood', *African Security Review* 17.3, pp. 98–124. Routledge.

Carothers, Thomas (2005) A Better Way to Support Middle East Reform, Policy Brief 3, Carnegie Endowment for International Peace.

Carre, Olivier (1995) 'From Banna to Qutb and "Qutbism": The Radicalization of Fundamentalist Thought under the Three Regimes' in Shamir, Shimon (Ed.), *Egypt from Monarchy to Republic: A Reassessment of Revolution and Change*, pp. 181–194, Boulder, CO: Westview Press.

Carter, B. L. (1986) *The Copts in Egyptian Politics 1918–1952*, London: Routledge.

The Carter Center (2012) Presidential Election in Egypt: Final Report, May–June 2012, Atlanta: The Carter Center.

Casanova, Jose (2006) 'Rethinking Secularization: A Global Perspective' *The Hedgehog Review*, pp. 7–21, Institute for Advanced Studies in Culture.

Cavanaugh, William T. (2009) *The Myth of Religious Violence: Secular Ideology and the Roots of Modern Conflict*, Oxford: Oxford University Press.

Cesari, Jocelyne (2014) *The Awakening of Muslim Democracy: Religion, Modernity and the State*, New York: Cambridge University Press.

Chandler, Adam (2015) 'Nigeria's Violent Year since "Bring Back Our Girls"' *The Atlantic Council*, 14 April 2015: www.theatlantic.com/ international/archive/2015/04/nigerias-violent-year-since-bring-back-our-girls/390510/ (Accessed on 1 January 2016).

Central Intelligence Agency 'Nigeria', *World Fact Book:* www.cia.gov/ library/publications/the-world-factbook/geos/ni.html (Accessed on 1 January 2016).

Clarke, Peter (2007) 'Islamic Reform in Contemporary Nigeria: Methods and Aims', *Third World Quarterly*, 10:2, pp. 519–538, Routledge.

Clarke, Steve (2014) *The Justification of Religious Violence*, Chichester: Wiley Blackwell.

Clausewitz, Carl Von (1976) *On War; Indexed Edition*, M. Howard & P. Paret, Princeton, NJ: Princeton University Press.

Collier, David (1993) 'The Comparative Method', in A. Finter (Ed.), *Political Science: The State of Discipline II*, Washington, DC: American Political Science Association.

Comolli, Virginia (2015) *Boko Haram: Niger's Islamist Insurgency*, London: C. Hurst & Co.

Connor, Jeffrey & Carol Rollie Flynn (eds.) (2015) Report: Lone Wolf Terrorism, Security Studies Program, Washington, DC: Georgetown University.

Cook, Steven A. (2011) *The Struggle for Egypt: From Nasser to Tahrir Square*, New York: Oxford University Press.

Cordell, Karl & Stefan Wolff (2010) *Ethnic Conflict: Causes, Consequences, and Responses*, Cambridge: Polity Press.

Craighead, W. Edward & Charles B. Nemeroff (2004) *The Concise Corsini Encyclopaedia of Psychology and Behavioural Science, Third Edition*, Hoboken, NJ: John Wiley & Sons, Inc.

Christian Solidarity Worldwide (2009) *Egypt: Religious Freedom*, London: Christian Solidarity Worldwide.

(2011a) 'Nigeria: Thousands Displaced in Bauchi State', 18 March 2011: www.csw.org.uk/2011/03/18/press/1137/article.htm (Accessed 1 January 2014).

(2011b) 'CSW Tribute to Forgotten Heroines', 8 March 2011: www .csw.org.uk/2011/03/08/news/1811/article.htm (Accessed 1 January 2014).

Dalsh, Amr Abdallah (2013) 'Five Die in Christian-Muslim Clashes in Egypt', *Reuters*, 7 April 2013: http://in.reuters.com/article/egypt-clashes-idINDEE93504U20130407 (Accessed on 1 January 2016).

Dawkins, Richard (2006) *The God Delusion*, London: Bantam Press.

Deutsche Welle (2015) '"We Are Importing Religious Conflict", Says Prominent Sociologist', 30 August 2015: www.dw.com/en/we-are-importing-religious-conflict-says-prominent-sociologist/a-18682373 (Accessed on 18 January 2016).

Diara, Benjamin & Nkechinyere Onah (2014) 'The Phenomenal Growth of Pentecostalism in the Contemporary Nigerian Society: A Challenge to Mainline Churches', *Mediterranean Journal of Social Sciences*, 5:6, pp. 395–402, Rome: MCSER Publishing.

Dion, Douglas (1998) 'Evidence and Inference in the Comparative Case Study', *Comparative Politics* 39, pp. 127–145.

Durkheim, Emile (1912) *The Elementary Forms of Religious Life*, K. Field (Trans.) (1995), New York: The Free Press (Simon &Schuster).

Ebeid, Mona Makram (1989) 'The Role of the Official Opposition', in R. Owen & C. Tripp (Eds.), *Egypt Under Mubarak*, pp. 21–53, London: Routledge.

Economist, (2000) 'Egypt's Vulnerable Copts', 6 January 2000: www.economist.com/node/271592 (Accessed on 1 December 2015).

(2010) 'Out on Patrol: Nigeria's Islamic Police Do Not Have as Much Power as Some Feared', 11 June 2010: www.economist.com/node/16311947 (Accessed on 1 April 2016).

Edkins, Jenny (2003) *Trauma and the Memory of Politics*, Cambridge: Cambridge University Press.

Egyptian Initiative for Personal Rights (2009) Freedom of Religion and Belief in Egypt: Quarterly Report, October–December 2009: http://eipr.org/sites/default/files/reports/pdf/FRBQ_Oct_Dec_09_EN.pdf (Accessed in December 2015).

(2010a), Naga Hammadi: Witnesses the Strife Fact-Finding Mission Report. January 2010: http://eipr.org/sites/default/files/reports/pdf/naga hammadi_witnesses_to_the_strife_report2010.pdf (Accessed in December 2015).

(2010b), Two Years of Sectarian Violence; What Happened? Where Do We Begin?: An Analytical Study of January 2008–January 2010: http://eipr.org/sites/default/files/reports/pdf/Sectarian_Violence_inTwo Years_EN.pdf (Accessed in December 2015).

Egyptian Organization for Human Rights (2007) EOHR Demands the Amendment of Articles Concerned with Torture in the Penal Code and the Criminal Procedures Code, 6 January 2007.

Ejiogu, E. C. (2011) *The Roots of Political Instability in Nigeria: Political Evolution and Development in the Niger Basin*, Surrey: Ashgate.

Ekwe-Ekwe, Harbert (1985) 'The Nigerian Plight: Shagari to Buhari', *Third World Quarterly* 7:3, pp. 610–624. Routledge.

El Gundy, Zeinab (2013) 'Angry Mog Kills at Least 4 Shias in Giza Village Including Leader', *Ahram Online*, 24 June 2013: http://english.ahram .org.eg/NewsContent/1/64/74773/Egypt/Politics-/-Angry-mob-kills-at-least–Shias-in-Giza-village-i.aspx (Accessed on 1 February 2016).

El-Houdabiy, Ibrahim (2012) 'Islamism Now; How the January 25 Revolution Changed Political Islam in Egypt' *Cairo Review of Global Affairs* 6, pp. 130–149, The American University in Cairo.

El-Naggar, Mona (2010) 'Egyptian Christians Clash with Police', *New York Times*, 7 January 2010: www.nytimes.com/2010/01/08/world/middle east/08egypt.html?_r=0 (Accessed on 1 January 2016).

Emon, Anver M. (2012) *Religious Pluralism and Islamic Law: Dhimmis and Others in the Empire of Law*, Oxford: Oxford University Press.

Fahmi, Georges (2014) The Coptic Church and Politics in Egypt, Carnegie Middle East Center, 18 December 2014.

Falola, Toyin (1998) *Violence in Nigeria: The Crisis of Religious Politics and Secular Ideologies*, Rochester, NY: University of Rochester Press.

(1999) *The History of Nigeria*, Westport, CT: Greenwood Press.

Falola, Toyin & Matthew Heaton (2008) *A History of Nigeria*, Cambridge: Cambridge University Press.

Fani-Kayode, Femi (2014) 'Boko Haram, Jonathan and a Nation without Empathy', *Premium Times*, 16 February 2014: www.premiumtimes ng.com/opinion/155155-boko-haram-jonathan-and-a-nation-without-empathy-by-femi-fani-kayode.html (Accessed on 14 January 2015).

Farneti, Roberto (2015) *Mimetic Politics: Dyadic Patterns in Global Politics*, East Lansing: Michigan University Press.

Fasua, Kayode (2013) 'Maitatsine: Tale of religious war in the North', *National Mirror*, 3 March 2013: http://nationalmirroronline.net/new/ maitatsine-tale-of-religious-war-in-the-north/ (Accessed on 1 January 2015).

Fayek, Mina (2014) 'Copts in El Sisi's Egypt', *Open Democracy*, 29 May 2014: www.opendemocracy.net/arab-awakening/mina-fayek/copts-in-el-sisis-egypt (Accessed 3 March 2016).

Fawzy, Samy (2000) 'Christian-Muslim Dialogue in Egypt', *Transformation: Journal of Holistic Mission Studies* 17:1 (2001), pp. 34–36, Oxford Centre for Mission Studies.

Felsberger, Stefanie (2014) 'Orientalism and Political Islam: The Western Analysis of Islamic Parties in Egypt post-Mubarak' in Hamed, Adham (Ed.), *Revolution as a Process: The Case of Egyptian Uprising*, pp. 244–275, Bermen: EHV Academic press GmbH.

Fielding, David & Anja Shortland (2010) 'An Eye for an Eye, a Tooth for a Tooth: Political Violence and Counter-Insurgency in Egypt' *Journal of Peace Research* 47(4), pp. 433–443, Sage.

Flemming, Chris (2004) *Rene Girard: Violence and Mimesis*, Cambridge: Polity Press.

Flower, Raymond (1972) *Napoleon to Nasser: The Story of Modern Egypt*, London: Compton Press.

Fox, Jonathan (1999) 'Towards a Dynamic Theory of Ethno-Religious Conflict', *Nations and Nationalism* 5:4, pp. 431–463. The Association for the Study of Ethnicity and Nationalism.

(2002a) *Ethnoreligious Conflict in the Late Twentieth Century: A General Theory*, Maryland: Lexington Books

(2002b) 'Ethnic Minorities and the Clash of Civilizations: A Quantitative Analysis of Huntington's Book', *British Journal of Political Science* 32:3, pp. 415–434, Cambridge University Press.

(2004) 'Religion and State Failure: An Examination of the Extent and Magnitude of Religious Conflict from 1950 to 1996', *International Political Science Review* 25:1, pp. 55–76. Sage Publications.

Fox, Jonathan & Shmuel Sandler (2004) *Bringing Religion into International Relations*, New York: Palgrave Macmillan.

Francis, Paul, Dierdre Lapin & Paula Rossiasco (2011) *Securing Development and Peace in the Niger Delta: A Social and Conflict Analysis for Change*, Washington, DC: Woodrow Wilson International Center for Scholars.

Freud, Sigmund (1929) *Civilization and Its Discontents*, England: Chrysome Associates.

(1957) 'Thoughts for the Times on War and Death', *The Standard Edition of the Complete Psychological Works of Sigmund Freud, Vol. 14 (1914–1916)*, pp. 275–300. London: The Hogarth Press.

Gadamer, Hans-Georg (2014) *Truth and Method*, London: Bloomsbury.

Gaiya, Muse (2004) 'Christianity in Northern Nigeria, 1975–2000', *Exchange – Journal of Missiological and Ecumenical Research* 33:4, pp. 354–371, Brill.

Gbasha, P. T. (1995) 'Religion' in G. Ashiwaju & O. Areola (Eds.), *Nigeria: The First 25 Years*, Ibadan: Ibadan University Press.

Geddes, B. (1990) 'How the Cases You Choose Affect the Answers You Get: Selection Bias in Comparative Politics', *Political Analysis* 2: pp 131–150.

Giddens, Anthony (1984) *The Constitution of Society*, Los Angeles: University of California Press.

Girard, Rene (1965) *Deceit, Desire and the Novel: Self and Other in Literary Structure*, Baltimore: Johns Hopkins University Press.

    (1979) *Violence and the Sacred*, Baltimore: Johns Hopkins University Press.

    (1986) *The Scapegoat*, Baltimore: Johns Hopkins University Press.

    (2010) *Battling to the End: Conversations with Benoit Chantre*, East Lansing: Michigan University Press.

Goldschmidt Jr, Arthur (2008) *A Brief History of Egypt*, New York: Infobase Publishing.

Gopin, Marc (2000) *Between Eden and Armageddon: Future of World Religions, Violence, and Peacemaking*, Oxford: Oxford University Press.

Gore, Charles & Pratten, David (2003) 'The Politics of Plunder: The Rhetorics of Order and Disorder in Southern Nigeria', *African Affairs* 102: pp 211–240, Royal African Society, Oxford University Press.

Gow, James, Fumi Olonisakin & Ernst Dijxhoorn (2013) 'Deep History and International Security: Social Conditions and Competition, Militancy and Violence in West Africa', *Conflict, Security & Development* 13:2, pp. 231–258, Routledge.

Gray, John (2015) 'Steven Pinker Is Wrong About Violence and War'. *The Guardian*, 13 March 2015: www.theguardian.com/books/2015/mar/13/john-gray-steven-pinker-wrong-violence-war-declining (Accessed in 1 April 2015).

Hanna, Michael Wahid (2013) 'With Friends Like These: Coptic Activism in the Diaspora', *Middle East Report* 43, Middle East Research and Information Project.

Harff, Barbara (2000) 'The Etiology of Genocides' in I. Wallimann & M. Dobkowski (Eds.), *Genocide and the Modern Age: Etiology and Case Studies of Mass Death*, pp. 41–59, Westport, CT: Greenwood Press.

Harris, Sam (2006) 'The Reality of Islam', 8 February 2006: www.samharris.org/blog/item/the-reality-of-islam (Accessed on 1 December 2015).

Harrison, Victoria (2006) 'The Pragmatics of Defining Religion in a Multi-cultural World', *The International Journal of Philosophy of Religion* 59:3, pp. 133–152, Springer.

Hasan, S. S. (2003) *Christians versus Muslims in Modern Egypt: The Century-Long Struggle for Coptic Equality*, Oxford: Oxford University Press.

Hasenclever, Andreas & Volker Rittberger (2000) 'Does Religion Make a Difference? Theoretical Approaches to the Impact of Faith on Political Conflict', *Millennium: Journal of International Studies* 29:3, pp. 641–674, SAGE.

Hellyer, H. A. (2013) 'The Scourge of Sectarianism in Egypt', *Foreign Policy* 26: http://foreignpolicy.com/2013/06/26/the-scourge-of-sectarianism-in-egypt/ (Accessed on 1 December 2015).

Henderson, Randall P. (2005) 'The Egyptian Coptic Christians: The Conflict between Identity and Equality'. *Islam and Christian-Muslim Relations* 16:2, pp. 155–166, Routledge.

Herskovits, Jean (1979) 'Democracy in Nigeria', *Foreign Affairs* 58:2, pp. 314–335, Council on Foreign Relations.

Hertzke, Allen (2004) *Freeing God's Children: The Unlikely Alliance for Global Human Rights*, Lanham, MD: Rowman & Littlefield.

Hervieu-Leger, Daniele (2000) *Religion as a Chain of Memory*, New Brunswick, NJ: Rutgers University Press.

Hibbard, Scott W. (2011) 'Egypt and the Legacy of Sectarianism' in T. Hisk (Ed.), *Between Terror and Tolerance: Religious Leaders, Conflict, and Peacemaking*, Washington, DC: Georgetown University Press.

Hickey, Raymond (1984) 'The 1982 Maitatsine Uprisings in Nigeria: A Note', *African Affairs* 83:331, pp .251–256, Oxford University Press.

Hill, J. N. C (2012) *Nigeria since Independence: Forever Fragile?*, New York: Palgrave Macmillan.

Hinton, A. Laban (ed.) (2002) *Genocide: An Anthropological Reader*, Oxford: Blackwell.

Hirst, David & Irene Beeson (1981) *Sadat*. London: Faber and Faber.

Høigilt, Jacob (2011) *Islamist Rhetoric, Language and Culture in Contemporary Egypt*, Oxon: Routledge.

Hoyle, Rich H., Monica J. Harris & M. Judd Charles (2002) *Research Methods in Social Relations*. Fort Worth, Texas: Wadsworth.

Human Rights Watch (2014a) 'Nigeria: Victims of Abductions Tell Their Stories', 27 October 2014: www.hrw.org/news/2014/10/27/nigeria-victims-abductions-tell-their-stories (Accessed on 1 November 2015).

(2014b) 'All According to Plan: The Rab'a Massacre and Mass Killings of Protesters in Egypt', 12 August 2014: www.hrw.org/report/2014/08/12/all-according-plan/raba-massacre-and-mass-killings-protesters-egypt (Accessed on 1 November 2015).

(2015) 'Egypt: Year of Abuses under Al-Sisi', 8 June 2015: www.hrw
.org/news/2015/06/08/egypt-year-abuses-under-al-sisi (Accessed on
1 November 2015).

Huntington, Samuel (1996) *The Clash of Civilizations and the Remaking of
World Order*, London: Free Press.

Hunwick, John. (1992) 'An African Case Study of Political Islam: Nigeria',
Annals of the American Academy of Political and Social Science 524,
143–155, SAGE.

Ibrahim, Jibrin (1991) 'Religion and Political Turbulence in Nigeria',
The Journal of Modern African Studies, 29:1, pp. 115–136.

Ibrahim, Saad Eddin (1996) *The Copts of Egypt*, London: Minority Rights
Group.

International Crisis Group (2006) Nigeria's Faltering Federal Experiment,
Africa Report No. 119, 25 October 2006.

Institute for Economics & Peace (2015) Global Peace Index 2015: Measur-
ing Peace, Its Causes and Its Economic Value: http://static.visionof
humanity.org/sites/default/files/Global%20Peace%20Index%20Report
%202015_0.pdf (Accessed on 1 April 2015).

Ihonvbere, Julius O. (1999) 'The 1999 Presidential Elections in Nigeria:
The Unresolved Issues', *A Journal of Opinion* 27:1, pp. 59–62, African
Studies Association.

Ikbe, Ukana B. Ikpe (2000) 'Patrimonialism and Military Regimes in
Nigeria', *African Journal of Political Science* 5:1, pp. 146–162, African
Association of Political Science.

Iskander, Elizabeth (2012) 'The "Mediation" of Muslim-Christian Relations
in Egypt: The Strategies and Discourses of the Official Egyptian Press
During Mubarak's Presidency', *Islam and Christian-Muslim Relations*
23:1, pp. 31–44. Routledge.

Jankowski, James (2002) *Nasser's Egypt, Arab Nationalism and the United
Arab Republic*, Boulder, CO: Lynne Rienner.

Joseph, Dave (2013) 'Common Ground, Common Good: As Nigeria battles
Islamist Boko Haram, an imam and pastor spread tolerance', *The
Christian Science Monitor*. 8 November 2013: www.csmonitor.com/
Commentary/Common-Ground/2013/1108/As-Nigeria-battles-Islamist-
Boko-Haram-an-imam-and-pastor-spread-tolerance (Accessed on 1 April
2015).

Joseph, Richard A. (2014) *Democracy and Prebendal Politics in Nigeria: The
Rise and Fall of Second Republic*, Cambridge: Cambridge University
Press.

Judah, Tim (2002) *Kosovo: War and Revenge*, New Haven, CT: Yale
Nota Bene.

Juergensmeyer, Mark (2001) *Terror in the Mind of God: The Global Rise of Religious Violence*, Los Angeles: University of California Press.

Kassab, Bisan (2012) 'Pope Shenouda: Enemy of Sadat, Friend of Mubarak', *AL Akhbar English*, 19 March 2012: http://english.al-akhbar.com/node/5385 (Accessed on 1 December 2015).

Kastfelt, Neils (1994) *Religion and Politics in Nigeria: A Study in Middle Belt Christianity*, London: British Academic Press.

Keman, Hans (2006) 'Comparing Political Systems: Towards Positive Theory Development', *Working Papers Political Science*, No. 2006/01, Department of Political Science, Vrije Universiteit Amsterdam.

Kepel, Gilles (1985) *Muslim Extremism in Egypt: The Prophet and Pharaoh*, Berkeley: University of California Press.

(2004) *The Revenge of God: The Resurgence of Islam, Christianity and Judaism in the Modern World*, Cambridge: Polity Press.

(2006) *Jihad: The Trail of Political Islam*, London: I. B. Tauris.

Kew, Darren (2010) 'Nigerian Elections and the Neopatrimonial Paradox: In Search of the Social Contract', *Journal of Contemporary African Studies* 28:4, pp. 499–521, Routledge.

Khalaf, Roula (2012) 'Morsi Code Reveals Stance on Army', *The Financial Times*, 8 October 2012: www.ft.com/cms/s/0/7e5bd1d4-1153-11e2-a637-00144feabdc0.html (Accessed on 1 December 2015).

Khalil, Magdi (2006) 'The Coptic Struggle after the Egyptian Revolution of 1952' in M. Thomas & A. Youssef (Eds.), *Copts in Egypt: A Christian Minority Under Siege*, pp. 36–45, Zurich: Vandehhoeck & Ruprecht.

Khater, Akram Fouad (2010) *Sources in the History of the Modern Middle East*, Boston: Wandworth.

Kingsley, Patrick (2014) 'Abdel Fatah Al-Sisi Won 96.1% of Vote in Egypt Presidential Election, Say Officials', *The Guardian*, 3 June 2014: www.theguardian.com/world/2014/jun/03/abdel-fatah-al-sisi-presidential-election-vote-egypt (Accessed on 1 December 2015).

Kirsch, Jonathan (2004) *God against the Gods: The History of the War between Monotheism and Polytheism*, New York: Penguin.

Kirwan, Michael (2004) *Discovering Girard*, London: Darton, Longman and Todd.

Komolafe, Sunday Jide (2013) *The Transformation of African Christianity: Development and Change in the Nigerian Church*, Cumbria: Langham Partnership.

Kraxberger, Brennan (2004) 'The Geography of Regime Survival: Abacha's Nigeria', *African Affairs* 103:412, pp. 413–430, Royal African Society.

Kukah, Matthew Hassam & Toyin Falola (1996) *Religious Militancy and Self-Assertion: Islam and Politics in Nigeria*, Aldershot: Avebury.

Laitin, David D. (1982) 'The Sharia Debate and the Origins of Nigeria's Second Republic', *The Journal of Modern African Studies* 20: 3, pp. 411–430, Cambridge University Press.

Lake, David A. & Donald Rothchild (1996) 'Containing Fear: The Origins and Management of Ethnic Conflict.' *International Security*, 21:2, pp. 41–75, Cambridge, MA: Belfer Center for Science and International Affairs.

Landman, Todd (2008) *Issues and Methods in Comparative Politics: An Introduction, Third Edition*, London: Routledge.

Lawal, Gbenga & Ariyo Tobi (2006) 'Bureaucratic Corruption, Good Governance and Development: The Challenges and Prospects of Institution Building in Nigeria', *Journal of Applied Sciences Research* 2:10, pp. 642–649, INSInet.

Levtzion, Nehemia (2000) *The History of Islam in Africa*, Athens: Ohio University Press.

Lewis, Bernard (1990) 'The Roots of Muslim Rage', The Atlantic 266:3, pp. 47–60, September 1990.

Liddle, James R, Todd K. Shackelford & Viviana A. Weekes-Shackelford (2012) 'Why Can't We All Just Get Along? Evolutionary Perspectives on Violence, Homicide and War', *Review of General Psychology* 16:1, pp. 24–36, American Psychological Association.

Lindber, Jo-Eystein (2008) "Running on Faith? A Quantitative Analysis of the Effect of Religious Cleaveges on the Intensity and Duration of Internal Conflicts", master's thesis, University of Oslo.

Longman, Timothy (2013) 'Conducting Research in Conflict Zones: Lessons from the African Great Lakes Region', in D. Mazurana, K. Jacobsen & L. A. Gale, (Eds.) *Research Methods in Conflict Settings: A View From Below*, pp. xv–xvii, New York: Cambridge University Press.

Lugard, F. D. (1922) *The Dual Mandate in British Tropical Africa*, London: William Blackwood and Sons.

Mahmud, Sakah Saidu (2013) *Sharia or Shura: Contending Approached to Muslim Politics in Nigeria and Senegal*, Lanham, MD: Lexington Books.

Maier, Karl (2000) *This House Has Fallen: Nigeria in Crisis*, Boulder, CO: Westview Press.

Malak, Magdy (2007) 'Copts in the Shura Council; Copts No Need to Apply', *Watani Newspaper*, 8 July 2007.

Makari, Peter E. (2007) *Conflict & Cooperation: Christian-Muslim Relations in Contemporary Egypt*, Syracuse, NY: Syracuse University Press.

Malnick, Edward (2013) 'The 'Almost Unremarked' Tragedy of Christians Persecuted in the Middle East', *The Telegraph*: www.telegraph.co.uk/news/religion/10264499/The-almost-unremarked-tragedy-of-Christians-persecuted-in-the-Middle-East.html (Accessed on 1 December 2015).

Mann, Michael (2000) *The Dark Side of Democracy: Explaining of Ethnic Cleansing*, Cambridge: Cambridge University Press.

Mazurana, Dyan, Karen Jacobsen & Lacey Andrews Gale (2013) *Research Methods in Conflict Settings: A View From Below*, New York: Cambridge University Press.

McDermott, Anthony (1988) *Egypt from Nasser to Mubarak: A Flawed Revolution*, New York: Croom Helm.

McMillan, M. E. (2013) *Fathers and Sons: The Rise and Fall of Political Dynasty in the Middle East*, New York: Palgrave Macmillan.

Meel, C. K. (1943) 'The Religions of Nigeria', *Africa* 14:3, pp. 106–117.

Meral, Ziya (2009) 'Muslim-Majority States and Human Rights: From the UDHR to Durban Conference', *Religion Compass* 3:5, pp. 876–886. Wiley and Sons.

Mertus, Julie A. (1999) *Kosovo: How Myths and Truths Started a War*, Berkeley: University of California Press.

Mohieddin, Mohamed M. et al. (2013) *No Change in Sight: The Situation of Religious Minorities in Post-Mubarak Egypt*, London: Minority Rights Group.

Moltmann, Jürgen (1993) *Theology of Hope*, Minneapolis, MN: First Fortress Press.

Momoh, Abubakar & Paul-Sewa Thovoeithin (2001) 'An Overview of the 1989–1999 Democratisation Process in Nigeria', *Development Policy Management Network Bulletin* 12:3.

Morrow, Adam (2006) 'Egypt: Attacks Raise Fear of Religious Discord' *Inter Press Service*, 24 April 2006: www.ipsnews.net/2006/04/egypt-attacks-raise-fear-of-religious-discord/ (Accessed in December 2015).

Munro, Sir Alan (2000) 'Egypt: The Post-Nasser Revival', *The Rusi Journal*, 145:5, pp. 66–72, Royal United Services Institute.

Naanen, Ben & Kialee Nyiayaana (2013) 'State Failure and Niger Delta Conflict', in M. Okome (Ed.), *State Fragility, State Formation, and Human Security in Nigeria*, Basingtsoke: Palgrave.

Newton, Kenneth & Jan W. Van Deth (2010) *Foundations of Comparative Politics: 2nd Edition*, New York: Cambridge University Press.

Nietzsche, Friedrich (1974) *The Gay Science*. Kaufmann, Walter (Trans.), New York: Vintage.

Nixon, Charles R. (1972) 'Self-Determination: The Nigeria/Biafra Case', *World Politics* 24:04, pp. 473–497.

Nnoli, Okwudiba (1995) *Ethnicity and Development in Nigeria*, Aldershot: Avebury.

Norton-Taylor, Richard (2015) 'Global Armed Conflicts Becoming More Deadly, Major Study Finds' *The Guardian*, 20 May 2015: www.theguardian.com/world/2015/may/20/armed-conflict-deaths-increase-syria-iraq-afghanistan-yemen (Accessed 1 June 2015).

Ogbondah, Chris W. (2000) 'Political Repression in Nigeria, 1993–1998: A Critical Examination of One Aspect of the Perils of Military Dictatorships', *Africa Spectrum* 35:2, pp. 231–242, Institute of African Affairs at GIGA.

Okereke, C. Nna-Emeka (2013) 'Anatomy of Conflicts in Northern Nigeria' in M. Okome (Ed.), *State Fragility, State Formation, and Human Security in Nigeria*, Basingstoke: Palgrave.

O'Mahony, Anthony (2008) 'Coptic Christianity in Modern Egypt', *The Cambridge History of Christianity*, Cambridge: Cambridge University Press.

Olick, Jeffrey K. (2007) *The Politics of Regret: On Collective Memory and Historical Responsibility*, New York: Routledge.

Omenla, Nicholas Ibeawuchi (2010) 'Blaming the Gods: Christian Religious Propaganda in the Nigeria-Biafra War', *Journal of African History* 51, pp. 367–389. Cambridge University Press.

Omotola, J. Shola (2010) 'Elections and Democratic Transition in Nigeria under the Fourth Republic', *African Affairs* 109:437, pp. 535–553, Oxford University Press.

Omotosho, A. O. (2003) 'Religious Violence in Nigeria – The Causes and Solutions: An Islamic Perspective', *Swedish Missiological Themes* 91:1, pp. 15–31. Swedish Institute for Missions.

Oren, Michael (2002) *Six Days of War: June 1967 and the Making of the Modern Middle East*, Oxford: Oxford University Press.

OSAC (2011) Egypt 2011 Crime and Safety Report, United States Department of State, Bureau of Diplomatic Security, Washington, DC.

Othman, Shehu (1984) 'Classes, Crises and Coup: The Demise of Shagari's Regime', *African Affairs* 83:333, pp. 441–461. The Royal African Society.

Paden, John N. (1986) *Ahmedu Bello: Sardauna of Sokoto: Values and Leadership in Nigeria*, Kent: Hodder and Stoughton.

(2005) *Muslim Civic Cultures and Conflict Resolution: The Challenge of Democratic Federalism in Nigeria*, Washington, DC: The Brookings Institution.

Palaver, Wolfgang (2013) *Rene Girard's Mimetic Theory*, East Lansing: Michigan State University.

Pantucci, Raffello & Sasha Jesperson (2015) *From Boko Haram to Ansaru: The Evolution of Nigerian Jihad*, London: Royal United Services Institute.

Pennington, J. D. (1982) 'The Copts in Modern Egypt', *Middle Eastern Studies* 18:2, pp. 158–179, Taylor & Francis.

Perego, Elizabeth (2014) 'Clampdown and Blowback: How State Repression Has Radicalised Islamist Groups in Egypt', *Origins: Current Events in Historical Perspective* 7:10, Ohio State University.

Pesta, Abigail (2015) '"I Believe in Miracles," Says "Bring Back Our Girls" Founder Obiageli Ezekwesili', *Women in the World*, *New York Times*, 23 April 2015 : http://nytlive.nytimes.com/womenintheworld/2015/04/23/i-believe-in-miracles-says-bring-back-our-girls-founder-obiageli-ezekwesili/ (Accessed on 14 January 2015).

Pew Research Center (2011) The Future of the Global Muslim Population; Region: Sub-Saharan Africa, 27 January 2011: www.pewforum.org/2011/01/27/future-of-the-global-muslim-population-regional-sub-saharan-africa/#nigeria (Accessed on 14 January 2015).

Philipp, Thomas (1988) 'Nation State and Religious Community in Egypt: The Continuing Debate', *Die Welt des Islams*, New Series, Bd. 28, Nr. ¼, pp. 379–391, Brill.

(1995) 'Copts and Other Minorities in the Development of the Egyptian Nation-State' in Shimon Shamir, *Egypt from Monarchy to Republic: A Reassessment of Revolution and Change*, Boulder, Colorado: Westview.

Philpott, Daniel (2007) 'Religion, Reconciliation, and Transitional Justice; The State of the Field', Social Science Research Council Working Papers, New York: SSRC.

Pinker, Steven (2011) *The Better Angels of Our Nature*, New York, NY: Viking.

Posen, Barry R. (1993) 'The Security Dilemma and Ethnic Conflict', *Survival* 35:1, pp. 27–47.

Price, Eric (2011) 'Selected Literature on Terrorism and Religion', *Perspectives on Terrorism* 5:1, pp. 64–75, Terrorism Research Initiative, University of Massachusetts.

Raine, Adrian (2013) *The Anatomy of Violence: The Biological Roots of Crime*. London: Penguin.

Rapport, David (2007) 'The Importance of Space in Violent Ethno-Religious Strife', *Nationalism and Ethnic Politics*, 2:2, pp. 258–285, Routledge.

Reno, William (1999) 'Crisis and (No) Reform in Nigeria's Politics' *African Studies Review* 42:1, pp. 105–124, African Studies Association.

Ruane, Joseph & Jennifer Todd (2011) 'Ethnicity and Religion' in Karl Cordell & Stefan Wolff (Eds.) *Routledge Handbook of Ethnic Conflict*, pp. 67–78, New York: Routledge.

Rubenstein, Alvin (1972) 'Egypt since Nasser', *Current History* 62:365, pp. 6–12.

Rubin, Barry (2013) 'Revolutionary Salafi Islamists in Egypt: An Analysis and Guide', *Middle East Review of International Affairs* 17:2, pp. 37–54. Rubin Center for Research in International Affairs.

Rutherford, Bruce K. (2006) 'What do Egypt's Islamist Want? Moderate Islam and the Rise of Islamic Constitutionalism', *Middle East Journal* 60:4, pp. 707–731, Middle East Institute.

Ryad, Umar (2014) 'Anti-Imperialism and the Pan-Islamic Movement' in D. Motadel (Ed.), *Islam and the European Empires*, pp. 131–150. Oxford: Oxford University Press.

Saleh, Heba (2011) 'Cairo Residents Fear for Security', *Financial Times*, 30 January 2011: www.ft.com/cms/s/0/2e3152bc-2c5b-11e0-83bd-001 44feab49a.html#axzz3wTOEZTlQ (Accessed in December 2015).

Sampson, Terwase Isaac (2012) 'Religious Violence in Nigeria: Causal Diagnoses and Strategic Recommendations to the State and Religious Communities', *African Journal on Conflict Resolution* 12:1, pp. 103–133, Durban: ACCORD.

Schmitt, Carl (1996) *The Concept of the Political*, Chicago: University of Chicago Press.

Scott, Rachel M. (2010) *The Challenge of Political Islam; Non-Muslims and the Egyptian State*, Stanford, CA: Stanford University Press.

Scruton, Roger (2008) 'Alexander Solzhenitsyn: The Line Within', *Open Democracy*: www.opendemocracy.net/article/alexander-solzhenitsyn-the-line-within (Accessed on 10 May 2015).

Sedra, Paul (1999) 'Class Cleavages and Ethnic Conflict: Coptic Christian Communities in Modern Egyptian Politics', *Islam and Christian-Muslim Relations* 10:2, pp. 219–235, Routledge.

(2013) 'The Copts Under Morsi: Leave Them to the Church', *Middle East Institute*, 1 May 2013: www.mei.edu/content/copts-under-morsi-leave-them-church (Accessed on 14 January 2015).

Shoneyin, Lola (2014) 'Nigeria Is Mired in Violence and Inequality. It's the Girls Who Suffer.' *The Guardian*, 11 May 2014: www.theguardian .com/commentisfree/2014/may/11/nigeria-boko-haram-education-school girls-kidnapped (Accessed on 14 January 2015).

Shortt, Rupert (2012) *Christianophobia: A Faith Under Attack*, London: Rider.

Sika, Nadine (2014) 'The Arab State and Social Contestation', in M. Kamrava (Ed.), *Beyond the Arab Spring: The Evolving Ruling Bargain in the Middle East*, Oxford: Oxford University Press.

Smith, Christian (1998) *American Evangelicalism: Embattled and Thriving*, Chicago: University of Chicago Press.

Soliman, Samer (2011) *The Autumn of Dictatorship: Fiscal Crisis and Political Chance in Egypt under Mubarak*, Stanford, CA: Stanford University Press.

Stacher, Joshua (2012) 'Why the Generals Back Morsi: The Invisible Hand in Egypt's Government', *Foreign Affairs*: www.foreignaffairs .com/articles/egypt/2012-12-20/why-generals-back-morsi (Accessed on 1 January 2015).

Stamboliyska, Rayna (2013) 'Sectarian Sweeps Over Egypt', *Jadaliyya,* 17 August 2013: www.jadaliyya.com/pages/index/13660/sectarian-vio lence-sweeps-over-egypt-(Accessed on 1 January 2015).

Stanton, Andrea L. (ed.) (2012) *Cultural Sociology of the Middle East, Asia & Africa; An Encyclopaedia,* Thousand Oaks, CA: Sage.

Stark, Rodney & Roger Finke (2000) *Acts of Faith; Explaining the Human Side of Religion,* Berkeley: University of California Press.

Stein, Sabina (2011) 'Competing Political Science Perspectives on the Role of Religion in Conflict', *Politorbis* 52:2, pp. 21–27, Federal Department of Foreign Affairs.

Stevenson, John (2015) Statistical Analysis of Event Data Concerning Boko Haram in Nigeria (2009–2013), Maryland: National Consortium for the Study of Terrorism and Responses to Terrorism.

Strathern, Alan (2013) 'Why Are Buddhist Monks Attacking Muslims?', *BBC Magazine,* 2 May 2013: www.bbc.co.uk/news/magazine-2235 6306, (Accessed on 1 January 2015).

Suberu, Rotimi (2010) 'The Nigerian Federal System: Performance, Prob- lems and Prospects', *Journal of Contemporary African Studies* 28:4, pp. 459–477, Routledge.

Sullivan, Denis J. & Kimberly Jones (2008) *Global Security Watch-Egypt: A Reference Handbook,* Westport, CT: Praeger Security International.

Swartz, David L. (2002) 'The Sociology of Habit: The Perspective of Pierre Bourdieu', *The Occupational Therapy Journal of Research,* Volume:22, Issue: 1, pp. 61S–69S, The American Occupational Therapy Foundation.

Tadros, Maryln (2014) 'The Not-So-Silent Minority: The Case of Egypt's Coptic Minority in Post-Arab Uprising Egypt', in M. Ennaji (Ed.), *Multiculturalism and Democracy in North Africa: Aftermath of the Arab Spring,* pp. 203–223, London: Routledge.

Tal, Nachman (2005) *Radical Islam in Egypt and Jordan,* Brighton: Sussex Academic Press.

Tanner, Marcus (2005) 'Three Die as Muslims Sack Church in DVD Pro- test', *The Independent,* 22 October 2005: www.independent.co.uk/ news/world/africa/three-die-as-muslims-sack-church-in-dvd-protest-321 601.html (Accessed in December 2015).

Taylor, Paul (2013) 'Two More Dead after Sectarian Clashes in Egypt', *Reuters,* 8 April 2013: www.reuters.com/article/us-egypt-clashes-idUS BRE93503A20130408 (Accessed on 1 January 2016).

Thomassen, Bjorn (2015) 'Thinking with Liminality: To the Boundaries of an Anthropological Concept' in H. Wydra, A. Horvarth & B. Thomas- sen (Eds.), *Breaking Boundaries: Varieties of Liminality,* pp. 39–58, Oxford: Berghahn Books.

Tilley-Gyado, Terfa (2012) 'Opinion: Why Are Nigerians Numb to Slaughter?' *CNN Opinion*, 5 October 2012: http://edition.cnn.com/2012/10/05/world/africa/nigeria–shooting-mubi (Accessed on 14 January 2015).

Tilly, Charles (2003) *The Politics of Collective Violence*, Cambridge: Cambridge University Press.

Timmer, Daniel (2013) 'Is Monotheism Particularly Prone to Violence? A Historical Critique', *Journal of Religion and Society* 15, The Kripke Center.

Torrey, Gordon H. (1965) 'Nasser's Egypt', *Current History*, 48:285, pp. 290–308. Current History Inc.

Thurston, Alex (2016) 'The Disease Is Unbelief': Boko Haram's Religious and Political Worldview. The Brookings Project on U.S. Relations with Islamic World, Analysis Paper, No. 22, January 2016. Washington, DC: Brookings Institute.

Turner, Jonathan et al. (2012) 'Chapter 3: The Sociology of Auguste Comte', in *The Emergence of Sociological Theory*, Sage: London.

Ukiwo, Ukoha 2003) 'Politics, Ethno-Religious Conflicts and Democratic Consolidation in Nigeria', *Journal of Modern African Studies* 41(1), pp. 115–138, Cambridge University Press.

Verkaaik, Oskar (2003) 'Fun and Violence: Ethnocide and the Effervescence of Collective Aggression', *Social Anthropology* 11: 1, pp 3–22, European Association of Social Anthropologists.

Volkan, Vamik (2006) *Killing in the Name of Identity: A Study of Bloody Conflicts*, Charlottesville, VA: Pitchstone.

Walsh, James (1981) *The Cloud of Unknowing*, Classics of Western Spirituality, Mahwah, NJ: Paulist Press.

Waterbury, John (1983) *The Egypt of Nasser and Sadat: The Political Economy of Two Super Regimes*, Princeton, NJ: Princeton University Press.

Weaver, Matthew (2012) 'Muslim Brotherhood's Mohammed Morsi Wins Egypt's Presidential Race', *The Guardian*, 24 June 2012: www.theguardian.com/world/2012/jun/24/muslim-brotherhood-egypt-president-mohamed-morsi (Accessed on 1 January 2015).

Weber, Max (1948) *From Max Weber: Essays in Sociology*, London: Routledge.

Weinbaum, Marvin G. (1985) 'Egypt's "Infitah" and the Politics of US Economic Assistance', *Middle Eastern Studies* 21:2, pp. 206–222, Taylor & Francis.

Welch, Claude (1995) 'Civil-Military Agonies in Nigeria: Pains of Unaccomplished Transition', *Armed Forces & Society* 21, pp. 593–614, SAGE.

Wentz, Richard E. (1993) *Why People Do Bad Things in the Name of Religion*, Macon, GA: Mercer University Press.

Wickham, Carrie Rosefsky (2002) *Mobilizing Islam: Religion, Activism and Political Change in Egypt*, New York: Columbia University Press.

Williams, Dodeye Uduak (2015) 'How Useful Are the Main Existing Theories of Ethnic Conflict?', *Academic Journal of Interdisciplinary Studies* 4:1, pp. 147–152, MCSER Publishing.

Williams, Pat & Toyin Falola (1995) *Religious Impact on the Nation State: The Nigerian Predicament*, Aldershot: Avebury.

Wilson, Michael L. et al. (2014) 'Lethal Aggression in Pan Is Better Explained by Adaptive Strategies Than Human Impacts', Nature 513:18, Macmillan.

World Bulletin, 'Hindus Attack Muslims in India, 15 Killed', 8 September 2013: www.worldbulletin.net/news/117297/hindus-attack-muslims-in-india-15-killed (Accessed on 5 January 2015).

Wrangham, Richard W & Dale Peterson (1996) *Demonic Males; Apes and the Origins of Human Violence*, New York: Mariner Books.

Wydra, Harald (2015) *Politics and the Sacred*, Cambridge: Cambridge University Press.

Wydra, Harald, Agnes Horvarth & Bjorn Thomassen (2015) *Breaking Boundaries: Varieties of Liminality*, Oxford: Berghahn Books.

Yohannes, Okbazghi (2001) *Political Economy of an Authoritarian Modern State and Religious Nationalism in Egypt*, Queenstown: The Edwin Mellen Press.

Zahid, Mohammed (2012) *The Muslim Brotherhood and Egypt's Succession Crisis: The Politics of Liberalisation and Reform in the Middle East*, London: I. B. Tauris.

Zeidan, David (1999) 'The Copts: Equal, Protected or Persecuted? The Impact of Islamization on Muslim-Christian Relations in Modern Egypt', *Islam and Christian-Muslim Relations* 10:1, pp. 53–67, Routledge.

Zollner, Barbara (2007) 'Prison Talk: The Muslim Brotherhood's Internal Struggle during Gamal Andel Nasser's Persecutions, 1954 to 1971', *International Journal of Middle East Studies* 39, pp. 411–433, Cambridge University Press.

(2009) *The Muslim Brotherhood: Hasal al-Hudaybi and Ideology*, Oxon: Routledge.

Zuhur, Sherifa & Marlyn Tadros (2015) 'Egypt's Conspiracy Discourse: Liberals, Copts and Islamists' *Middle East Policy* 22:3, Middle East Policy Council.

Index